No Featherbed to Heaven

No Featherbed to Heaven

A BIOGRAPHY OF MICHAEL WIGGLESWORTH, 1631-1705

by

Richard Crowder

Nor must we think to ride to Heaven
Upon a Feather-bed.

Meditation I,
Meat Out of the Eater, 1669

Michigan State University Press

For Avis

Preface

This is a book about a poet, one of the three major poets of the seventeenth century in New England—how he was educated, who his friends were, what part he took in the life of his community, what he wrote. That his most productive period was limited to a decade is as nothing compared to the wide reception his books enjoyed, for his verse was bought, read, memorized, recited, and absorbed for a hundred solid years.

True, he was a teacher whose pupils became men of more than passing influence, a physician consulted by people of distinction, and a clergyman eventually esteemed by laymen and colleagues alike. The fact remains, however, that in his time, and ours, his verse writing was his most salient contribution to American civilization.

In preparing this biography, I have incurred more debts than it is possible to enumerate. The Modern Language Association provided funds for photostats. Purdue University granted a year's sabbatical leave. Librarians everywhere were generous and helpful. Especially do I appreciate the aid of John H. Moriarity, Director of the Purdue University Libraries; Zoltán Haraszti, Keeper of Rare Books in the Boston Public Library; Robert H. Haynes, Assistant Librarian of the Harvard College Library; and Caroline Jakeman of the Houghton Library at Harvard. I could not have completed the book without the assistance of the staffs of the Massachusetts Historical Society, the New England Historic Genealogical Society, the Boston Athenaeum, and the Malden (Massachusetts) Public Library.

I am happy to acknowledge the courtesies of William Moulding of Mill Hill, London, England, in trying to find traces of the Wigglesworths in Hedon. My colleague, Virgil L. Lokke of Purdue University, gave the entire manuscript a patient and astute reading, pointing out irrelevancies and misinterpretations. Norman S. Grabo of Michigan State University gave generously of his time, talent, and knowledge in bringing my work into line. What error remains can most assuredly never be laid at the doors of these scholars.

Without the help of Frances Teeling and Maryann Bache and of my wife, Esther, the rough draft would still be lying on my desk.

An essay on the material of part of Chapter VI, based on the study of a copy of *Meat Out of the Eater* (1689 edition) in the Rare Book Department of the Boston Public Library, has been published by Mr. Haraszti in the *Boston Public Library Quarterly.*

Chapters VII and VIII interrupt the narrative to give an account of Wigglesworth's orthodox ideas. Admittedly, they say nothing new, may in fact often be somewhat repetitious, but for the record they bring together in one place the poet's version of the Calvinist doctrines received by the Puritans in Massachusetts. In constructing them, I was following—with patent modification and at a respectful distance—the method of Perry Miller in *The New England Mind: The Seventeenth Century* (New York, 1939).

The poetry of Michael Wigglesworth has never been collected.

Contents

The following abbreviations are used in the references:

Buncker: "Upon the much lamented Death of . . . Mr. Benjamin Buncker"
Christe: *"Christe, parum doleo"*
Con: "In Confinement Liberty"
D: Michael Wigglesworth's "Diary"
DD: "The Day of Doom"*
Eternity: "A Short Discourse on Eternity"
Foster: "Upon the return of . . . Mr. Foster . . . out of captivity"
God's Con: "God's Controversy with New-England"
Heaven: "Heavenly Crowns for Thorny Wreaths"
Ira: *"Ira premit"*
Joy: "Joy in Sorrow"
Life: "Life in Deaths"
Light: "Light in Darkness"
Meat: "Meat Out of the Eater"*
Mole-hill: "I walk'd and did a little Mole-hill view"
Poor: "Poor Men's Wealth"
Prayer: "A Prayer unto Christ"
PS: "A Postscript unto the Reader"
Reader: "To the Christian Reader"
Riddles: "Riddles Unriddled"
Sick: "Sick Men's Health"
Sol: "In Solitude Good Company"
Strength: "Strength in Weakness"
Vanity: "Vanity of Vanities"
When as: "When as the wayes of Jesus Christ"

* A distinction is made between *The Day of Doom* and *Meat Out of the Eater* as volumes and "The Day of Doom" and "Meat Out of the Eater" as poems.

No Featherbed to Heaven

I. Transplanted

On Monday night, October 24, 1653, Michael Wigglesworth had an elaborate dream of the Last Judgment.[1]
God was on His glorious throne, the saved rejoicing on His
right hand, the doomed cowering and whimpering on His
left. Dread and awe permeated the vision, which so impressed the young man that next day he vowed anew to try
to follow the paths of the Lord in tearful penitence.

Michael had just turned twenty-two the week before. As a
teaching fellow at Harvard, he was studying in his spare
time in preparation for taking the degree of Master of Arts.
He had belonged to the church in Cambridge about two
years, but membership in the church, trying as was the
ordeal of initiation, did not guarantee entrance to heaven. A
man could sense that he was of the elect, but paradoxically
he should never feel secure, for security of the soul was
rooted in pride, a deadly sin.

Michael's whole life was defined by a sense of finitude and
its accompanying dread. He had been reared in the strictest
sort of Puritan family; he was to go on into a ministry
based on a severe and unyielding theology and to write
poetry sometimes frighteningly graphic. Withal, he was to
mollify the fierceness of his beliefs with a gentleness and
love that eventually earned him veneration worthy of a
Catholic saint, staunch Protestant though he was.

Michael was born in Yorkshire in 1631.[2] Wigglesworths
had been long in the land. Soon after the Normans had over-

powered Harold in 1066, the records of the county had been dotted with "Wiclesfords," and "Winchelswrde," and out-and-out "Wigglesworth."[3] Michael's father, Edward, a thriving business man, must have felt himself deep-rooted here.

All England, however, was alive with controversy.[4] The first Charles Stuart had been on the imperious and high-handed throne six years. Refused monies for his extravagant purposes, he had dissolved Parliament two years before and had given no indication that he would ever reconvene that body. Instead, he was collecting forced loans directly from the taxpayers themselves. Moreover, he had married a Catholic, a Papist.

Under Elizabeth a state church based on moderate Calvinist theology had evolved, a church that most Englishmen could accept. Her successor, James Stuart, had permitted, nay, nurtured, an Arminian heresy: that man, through good works, could deserve, and attain, election to eternal happiness. And now his son had proceeded from there, had brought to the throne Henrietta Maria, who had given birth to a son, another Charles. It appeared that this arrogant, presumptuous state of affairs would continue on into the next generation.

Contention, turmoil, dissension were rife. Every Englishman felt the magnetism of the struggle, from goodman to lord. Parliament had been against the Crown; Anglicans were feeling the threat of Roman Catholicism; Puritans, who had thought that their point of view might find at least tolerant reception, were suffering from pressures. The year before Michael's birth, John Winthrop and other influential Puritans had led a company to the savage wilderness of Massachusetts in New England to establish "a city upon a hill" in order to show the world, and especially England, what an ideal civilization could be like, purged of the frivolities and abominations of Popery.[5] These were

men that prized libertee
To walk with God according to their light,

[2]

To be as good as he would have them bee,
To serve and worship him with all their might. . . .
(God's Con)

In this year of 1631 died Michael Drayton, author of
sonnets and odes, of a stylish poem called "To His Coy
Love." In this year died John Donne, inspired preacher with
a lively past, never quite sure that Anglicanism was the answer; poet who had early written "For Godsake hold your
tongue, and let me love" and later had called out "Death be
not proud"; clergyman who had begun in the Romanist tradition but had ended as the dean of London's cathedral, St.
Paul's. George Herbert was composing verses to the greater
glory of God and His Church. Sir John Suckling was assuring lovelorn courtiers that women are not worth the worry.
Thomas Carew was praising or deploring his "Divine Mistress," his "Beautiful Mistress," his "Cruel Mistress." Robert Herrick was encouraging his readers to seize the day.
John Milton, Puritan, at twenty-three was still at Cambridge
University, where he would take his Master of Arts degree
the following summer.

In the North, in Yorkshire, the Puritan principles had
taken a strong hold, even among the modest, who included
Edward Wigglesworth, about twenty-seven, residing in
Hedon near Hull on the coast in the East Riding. (It probably was Hedon: the records show a great fire there after
Edward had migrated,[6] his son later reported such a fire,[7]
and the family did have Yorkshire relatives.) After October
18 of this year, when Edward's wife, Esther (Hester), presented him with his son, Michael, would come the problems
of education, of religious training. Already the tension of
the medieval trying to restrain the new and modern was
furrowing even the custom-smoothed details of everyday
living: reliable superstitions were being questioned by skeptics; reliable authority was being called to the bar by reason; reliable religious beliefs were being tested by embryonic
science. The main problems for men like Edward Wigglesworth were economic and religious.

[3]

Hedon had had a long history. Probably once a thriving port and business center, it had figured in authentic records in the time of Henry II, in the middle of the twelfth century.[8] During the reign of King John the men of Hedon had paid four pounds for the right to sell cloth. To judge from the size of its tax, it was the third largest port in Yorkshire —Hull, its very near neighbor, and the city of York itself surpassing it by a good margin.[9] In 1295, under Edward I, Hedon had sent two representatives to the Parliament in London.[10]

In spite of a long family history, current events were becoming increasingly unbearable for Edward and Esther. In 1633 Charles and his Queen had another son, James, insuring a continuance of the Arminian ascendancy in all probability. But worse, in this same year, the Bishop of London, William Laud, a close friend of the King, became Archbishop of Canterbury. Encouraged by his sovereign, Laud was determined to bring destruction to all organizations opposing the doctrine that any man could get to heaven through his own will power. To achieve this house-cleaning, he resorted to tactics of a reign of terror by restoring the unconstitutional Star Chamber and the Court of the High Commission. Charles had virtually turned the control of both church and state over to the Archbishop.

In doctrine Laud contended—indeed, actually insisted—not only that man's works could gain him eternal salvation, but that it was possible on the contrary for a man who had once held the faith to lose it and, consequently, his reward before the throne of God. Simply to trust in the merit of Jesus and the infallibility of God's plan and selection before the world began was out of the question.

What was more, since good works were a sign of man's desire for salvation, it followed that the most beautiful service of worship possible was necessary to the proper honoring of the Lord. Candles, flowers, crucifixes, fair linen, processionals, choirs, the set language of *The Book of Common Prayer*—every visible symbol that would enhance the loveliness of man's relation to his Creator was put to use. Even the symbolism of location was stressed: the table of the Holy Communion, no longer in the center of the chancel, was moved to the east wall and separated from the congregation by rails.

Unquestionably Archbishop Laud was the great power. He despised the Puritan concept of the Sabbath and supported the reissue of *The Book of Sports*. Furthermore, he was determined to restore the priests and bishops of the Anglican Communion to what he insisted was their rightful position as statesmen of the highest order and privilege.

As the decade wore on, the indignities and injustices piled up. In 1635, with no Parliament to approve or disapprove, the King levied taxes to support his Navy. Yorkshire's portion was twelve thousand pounds, Hedon having to give over an exorbitant assessment of something more than twenty pounds.[11] Men like Edward, hard-working tradesmen, would feel the burden.

Moreover, whenever spies of the High Commission uncovered a group worshiping in a way different from the rites of the state church (in a "conventicle"), not only the dissenting clergyman but the laymen themselves were thrown into prison until they took an oath to follow the Anglican tradition or until, with apparently whimsical irresponsibility, the Court decided to set them free again.[12] In 1637 Laud issued a proclamation forbidding such non-conformists to leave England unless they could show testimonials from reliable persons that they were, after all, *bona fide* observers of the rites of the Church of England. During this decade Englishmen by the thousands had been following the trail of John Winthrop over the Atlantic to Massachusetts, not to find religious tolerance, but to practice their own kind of strictness: to let no one celebrate the pagan-related feast of Christmas, to allow no clergyman to wear a surplice, to permit only extempore prayer in the meeting houses, to eliminate a thousand Romish practices.

Edward and Esther Wigglesworth, godly folk of the Puri-

[5]

tan persuasion, could not support the formalities of their parish church and went outside to a conventicle to hear the word of God preached according to their likes and to receive the "ordinance" of the Lord's Supper according to their plain principles. For this they were pursued by Laud's men. For this they sought and found (probably without benefit of the Archbishop's required testimonials) passage to the shores of Governor Winthrop's Massachusetts Bay.[13] During that summer of 1638 three thousand people joined the Great Migration. John Winthrop's government, the city upon a hill, offered them unparalleled opportunity for the practice of Christian virtue as they saw it, as they were certain God intended:

> men that erst at my command
> Forsook their ancient seats and native soile,
> To follow me into a desart land,
> Contemning all the travell and the toile,
> Whose love was such to purest ordinances
> As made them set at nought their fair inheritances.
>
> (God's Con)

It was not easy to pull up stakes, to leave a new house and a fine trade, to part from warm and cordial relatives and friends, to require a wife and six-year-old boy to endure the tribulations of a long and uncertain sea voyage and the unknown hardships of life in a wilderness. But Edward was a man of staunch beliefs. The stinging persecutions of the King and the Archbishop had gone beyond bearing, especially since a way out offered itself at the end of an ocean journey. One had only to trust God:

> Are these the folk whom from the brittish Iles,
> Through the stern billows of the watry main,
> I safely led so many thousand miles,
> As if their journey had been through a plain?

Four years before Thomas Shepard had left Yorkshire for the new colony, glad to bring his wife and child out of "that rude place of the North where was nothing but barbarous wickedness generally. . . ."[14] Years later Edward's son

[6]

Michael was to call the Yorkshire his family had left "an ungodly place." These epithets are a matter of definition, for one man's "ungodly" is often another man's "righteous."

The details of the Wiggleworths' voyage are lost: the name of the ship, the list of passengers, the date of sailing. The company landed at Charlestown in Massachusetts in August, 1638, having been preceded in June by another group of Yorkshiremen under the leadership of the Reverend Ezekiel Rogers, rector of St. Peter's Church in Rowley. Highly esteemed in Yorkshire, Rogers had nevertheless come down to London, whence, after engaging a ship, he had left for the New World with his little company, patently all dissenters.[15]

So there were Yorkshiremen to greet the Wigglesworths in Charlestown. The colonists were probably still discussing the wonder of God in the great earthquake that had struck about noon on the first of June, rocking the ships on the Charles River and upsetting their cargo—an earthquake so violent that the townsmen had had difficulty remaining on their feet.[16] Even now they were still talking of the banishment, over two years before, of Roger Williams, who could not believe that baptism before an age of understanding and consent was valid, and, more recently, of Anne Hutchinson, that bright and witty heretic of Boston who held to her belief that the Bible was not the only channel of the divine Word to man, that God could speak to her "by an immediate revelation," that communication was direct between the Spirit of the Almighty and the human soul, hers in particular.[17] Two such heresies, if left to spread in Massachusetts Bay, would have undermined the entire basis of organization of the colony: there would be no more faith in God's selection of citizens of His eternal kingdom and no more need for pastors and teachers to interpret the Word. All-important structure and authority would be drowned in a sea of anarchy.

On September 14 occurred the death of the young Reverend John Harvard, pastor of the church in Charlestown.

[7]

The Wigglesworths were still there and no doubt attended the funeral of this youthful divine,[18] who generously left in his will his library of four hundred books and a substantial sum of money to a struggling little college which the General Court had decided to establish in "Newtowne" up the twisting Charles River a few miles.[19]

Charlestown, however, could not hold Edward Wigglesworth. With a group of others from Yorkshire he set out with Esther and Michael early in October for Quinnipiac on Long Island Sound. Ezekiel Rogers chose not to accompany this expedition, but soon went to the country north of Charlestown to found a community named for his English home, Rowley. Early the following spring some of his original followers returned from Quinnipiac to join him in the little settlement. But not Edward Wigglesworth.[20]

The winter had been a hard one. First of all, on the long trip around Cape Cod the ship had been thrown up on the shore by a rigorous storm and had been forced to remain there until high tide had produced sufficient force to release it. Next, it was necessary for the newcomers to spend the winter in cellars built partly underground. Fairly substantial, supported by timber sides, roofs, and floors, a few were divided into rooms. Probably several extra cellars had been prepared in expectation of such new people as the Wigglesworths, whose own pit, despite supports, fell partly to pieces during a heavy rain that winter so that young Michael was thoroughly drenched in his sleep and consequently languished in a severe sickness, from which, however, with the resilience of childhood, he made total recovery.[21]

Quinnipiac, re-named New Haven by its English settlers, was small and extremely conservative. Unimpeded by a royal charter, far removed from the organization dominated by the bishops of England, it was an almost ideal place to try out the theories of the Puritans concerning church and government. Without question its two leaders were John Davenport, eventually the pastor, and Theophilus Eaton, a business man who had made a fortune in trade.[22]

[8]

Davenport had been vicar of St. Stephen's, Coleman Street, London, but had run afoul Archbishop Laud because he had persisted in the claim that kneeling and idolatry were blood relatives. He had fled to Holland, had returned in disguise to England, had arranged with his boyhood friend Eaton to organize a party to sail to New England, had hired a ship (the *Hector*), and, after further difficulties, had arrived at Boston on June 26, 1637. Late that summer, having heard that Quinnipiac was a promising spot, Eaton had led an expedition of investigation, had found the place indeed likely, and had returned to Boston full of hope, having left behind seven men to make ready over the winter for the coming of the whole group when the weather would be more favorable.

On March 30, Eaton, Davenport, and the rest had left the Bay. The voyage, of about two weeks' duration, had been tiresome and trying. They had heard, though, that King Charles might send a governor to Massachusetts that summer, and they had had enough interference from the Crown. Here they would be away from the crowded districts around Boston. Here they could look ahead to prosperity on the land and on the sea, for it was a part of the Puritan complex of faith that full development of one's talents and physical resources was a debt one owed the Creator.

Not long after landing, the company had observed a day of fasting and humiliation and had put their names to a covenant: "thatt as [in] matters thatt Concerne the gathering and ordering of a Church, so Likewise in all publique offices which concerne & wil order, as Choyce of magistrates and officers makeing and repealing Lawes devideing allotments of Inheritance and all things of Like nature we would all of us be ordered by those Rules which the Scripture holds forth to us."[23] There was to be none of Anne Hutchinson's "immediate revelation" here. The law would be the Bible, its ambiguities interpreted by the leaders.

There had been worship services from the beginning, though the church itself was not "gathered," according to

[9]

the New England way, for many months. Until this organization could be effected, theirs would be simply "a plantation covenant," not a "church covenant," the ideal in government.[24] The first written agreement with the Indians was signed on November 24, 1638, after the Wigglesworths had settled in their cellar. The Indians having conveyed even more land to the English in the next month, the assignment began of home lots and meadowland and acreage for crops.

Every man was expected to erect his house near the church building. In the spring Edward began work on his dwelling, next west to that of John Cockerill, probably a Yorkshireman also.[25] His estate being valued at three hundred pounds, Edward was assigned twenty-two and a half acres in the "first division," that is five acres for each hundred pounds and two and a half additional acres for each member of the family (himself, Esther, and Michael). The same allotment was to be his in the meadowlands. Though he came out an acre and a half short, he was later assigned sixty-six acres in the "second division," farther from home.[26] In spite of the fact that Eaton and Davenport and some of the others were given larger holdings, Edward's property totaled a sound, substantial average.

With the other planters he invested in livestock and grain. His horses and cattle were marked, for they shared common pasture under the eye of hired herdsmen. He no doubt was as vigilant as the rest in ridding the settlement of wolves, foxes, and bears, for whose heads the town offered bounties.[27] In the cultivation of his property he was assiduous and astute.

His careful husbanding of his estate was balanced by his vigorous warfare against sin. The town church was finally gathered in the summer of 1639, after much soul-searching in "private meetings." On June 4, some twelve people were selected as worthy to organize the church. At length, on August 21 or 22, seven people, including Davenport and Eaton, and, very soon after, three more, including the schoolmaster, Ezekiel Cheever, were chosen to form the nucleus of the group. In the Congregational manner, Davenport was selected from their own number and was ordained as the pastor, for, having been a clergyman in England, he had had more theological training and experience than the rest. Services were held either out of doors, in good weather, or in Robert Newman's barn, when the rains and snows came.

Strictly speaking, the membership was never very sizable, for each candidate was required to provide undeniable proof of his conversion from wickedness by passing a rigorous oral examination and to confess in open meeting the tenets of his faith. Edward and Esther Wigglesworth, however, were soon admitted to the central group. After the construction of the meeting house in 1640 (at a cost of five hundred pounds), they were assigned seats of considerable dignity, "Goodman Wigglesworth" in the middle of the men's section and "Sister Wigglesworth" in the middle of the women's.[28] Presumably Michael sat with the young boys under the surveillance of a disciplinarian.

Attended by everybody in town, member or not, the services were long from the earliest days and convened twice on Sunday, at nine in the morning and again at two in the afternoon. Following prayer by the pastor and Scripture reading, there would be singing from *The Whole Booke of Psalmes Faithfully Translated into English Metre* (after it had been printed in 1640), a two-hour sermon, another prayer, and at last the benediction. The people were never far away from theology. On Tuesday nights, as a general rule, came the town meetings, held in the meeting house, for church and state were inseparable. On Wednesday nights came lectures, on godly topics. On other evenings came private meetings, neighborhood gatherings where the participants repeated the matter of the lectures and the sermons and engaged in lively discussion of the issues raised therein. No pagan toleration could creep in here; this, and nothing else, was what the spiritual life was meant to be in New Haven.

Edward had been present at the meeting of June 4, 1639,

[11]

at which the first little company of church members had been determined. He had signed the agreement "thatt church members onely shall be free burgesses, and they onely shall choose among them selves magistrates and officers to have the power of transacting all publique civil affayres of this plantation, of makeing and repealing lawes, devideing inherritances, decideing of differences thatt may arise, and doeing all things and businesses of like nature. . . ."[29] Sixty-three men affixed their signatures to the pact. The plantation covenant was no more; a church covenant of the strictest sort would now guide their thinking and doing. Edward's turn to sign brought his name about half way down the list. In spite of his position, however, to the end of his days he remained "Goodman Wigglesworth," not being eligible for the title "Mr." because he had worked in his fields along with any laborers he might employ.

Life in the new settlement was tempered by godliness, it is true, but there developed such diversions as weddings, house-raisings, husking-bees, election days, military-training days, and great feasts of thanksgiving. Liquor was not forbidden; beer was looked on as a proper beverage for nearly any occasion. But, if a man—or woman—was found guilty of taking too much, the penalties were sometimes more than just embarrassing. The idea that one should learn to meet temptation with bravery well fortified by principle was central to the life experience. To remove temptation would be to take the place of God Himself, a blasphemy no Christian would care to commit. Though they must live in the world and cultivate what good the world could offer, the Puritans knew that their very salvation depended on keeping an eye on eternity.

> To kick against the bowels of his Love,
> Is this aright his bounty to improve?
> (PS)

Now that Michael was nearly eight years old, his parents decided to send him to school. The Puritans believed in edu-

[12]

cation, many of them being college men themselves. They had early passed a law in the colony requiring all parents to see that their children were taught to read and write. By this summer of 1639 Michael had mastered the rudiments of communication, though the quality of the instruction in spelling may not have been first rate considering his father's seventeenth-century way with his own name, which came out sometimes "Wiglesworth," sometimes "Wigleswor," or even "Wiggleworth."

Whatever his first instruction was before he was eight, Michael began learning Latin under Ezekiel Cheever, twenty-four-year-old schoolmaster who taught—and punished—pupils in his own house until a proper school building was constructed. The New Haven settlers were as eager as the Puritans around Boston to bring their children up not only literate but actually acquainted with learning. Cheever's school had been established very soon after Eaton and Davenport had led the company down from Boston, for in 1639 Thomas Fugill, who was serving a rather shaky term as town clerk, was ordered "to keep Charles Higinson, an indentured apprentice, at school one year, or else advantage him as much in his education as one year's schooling comes to."[30]

Cheever himself was one of the early members of the New Haven Church. A sound Christian, at least for a time, he was also a trained scholar, having been educated at Emmanuel College, Cambridge, as had John Harvard, Thomas Shepard, John Cotton, Thomas Hooker, and Nathaniel Ward, all prominent in the New England settlements. Cheever's personality, scholarship, and birch rod had a great influence on the second and succeeding generations not only in New Haven but elsewhere, for in 1650, having been summarily and without warning dismissed from the New Haven church for objecting to what he felt was too much power among the elders, he moved up to Ipswich for eleven years, to Charlestown for nine, and eventually to Boston, where he was head of the Latin School for twenty-eight years. His *Latin Acci-*

dence, in manuscript until the year after his death, was to be a standard textbook for nearly a century and a half.[31] An excellent and in-the-long-run beloved teacher despite the physical violence of his discipline, when he died in 1708, he was honored with a witty elegy by one of his former pupils, Benjamin Tompson. In this poem the mourners are the eight parts of speech, Cheever's servants and companions at his funeral:

> The Clouds of Tears did overcast their faces,
> Yea all were in most lamentable *Cases,*
> We five *Declensions* did the Work decline,
> And *Told* the *Pronoun Tu,* The Work is thine. . . .[32]

But all this occurred many years after the boy Michael Wigglesworth had sat in his classes.

The General Court at New Haven had given its sanction to a Latin school: "For the better trayning upp of youth in this towne, that, through God's blessing they may be fitted for publique service hereafter, either in church or commonweale," a free school was ordered, the master to be paid from town funds. Cheever received the appointment at twenty pounds a year until August, 1644, when he was voted an increase of ten pounds.[33]

Michael was his pupil for about two years at first. As was common practice, the boy studied Latin, and Latin only. A very industrious student, even at his unripe age he made rapid progress in the declensions and conjugations, in the reading, writing, and speaking of this ancient tongue. This was, however, the normal program for a boy of the seventeenth century.

After Michael had been in school about a year and a half, his mother had another baby, a daughter, who was named Abigail. The date of her birth is not recorded, but, since she was baptized on December 1, 1640,[34] it is safe to assume that she was born in the latter part of November, for no orthodox Puritan would run the risk of eternal damnation of his child because of careless postponement or omission of the "ordinance" of baptism.

[14]

On March 17, 1641, at a town meeting, Edward, through the casting of lots, was one of twenty-eight freemen selected "to have their meadow" in the land east of town. Every effort was made to be fair in the distribution of land. Industrious and thrifty, Edward was to be awarded his just share. His name was tenth on the list.[35]

Misfortune struck one cold day. Overheated from working very hard, Edward bent over to pick up something, strained his back, and took cold in it. And he never recovered. Though he felt little pain, for the rest of his life he suffered from weakness and vertigo. During the summer he grew worse. That fall he tried hot baths, and the following spring he applied oils, ointments, and plasters, but all to no avail.[36]

The farm work being heavy in the summer months, there seemed to be no solution but to take Michael from his studies and put him to work, though this was hard on the parents, for they had hoped their son could become a cultivated gentleman. But what was to be done? The baby, Abigail, would be growing and would need more attention and more food; the lands could not lie fallow; hired help was not plentiful. So, not yet ten years old, Michael left school to work in the fields. Needless to say, what he had learned of Latin—and he had done very well—was soon entirely lost.[37]

During the next few years, despite his disabilities, Edward continued as voting freeman in the plantation. When in 1644 Theophilus Eaton was again sworn in as governor, Edward signed the instituting document, along with many others, as a kind of oath of fidelity.[38] In this same year he helped elect Robert Newman "ruleing elder" and gave his nod of approval to the ordination of William Hooke as "teacher" in the church. John Davenport remained as "pastor." Hooke's duties were to lecture, to explain the doctrine, and "to administer a word of knowledge."[39] The pastor, on the other hand, was to call on his flock, to exhort, and "to administer a word of wisdom." These were only technical differences, however, for both were preachers, and both administered the ordinances of baptism and the Lord's Supper. The two offices were common throughout the Massachusetts churches

[15]

(and New Haven was still a part of Massachusetts, though geographically distant).

Since these were the years of the Civil Wars in England, years of non-interference in American colonial affairs, Massachusetts Bay and New Haven were left to develop as they saw fit. Though the first fine glow of the Great Migration had faded, the problems created by the deaths of the original leaders, the rule of Oliver Cromwell, and eventually the Restoration were still to come.

> While almost all the world beside
> Lay weltring in their gore:
> We, only we, enjoyd such peace
> As none enjoyd before.
>
> . . .
>
> No forrein foeman did us fray,
> Nor threat'ned us with warrs:
> We had no enemyes at home,
> Nor no domestick jarres.

. . .

Are these the men whose gates with peace I crown'd,
    To whom for bulwarks I salvation gave,
Whilst all things else with rattling tumults sound,
    And mortall frayes send thousands to the grave?
Whilest their own brethren bloody hands embrewed
    In brothers blood, and fields with carcases bestrewed?
                                                    (God's Con)

Early in 1645 the General Court ordered the minutes of its meetings from the beginning carefully checked, for it had discovered that the clerk, Thomas Fugill, was unreliable. There was considerable recopying of the records with some changes and such additions as would bring the accounts up to date. Among other items, however, Edward's rights in the east meadows were confirmed.[40]

In this year, too, Eaton's wife, Anne, was excommunicated on April 20 because she could not bring herself to have faith in the efficacy of infant baptism. She maintained that, because she had not been baptized after she had reached an age of choice, she was as good as baptized not at all. Her

[16]

convictions had resulted in her remaining away from the Lord's Supper—a serious disregard of the law.[41] Even the Governor's wife was not above reproach. Her membership in the church community was revoked, in spite of her husband's position. God's church could not afford to be a respecter of persons.

Meanwhile, Michael had been trying manfully to do his part in supporting the family, but, because he simply had no talent for farming and showed no promise of cultivating any, his father decided to get along without him and to send him back to Cheever. Michael objected, for he was a proud boy and disliked having to start again, this time far behind his contemporaries,[42] having been away from the schoolmaster's tutelage a good three years. Because in a Puritan family, however, the father's word was law, when he was almost fourteen, Michael began the learning of Latin once more, this time with the addition of Greek grammar. A good deal of what he had known three years before came to mind as he pursued his studies. If he was going to school at all, he was going to excel. Since he enjoyed having the approval of his schoolmates and of his elders, he worked hard.

In August, 1646, Edward sold his house and home lot to Samuel Wilson,[43] for it was impossible for him in his lameness to maintain his property. He would need money for food and clothing, too. It is not clear where the Wigglesworths lived for the next year and a half, except that they were some distance from the church. On February 14, 1648, however, Robert Newman, the ruling elder, proposed in General Court "that they would grant brother Wiggelsworth a small pec of ground neare the meeting-house, to sett him a little house upon and make hime a garden, because he is so lame that he is not able to come to the meeting, and so is many times deprived of the ordinances, when if he was neare he might enjoye them. The courte considering and pittying his case, inclined to doe it & left it to the dispose of them whoe are intrusted to dispose of lotts in the towne."[44]

Three weeks later Edward was selling more of his property—"six acres of upland ground lying in the Yorksheir quarter within the two myle. . . ." Edward's shrewdness as a business man now appeared: ". . . whereas in the towne books their is but 22 acres and a halfe of land placed upon Ed. Wigglesworths lott, bothe for estate and persons, and yett he had layd oute and hathe sould 24 acres, he declared that the acre and a halfe, which makes it 24 acres, was given him in allowance for shortnes in his home lott."[45] Actually the record of July 5, 1643, shows the shortage to have occurred in the apportionment of meadowland, but Edward was going to have his due, even though his memory in some respects was not exactly trustworthy.

In this year of 1648 Ezekiel Cheever having declared Michael prepared for college, Edward decided to send him, no matter what the cost. In the two and three-quarters years since Michael had resumed his studies, he had learned to understand at sight any passage from Cicero (the orations against Cataline, the essays *De Amicitia* and *De Senectute*); he had developed skill in writing Latin, not only ordinary prose, but verse as well; and he was able to speak Latin fluently, both in prepared oration and in extempore conversation. In addition to all this, he had mastered Greek paradigms: he could decline the nouns and conjugate the verbs without mistake in that richly inflected language. Counting the time before he had dropped out to help his father, this had all been accomplished in less than five years. And he was not yet seventeen. Cheever had been strict with him and solidly religious, had given him incidental high moral instruction. The credit, however, rested with the boy himself. He was determined to catch up to and, if possible, outshine his peers, for he was somewhat vain and needed the plaudits of his companions.

His was not altogether an unusual performance. Many youngsters both in New England and in Old entered college in those days even before the age of seventeen. Increase Mather, for example, was to be only twelve. No doubt, if

[18]

Michael had not been required to help out at home, he would have been able to equal this record. In behavior he was an average good boy, guilty of no "scandalous sins," but he admitted later that he was self-centered, that he sought promotion and pre-eminence above everything else to satisfy his self-esteem.[46] He knew he was bright, and he wanted everyone else to know it, too.

Ever since September, 1645, most New Haven citizens had been contributing to the college at Cambridge near Boston. Soon after John Harvard's bequest the college had been called "Harvard" and its town—"Newtowne" at first—had been renamed. In a session of the commissioners of the United Colonies, the Cambridge pastor, Thomas Shepard, had suggested that every able family in the area be asked to send in a quarter part of a bushel of grain each year for the support of the poor scholars at the college. New Haven wanted its boys to have more than a Latin school education; therefore the contributions were regular.[47] And it sent some of its sons to the college: Nathaniel Brewster of the first graduating class; Robert Johnson three years later; and Isaac Allerton, in the class before Michael's.[48] Several others began their studies, but for one reason or another dropped out without taking their degrees. The desire for cultivated leaders was in the air. It is to Edward's credit that, no matter at what expense, he would send Michael to college.

Michael was leaving the most conservative kind of Puritan environment. He himself was not yet a professing member of the church, but his upbringing had been of the most careful order, and he was familiar with the long sermons twice on Sunday, the lectures, the private meetings, and the catechizing. His father and mother were orthodox and strict. On the other hand, the world he was about to enter was beginning to show signs of being otherwise.

In December, 1641, the General Court of Massachusetts Bay had accepted the "Body of Liberties" which they had authorized Nathaniel Ward of Ipswich, the humorous but somewhat irascible "Cobbler of Aggawam," to draw up.

[19]

Among its hundred provisions were statutes against monopolies and against the restriction of lands that the medieval feudal system had imposed. It provided for much less red tape in processes of court than the colonists had known in England. Though it assured these settlers that they would still be guaranteed trial by jury and the justice of due process of law, there was still medieval influence in the enumeration of crimes which in the eyes of these New World Puritans justified death according to the Word of God: treason and murder were listed, of course, and sex crimes such as bestiality, sodomy, and adultery; the others were man-stealing, false witness, idolatry, witchcraft, and blasphemy.[49] How blindingly glow the Ten Commandments in this catalogue! This was a Bible state, and the Bible was law.

For a decade after the first migration in 1630 the citizens on John Winthrop's hill appeared to be flourishing, but with the outbreak of the wars in England fortune had shifted its weight.[50] Massachusetts Bay would inevitably remain neutral in the battles between the Cavaliers and the Roundheads, though the latter elicited the sympathy of the colony because they were against papistic practice. Following the faith of Governor Winthrop, the Bay plantations considered themselves still part of the Church of England, but a "purified" part. Further, the Governor did not think of himself at all as a Separatist like the Plymouth Pilgrims. In England the Roundheads were divided into two camps: those that stayed loyal to the Established Church unfortunately (for Massachusetts) shifted from a hierarchy of bishops to a governing presbytery; on the other hand, those who declared themselves independent of the Established Church grew tolerant of any sect so long as it was Protestant and unattached. The position of the churches in Massachusetts Bay was that, though considering themselves still a part of the Church of England, they were unwilling to be governed by any organization outside their individual selves and that, having found a place where they could keep their light glowing, they were set on proving theirs the only true beacon, to permit no distracting, competing flame. Toleration would lead to admission into the inner circle of anyone who had not committed an open sin; public profession and proof of faith would no longer be necessary. Such loosening of the tests would mean eventual defeat of the cause.

As the Roundheads began to demonstrate their strength in the English conflicts, not only did migration to the new colony come almost to a halt, but colonists, discouraged by the rugged life in the wilderness and full of hope for the future back in England, began going home in alarming numbers. The result was serious economic depression. Since there were no longer newcomers to buy goods manufactured in Massachusetts, there was a scarcity of money for the purchase of foreign materials. As much as possible now had to be made at home: the weaving of textiles became a household chore; Nathaniel Ward's law against monopolies had to be relaxed to allow for the manufacture of iron and salt. Products of natural resources, formerly sold to English immigrants, had to find other markets: fish, hides, lumber, cattle—all eventually found sale in the West Indies, in Nova Scotia, even in Spain, Portugal, and the Azores. Such a widening market required the building of more ships. Here was the beginning of the impressive world-wide trade that was to bring wealth, culture, and sophistication to New England.

Other changes were taking place in the world outside Michael Wigglesworth's tight little New Haven. On May 6, 1646, Robert Child, physician of Cambridge University and continental education who had a genuine interest in Massachusetts even though he spent all told very little time there, was the first of seven petitioners to sign a document making a plea for greater toleration. Two weeks later it was rejected by the General Court and the Assistants (judges and magistrates), who felt that it would be the devastation of the government, the undoing of the hard-achieved New Jerusalem, to admit the clauses of this *Remonstrance and Petition to the General Court.* The doctrine of predestination and its accompanying privileges had been attacked as a suppression of liberty. Its authority based on closely argued interpretation of the Word of God, the Bible state had been denounced as arbitrary, possibly inhumane, subject to man's own fallibility. When the *Petition* made the forthright request that "all truly English" be permitted either to join existing churches or to form congregations of their own in accordance with practices now current in England, the Court was aghast. A government based on impartial law, the right to vote extended no telling how far, toleration of sects of varying degrees of unorthodoxy—no, such radical departure from principle would wreak havoc, total havoc, on God's clear purpose in New England. Fines were levied. Dr. Child paid fifty pounds (equal to two and a half years' starting salary for Ezekiel Cheever in New Haven). Later, when it was learned that Child was about to carry the *Petition* to England, fearing lest they lose stature in London, the Court clapped the doctor in jail and fined him further. One of his colleagues, Thomas Fowle, however, did get away to England with a copy of the fiery document.

The General Court would never have admitted that Child's paper had made any difference in the least. Non-freemen had none the less been brought to realize that they might have rights. After all, they were made to attend a church they could not be admitted to membership in, and they were being taxed to support a government they had no voice in. Political consciousness was beginning to bud.

In the very next year, modern democracy began a modest break-through into the medieval authoritarianism of the founding fathers. Seventeen years after John Winthrop and his followers had set up the Bible state with its stringently restricted electorate, the General Court, though closing its eyes to the influence of Child, passed a township act by which non-freemen, if they had attained twenty-one years and were willing to swear a loyalty oath to the colony, could take a more active part in the managing of local affairs. Now they could serve on juries; they could even stand for election as selectmen for their towns; and in town meeting they could have their say and cast their ballots on such matters as the herding of cattle, the assessment of local taxes, the organization of schools, the distribution of land, and the laying out of roads. In the matter of age there was little likelihood of cheating, but what about the loyalty oath? Eager for power, any hypocrite could swear fealty to the government—and then go about his selfish, undermining business, for loyalty oaths never have to have any value. But even so, in 1647 the liberalizing movement toward recognition of the rights of man was gathering momentum in Massachusetts.

In the early summer of the next year the ministers of the colony came together at Cambridge to decide on the entire matter of church discipline—how far the churches could safely go in relaxing their hold on the life of the whole community. A synod drew up *A Platform of Church Discipline,* in which, by a move that would help their case in the now-established powerful grip of the Roundheads on the reins of England, they agreed in matters of faith with the Westminster Confession. The *Platform,* however, differed from the Confession concerning the relation of the churches to each other and to the civil government. There was mutual agreement that pastors and teachers in the churches should not interfere with civil business and in turn would have full control over the affairs of their individual organizations. As it worked out, the ministers were able to wield considerable influence in government, for they were often the men with the best education in a town. As a result, though without formal authority, they could, and did, sway the thinking of the townsmen through sermons, counseling, and mere passing conversation, but the situation was not the same as when the minister through divine will and interpretation of God's Word had been obeyed without question.

The Cambridge *Platform* also dealt with the knotty problem of church membership. The "visible saints" who had gathered the original churches and—here a dozen or so years later—those of their children who had made public profes-

sion of faith could be classified as "holy." Nothing was said
of those honest young people who could not bring themselves to admitting complete agreement with the Puritan
tenets as held in Massachusetts, and no mention was made
of what would happen to *their* children. Nevertheless, the
churches had to go on. They would have to depend on these
descendants of the original "saints" for continuing strength.
The ministers assembled agreed that leaning on sons and
grandsons of the founders could lead to some hypocrisy, but
what to do? This was a contingency unforeseen in 1630. If
men wanted a part in the government and had to belong to
the church to get it, now after the first wave of enthusiasm
and sincerity had broken and drawn back, the unscrupulous
could conceivably swear to any loyalty oath to gain their
ends.

The synod's problems were complex. There had to be men
and women to take the place of those who through infirmity
and death were no longer available for maintaining this
utopian experiment in Christian living. Whether thoroughly
convinced of all the original tenets or not, succeeding generations had to be brought into the fold. There were other
problems. Presbyterians, Anabaptists, and other deviators,
who were becoming more and more vocal, had to be met.
The doctrines of predestination and its accompanying atone-
ment only for the select few had to be carried high and
assuredly. Further, it was necessary to guard against sugges-
tion of any magical qualities in the ordinances: baptism and
the Lord's Supper were signs only, outwardly demonstrating
inner grace, seals of a covenant between God and His elect.

This was the situation when Michael Wigglesworth came
up to Harvard. Because of the economic setbacks produced
by the return of settlers to England, money was not easy to
come by, but Edward was willing to make any sacrifice to
give Michael an advantage. Partly because of the admission
of non-church members to the administration of local governments, the clergy, at least on the face of things, were beginning to lose their old prestige. Other vocations were

offering attractions to young men. The idea of becoming a minister did not occur very seriously to Michael. Rather, he was inclined toward the practice of medicine. According to the Cambridge *Platform,* he was not even "holy," for he had not made a public profession, nor had he offered proof to the New Haven church that he had been foreordained for salvation. He had had a strict family upbringing, however, and he had had Ezekiel Cheever's thorough college preparatory course in Latin and Greek. In the summer of 1648, not yet seventeen, he left his badly crippled father, his mother, and his seven-year-old sister to enroll as a freshman at Harvard.

II. Harvard Yard

Cambridge was a long way from New Haven. Michael had never been separated before from his family and friends. At Harvard he knew no one except the three or four New Haven boys enrolled there, including John Davis, in his class. The others in the entering group were from towns near Cambridge: Dorchester, Scituate, Newbury, Boston.

Having been an assiduous and bright scholar under Cheever, Michael passed the oral examination administered to all would-be freshmen by President Dunster and the college tutors.[51] Like other beginning students he made a list of the laws of the college, copying them out to make them stick in the mind, and presented them for the President's signature. Tuition amounted to one pound six shillings eight pence a year, and students were charged for room and board and for the making of their beds.

Michael was assigned to a room on the second floor of the college building with two or three others. Then, having paid the steward a shilling to have his name posted in the buttery, he was ready for three years of undergraduate life. Food and drink he would pay for in quarterly assessments. He would be expected as freshman to run errands for the upperclassmen and to do menial duties in the hall. For one thing, he would bring from the buttery to his elders their "morning bever," the bread and beer on which they breakfasted.[52]

The structure in which he would live and study had been completed in the summer of 1642, just before commencement. It was shaped like a large E, the long hall being used for meals, for prayers, and for lectures, the long room above being generally assigned to freshmen. The wings contained the kitchen and five large rooms for students. The staircase was at the center of the court. The building had not been sturdily constructed, however, for even by the time of Michael's matriculation, though only six years old, it was beginning to deteriorate.

In fact, the twelve-year history of the college had been a story of struggle, of sinking and recovery. Nathaniel Eaton, a younger brother of the Governor of New Haven, had been the first master, but had lasted only a little over a year, for he and his wife not only had mismanaged the scanty funds but had been cruel to the students. For a whole year following Eaton's dismissal in August, 1639, the college had been deserted.

On August 27, 1640, the Overseers had invited Henry Dunster to become the first President. This had proved to be a fortunate move. In spite of the depression of the 1640's Dunster had made progress in the development of the institution. He had only just arrived from England when he had been approached by the Overseers. Reared on a farm in Lancaster, he had worked his way through Magdalene College, Cambridge, and had served variously as curate and schoolmaster after graduation. Now at thirty-one he had tackled this challenging job of making firm the establishment of a college in New England, which he naturally modeled, with necessary departures, on the colleges at Oxford and Cambridge.

At first he had done all the teaching as well as the fundraising. Several of Eaton's disillusioned students had returned for their second year's study, and a class of four had been matriculated as freshmen. Dunster had introduced a three-year course leading to the Bachelor of Arts degree, the subjects being roughly related to those of the universities of Europe: the medieval liberal arts and philosophies, the Renaissance addition of the classical *bonae litterae,* and the "learned" tongues.[53] That he should have dared to grant degrees at all had been bold, for this was a prerogative in England accruing to King Charles alone.[54]

Besides the fees paid by the students, the income of the little college was not abundant. Dunster had financial problems during his entire term. His average budget was one hundred seventy-five pounds, his own salary amounting to fifty-five pounds. Between thirty and forty pounds came in each year from the Boston-Charlestown ferry, this source having been granted the college at the time of Dunster's installation. Back in October, 1636, when the General Court had legislated the college into being, four hundred pounds had been allocated to the construction of the building, two hundred within the ensuing year, the rest at its completion. Because of other problems—Anne Hutchinson's trial and a war with the Pequot Indians—it had not been until November, 1637, that six magistrates and six ministers had been appointed as the first Board of Overseers and not until the following May that Nathaniel Eaton had been selected as master. So the first building had not been finished until Dunster had been in office almost two years.[55]

In this trying time Dunster had had the guidance and inspiration of Thomas Shepard, pastor of the church in Cambridge. Himself a truly godly man, Shepard had exercised a steadying influence over the students, who, of course, were required to attend his services on Sunday, and he had worked unceasingly for the prosperity of the college, as when in 1644 he had requested and secured the collection of "college corn" for the poor scholars. But by the time young Wigglesworth came to Cambridge, the first excitement about the founding of the institution was abating. For one thing, with the ascendancy of the Puritans in England some of the graduates were returning with many other men across the Atlantic in pursuit of what they felt were more rewarding careers. Taxpayers who remained in New England could not see any wisdom in parting with good grain for the education of young men who would desert them as soon as they had

[28]

received their degrees. Things had come to such a pass, indeed, that in the summer in which Michael entered Harvard there was no commencement, for there were no seniors at all, and at the end of his freshman year there were only five graduates.[56] Clearly, the college was losing ground again. Not only was the building in bad need of repair, but Dunster announced that the library was weak all around, especially in the subjects of physics, philosophy, and mathematics.

This report reflected the point of view of the founders, who did not intend their college to be a theological school, but rather a place for both the preservation and the advancement of learning—in other words, the education of gentlemen. True, *New Englands First Fruits,* published in 1645 as propaganda in London, had expressed their dread of leaving "an illiterate Ministry to the Churches." Furthermore, one of the college laws, which all freshmen were expected to make copies of, made it clear that Chirst should come first, that the pursuit of knowledge without primary intention of glorifying God was sinful. Still, however emphasized throughout this holy commonwealth, religion was considered in the curriculum as simply one of the disciplines in which a young gentleman should be well versed, even though he did not intend to prepare himself for the clerical profession. In his petition for more books for the library Dunster explained that he wanted to supply background material for "all professions." Further, when he achieved the charter of 1650, it did not mention specific ministerial training, but made a point of "the advancement of all good literature artes and Sciences."[57]

Michael was not headed for the ministry. Rather vaguely he thought of himself as a physician, but first of all he was intent on acquiring a sound general education. His motives, he confessed later, were not altogether pure: he may have perjured himself in copying out the college law about Christ as the foundation of all learning, for he had not yet been made a member of the church and was the haughty victim of the sin of pride—to hear him tell it. Several years later he

[29]

was to write: "When I came first to the College, . . . I had a naughty vile heart and . . . could propound no Right and noble ends to myself, but acted from self and for self. . . ." He was not a bad boy, as boys go; yet his chief preoccupation was in "honor & applause & Preferment & such Poor Beggarly ends." Because of this compulsion he applied himself prodigiously and was the intellectual leader of his class.[58] He had later to learn that excessive pride in scholarly attainment was risky in the prospect of eternity.

> Go on you nobler Brains, and fill your sight
> As full of Learning as the Sun's of light;
> Expand your Souls to Truth as wide as Day,
> Know all that Men, know all that Angels say,
> Write shops of Volumns, and let every Book
> Be fill'd with lustre as was Moses look:
> Yet know, all this is but a better kind
> Of sublime vanity, and more refin'd:
> Except a saving knowledge crown the rest,
> Devils know more, and yet shall ne'r be blest.
>
> (Mole-hill)

The three-year curriculum emphasized logic and rhetoric, Greek and Hebrew, and ethics and metaphysics. Its weaknesses lay in the areas of natural science and mathematics. (Isaac Newton was just six years old when Michael entered college.) Since all students had been prepared in Latin schools, a knowledge of Cicero was taken for granted. Through logic they were taught how to think; through rhetoric, how to be compelling in communication. Their Greek studies introduced them not only to the New Testament, but to Isocrates, Hesiod, and Homer. They were given a thorough grounding in Hebrew partly because the Old Testament played a large part in Puritan theology and partly because Dunster knew and enjoyed the language! In ethics they were guided largely by Aristotle.[59] Generally speaking, to Dunster's credit, the approach to these studies was temperate, though not skeptical. There was, however, room for some differences of opinion.[60]

For six hundred years the universities of Europe had fol-

[30]

lowed such a curriculum. Even the commencement theses were identical. Harvard students were also required to emulate their European predecessors by using Latin constantly, even in informal exchange, except during stated periods of recreation.[61] The college was doing its utmost, in the wilderness that was New England, to give its students the best that had been thought and said in the world up to that time. Limited though it was in science, it was laying the foundation for eighteenth-century acceptance of Newton's mechanical view of nature.[62]

In setting up the week's program for his students, Dunster tried to follow the plan of Petrus Ramus at the University of Paris in the preceding century, that is, devoting an entire day to a single subject. This was not easy, because Dunster for several years was himself the only teacher, and it was a serious problem to juggle successfully the programs for all three classes. He did not have to endure the drudgery of paper grading, however, for all examinations were oral. Scholars were then judged by his opinion of their ability and earnestness.

The student was expected very early in the course to compile or copy a "system" or outline. Such practice gave him a preview of the subject as well as pegs on which to hang notes as he proceeded through the study. A synopsis was often extremely complex, following Ramus in classifying, defining, and making neat branches.

Then came the digestion of the textbooks, purchased either from former users or from the bookseller in Boston. Most of them were in Latin, which every student was supposedly fluent in. Dunster would read aloud from the texts; the boys would read the books for themselves; there would follow questions and answers and, finally, debate, all based on the matter of the texts. It was in debate that varying attitudes were tolerated, philosophical differences aired. Then in the art of communication great emphasis was placed on declamation.[63] There were no electives; all members of a class studied the same subjects; so there was ample common ground for discussion and intellectual exercise. Dunster's medieval system of no electives had its limitations, but what his best pupils learned was solid; they emerged well disciplined, no mere superficial dilettantes.

By the time Michael came to Harvard, Dunster had found funds to employ two or three tutors, who could relieve him of the heavy teaching load. As a rule a tutor had recently acquired his Bachelor's degree and was staying on only until he was called to ordination by some church. His pay was small—eight, ten, twelve pounds a year. Even more than masters in our own preparatory schools, he was with his charges almost constantly, being responsible for both their intellectual growth and their spiritual and moral well-being, too.[64] Michael's class was assigned to Jonathan Mitchell as tutor. It was Mitchell's responsibility to teach his pupils every subject. (There were no specialists segregated into departments in this seventeenth-century institution. Rather there was quietly achieved a cutting across disciplines to get at the whole of knowledge.) Michael became fondly attached to his tutor. In after years when Mitchell was a famous preacher, the friendship continued.[65] The fact that Mitchell too was originally from Yorkshire may have helped make the bond a close one.

Mitchell, then, led his little flock through the devious paths of logic for the first three quarters of their freshman year, physics for the fourth, or summer, quarter; through Greek grammar, emphasizing chiefly the derivation of words and the structure of sentences; through Hebrew grammar and readings from the Old Testament; and through rhetoric with its accompanying practice in declamation. This was a rigorous six-day schedule, for on Saturday morning the boys were expected to be skilled in answering questions from the catechism and in the afternoon, spring and summer, to study botany; fall and winter, history. Monday afternoons were given over to preparations and to debate, in which the pupils practiced what they had learned of logic in the morning.[66]

In 1649 death took away men of great, though differing,

influence in Massachusetts Bay. On March 26—Michael was still a freshman—John Winthrop died. Winthrop had been the leader of the original migration in 1630. It had been he who described the experiment in New England as "a city upon a hill" which would set an example of the ideal government for Puritans everywhere. John Hull, the Boston merchant, reflected on the esteem with which Winthrop had been almost universally regarded, "our honored governor, Mr. John Winthrop, departed this life,—a man of great humility and piety, an excellent statesman, well skilled in law, and of a public spirit."[67] Winthrop had had his differences with other Puritan leaders, but he would be genuinely missed from the community. Already, of course, the light of his ideal Bible government was beginning to dim. Though Michael probably had had no contact with Winthrop, the Bay area, where Michael was to live, had been profoundly influenced by this Governor's thought and action. A dozen years later Michael was to write his own tribute to Winthrop and his colleagues:

> Our governor was of our selves
> And all his Bretheren,
> For wisdom & true piety,
> Select, & chosen men.
> Who, Ruling in the fear of God,
> The righteous cause maintained,
> And all injurious violence,
> And wickedness, restrained.
>   (God's Con)

The second death of an influential New Englander came after the Harvard commencement in August. Michael was now a junior sophister. Thomas Shepard died on August 25, fourteen years after his arrival in Boston in 1635. He had been invited immediately to Newtowne (Cambridge), where early in February, 1636, a church had been gathered and Shepard had been ordained as pastor. He had remained there for the rest of his life. Not physically impressive, he nevertheless had been a persuasive preacher, greatly beloved by his congregation. His had been the church Harvard students attended. Michael Wigglesworth had been under his irresistible power for his entire first year at college. Though the boy was not yet nineteen and not yet ready to make open profession and be accepted into full membership in the church, the seed of his ultimate "conversion" had surely been sown by this saintly man.

In May, Boston had heard of the beheading of Charles I on January 30. That the news had taken so long to reach New England may be explained by the wintry seas and by the probably more significant decrease in interest in westward migration now that England was in the hands of the Puritans. John Hull had not been sure that the execution of the King had been based on sound reasoning: "God alone can work good by so great a change, both to the nation and to the posterity of the King."[68]

In Michael's second year the schedule was no easier. Aristotle and various traditional manuals guided him and his classmates through the mazes of ethics and politics. In Greek he mastered the principles of prosody and of the varying dialects, translated the poets into Latin, and practiced the writing of Greek verse himself. From the Hebrew of his first year he now moved to the study of Aramaic with readings in the books of *Ezra* and *Daniel*. Fridays were devoted to further studies in rhetoric and the hour of declamation in which the entire student body participated. Second-year students too, like freshmen, were responsible for the catechism on Saturday mornings, and they too, like the other two classes, had their hour of debate ("disputations") on Monday afternoons.

To conquer these formidable foes, fairly rigid discipline was necessary. Though the young men were not allowed to light their candles before four o'clock in the morning, they were expected to be up and about at five. After prayers came breakfast, the bread and beer of "morning bever." Before the first lecture at eight o'clock there was time for about an hour of study. Each of the three classes had a lecture during

[34]

the morning. They heard their tutor read to them from the required text, on which they took notes if they did not follow the reading with a book of their own. At eleven came the mid-day meal, more bread and beer with the addition of meat—chiefly beef, varied with veal, pork, lamb, and mutton. Now and then apples appeared on the tables, and occasionally peas. The meal began with asking God's blessing and ended with thanks. The Fellows in residence and the Fellow-Commoners (well-to-do young men who did not intend to take degrees) sat at the head table decorated with silver and marked by the presence of the "great salt," gift of Richard Harris of the class of 1644, still to be seen at Harvard. The undergraduates ate from wooden trenchers and drank their beer from pewter cups. They were expected to bring their own knives and spoons. No one used forks. Since it was the custom to dine with hat on head, to be required to sit at table with head uncovered was a natural device for punishment. After the meal came an hour of recreation, which the boys passed usually in conversation—probably in English rather than the classroom and study Latin—and walking about the Yard. In the afternoon were oral quizzes in the tutor's room on the morning's lecture and more classes and debates. Late in the afternoon they enjoyed another bever followed by evening prayers and another study hour. After supper, from half past seven to nine, the students were free to relax. With permission they could "watch," that is, sit up till eleven reading by candlelight.[69]

There was not a great deal of variety in their extracurricular activities, none of the highly organized sports or student governments or specific-interest clubs that tempt modern-day students to waste too much of their time. For the most part, they were expected to stay within the confines of the Yard, though in summer they did go swimming and in the winter skated on the Charles River or on nearby ponds. To play cards was a serious offense, for it smacked of the sin of idleness. They sang ballads and played on musical instruments, but were not encouraged in such practice: no glee clubs or

[35]

orchestras would have been countenanced. But there was some mischief. After all, these youngsters, many of them younger than college boys of this century, were not devoid of animal spirits, even though they had heard all their lives of the evils of the flesh. Seaborn Cotton, one of Michael's classmates, actually wrote out some bawdy verses in his notebook. An occasional practical joke or broken window or even a brawl with the town folk punctuated the routine. In spite of rules against entering taverns, against associating with soldiers, drunkards, and prostitutes, there were occasional transgressions. College was in session twelve months a year, without vacations. Now and then a student would be allowed to go home to visit his parents, but generally the boys remained in Cambridge in the college Yard.[70] There is no record that Michael ever left town during his three-year course or that he ever disobeyed a college law. It is hard to believe that he never enjoyed any of the gaieties of youth despite his patent seriousness, but there is nothing to show that he did.

In the spring of Michael's second year, President Dunster was able to secure approval from the General Court of a stabilizing charter for Harvard. Signed by Thomas Dudley, the Governor, it provided for an organization composed of the President, a Treasurer, and five Fellows, known formally as the President and Fellows of Harvard College, "The Corporation," and given perpetual succession. Since 1642 there had been a board of Overseers, ministers and magistrates who had had more control than Dunster thought right. The Overseers, however, even under the charter, continued to exercise their power by paying the teaching Fellows, giving orders to the Treasurer, and telling the college servants what their duties were. It was to be the Overseers who would select and install Dunster's successors, Presidents Chauncy and Hoar.

Dunster, though, had put the college on a more businesslike basis than it had known before. He had probably drafted the wording of the charter himself. The holding of teaching

Fellows was not altogether easy, for they were inclined to stay only until something better came along. Samuel Mather and Comfort Starr resigned before the first year under the Corporation was over. Samuel Danforth and Samuel Eaton stayed three or four years. Late in 1650 Urian Oakes was appointed to fill one of the vacancies. The Fellows were not always teachers, however. Jonathan Mitchell remained a Fellow until 1668, even while he was pastor of the church at Cambridge.[71]

From the scant records it would appear that in Michael's senior (third) year about forty undergraduates were in residence at Harvard and about ten candidates for the Master of Arts degree. Michael continued his pursuit of the medieval curriculum. For the first three quarters he studied arithmetic and geometry; in his last summer quarter before commencement he tackled astronomy. (Music, the fourth member of the Quadrivium, was omitted from the course, possibly because of its frequent relation with sin.) On Wednesdays he worked at Greek, seniors being required to have their theory polished "before noone." He was expected in the afternoon to turn out accurate and smooth compositions in Greek, both poetry and prose. The Oriental languages this year were represented by Syriac; after a grounding in grammar he and his classmates were given passages from the Syriac New Testament to flex their minds on by translating them into Latin. As usual, Fridays were devoted to rhetoric and declamations and Saturdays to the catechism ("divinity catechetical").

In addition, seniors on Saturday mornings delivered "commonplaces," short practice sermons in which they drew on all their learning, both in content and delivery. These might be said to have paralleled the courses in synthesis of learning given to many senior classes today. In constructing their sermons, the students followed the procedure set down in the preceding century by Petrus Ramus. Having started with a text from the Bible, they separated it into "arguments," which in turn were rearranged to present the "doctrines"

[37]

the sermon proposed to teach. After each doctrine came the "reasons," which were driven home, made pertinent and personal, by "uses," "exhortations," and "applications."[72] This logical pattern was serviceable in communicating that element of Puritanism which its followers tried to keep under control, that is, the subjective Augustinian piety that, when allowed to have full sway, could lead to such intolerable heresies as Anne Hutchinson's direct contact with her God. But the Puritans recognized a certain degree of inwardness as well as the Calvinist belief in God's election of souls for salvation beyond man's power to say yea or nay. It was the influence of Augustine that led many Puritans to agonize in searching their souls for lurking evil. On the other hand, it was the influence of objective predestination that led Puritan preachers to pursue the logic of Ramus and to cultivate the "plain style," a combination of controlled delivery and content not relying on complex metaphor and conceit but on reason, example, and, where helpful, literary allusion.[73]

In his senior year Michael delivered two declamations on the subject of eloquence, applicable not only to speech but to writing. He copied them later into his notebook,[74] completing the second not until the end of August, 1655, over two years after delivering it. Every student kept a notebook of some sort. Michael's evidently was begun during his last undergraduate year. Into it he copied a number of "systems," some of them with the original author's name. The first entry, in Latin, was probably composed by his classmate from New Haven, John Davis. It consists of a set of preliminary observations on the liberal arts. There follow other Latin outlines—commentaries on dialectics and a comprehensive outline of physics. He copied someone's commencement dissertation of the year before, defending a centuries-old scholastic saw that the reasoning mind or soul is a created thing. Michael entered notes on a book by Scaliger, the Italian-born physician and scholar who had died forty years before, and on several chapters from a book on disputation by the master, Ramus. He began a Greek vocabulary (the

[38]

definitions in Latin), but abandoned that project before finishing the letter *alpha*. Other orations helped to fill over a hundred fifty closely written pages.

The first of his orations on eloquence, probably delivered at nine o'clock on a Friday morning toward the end of 1650, he called "The prayse of Eloquence." Though the ideal, he said, is an unadorned and direct style, the speaker must use enough colorful diction, imagery, and emotional appeal to move his listener. "Look as a mighty river augmented with excessive rains or winter snows swelling above its wonted channel bear's down banks and bridges, overflows feilds and hedges, sweeps away all before it, that might obstruct its passage: so Eloquence overturn's, overturn's all things that stand in its way, and carrys them down with the irresistible stream of its controuling power. . . ." Here by means of adjectives and verbs of force and by repetition of *overturn's,* the young orator (age nineteen) was demonstrating the method of drawing the audience toward emotional reaction. Such style is not an off-hand, easy product, he said; nor is delivery, though not depending on elaborate gesture or the shouting of an enthusiast, to be toned down to the point of inaudibility. "A good oration is not made at the first thought, nor scarce at the first writing over. Nor is true Eloquence wont to hurry it out thick and threefould, as if each word: were running for a wadger; nor yet to mutter or whisper it out of a book after a dreaming manner, with such a voice as the orator can scantly heare himself speak; but to utter it with lively affection, to pronounce it distinctly with audible voyce." Michael had read his books well and had all his life listened carefully to excellent preachers: John Davenport in New Haven, President Dunster at the college, Thomas Shepard at the Cambridge church, now succeeded by Michael's friend and tutor, Jonathan Mitchell. Though his oration had made no mention of sermons, in the Puritan community oratory and the pulpit were inseparable.

A few months after his first oration on the subject, he delivered another, this one designed not just to show the

[39]

value of eloquence, but to tackle the practical problem of its consistency and the ways of attaining it. No public speaker, he told his listeners, can be successful unless he "suits his matter to his Auditors, his style to his matter, and his pronunciation to them both." Michael insisted again and again upon the simple truth that, to be effective, an oration must be heard and understood. Though eloquence is "a more refined and noble kind of speech" than one would use in everyday conversation, he should remember that "two plain words are of more worth than 20 that cannot be understood." On the premise that teaching is his main purpose, an orator should present a logical expression of what he has in mind, should appeal to the emotions of his audience, and should take pleasure in winning "the good will and attention of his hearers."

Michael had absorbed the Puritan faith in the efficacy and therefore the sacredness of the word, but the word spoken—and, as it turned out for him, written—clearly and vigorously. "Some there are that treat of great and weighty matters after a careless, slothful and supinely-negligent fashion, as if they were indifferent whether they speak it or left it alone. It would grieve any man to see how by their ill handling they mar all they meddle with. Where there should be nothing but lightning and thunderbolts of logical Argumentation discharged against Engines of Rhetorical figures and Dialogismos, where there should be tempests and earthquakes of vehement affections, why there they are as lifeless as a frozen snail in the dead of winter. There's no strength of reason, no flourishing invention, no structure of words, no choice of expression, no vigor of affection in what they say. . . ." Oratory—and writing—placed serious obligations on the sincere man.

Michael had more to say. There was no place for obscurity in public speech and no place for the long and distracting narrative illustration. If the poets of the time (he would be referring to such men as Donne, Herrick, Vaughan, Herbert, Crashaw, Quarles) resorted to "catachrestical and strained metaphors, far-fetched allusions, audacious and lofty expression," that was their privilege. Distortions and conceits had no part in the language and sentence structure of persuasive discourse. "Such lincy-woolsy wil never pass currently in the room of broadcloth." (He was using here a homely reference that all could understand.) A speaker must guard against "newcoined, uncouth, exotic allusions. . . . Such as these bewilder the auditor amongst their winding, crooked, periphrastical circumlocutions, and dark allegorical mysteries, like a poor traveler that's benighted in a thick wood, and hath lost his aim so that he knows not East from West."

The second part of this senior dissertation Michael devoted to explaining that a student will achieve eloquence only "by precept, practice, and imitation." Naturally, Ramus would be the best guide.

Lest his fellow students feel that the order was too large, he followed this elaborate discussion with exhortation and encouragement. "Gird we up our loins then, and pluck up our spirits, that we may tread in the steps of such as have gone before us. Those that have been famous as for other endowments, so for their skill to speak well, let us follow after them as far as we can, though at a great distance. Away then with sloth and negligence, we have examples to quicken us: Away with despondency, we have examples to encourage us. Object not to difficulties; difficulties may be mastered. The fragrant rose grows upon a thorny bush; the sweetest nuts have a shell to break before you come at the kernel. *Difficilia pulchra.*" Even difficulties can be beautiful, if only one will realize that they make the goal worth while.

After such a flight of emotion and imagination, Michael concluded gently, if a little ungrammatically: "Finally (my courteous Auditors) & with this word I shall close, Consider that not so much I press you to these things, as your own welfare: which if they be duely attended the profit & credit, & comfort wil be your owne." The Puritan was concerned with the glory of God, yes, but he was duty-bound to cultivate his God-given talents and thus incidentally accumulate honors for himself.

This oration would appear to support a Puritan *credo* of

moderation in everything except the love of God: mediocrity had no place, but neither did excess. Consumption of beer and wine was taken for granted; satisfaction of biological urges was natural; the pursuit of material comforts was the sensible course; and, as here, even oratory should seek emotional appeal. All these matters, however, should be undertaken with balance; emotion and reason should meet on equal terms. The modern tendency to assign a harshly restrictive zeal to New England's Puritans is based on false assumptions. There was instead a possibly surprising relation among them to the Greek ideal of temperance in all things: nothing too much. The eighteenth century is often considered the period of neo-classicism, but its roots were firmly implanted in Wigglesworth's seventeenth century. The Puritan concept of sin was, therefore, two-fold: excess in love of the worldly, and moderation in the love of God, in which there could be no excess.

Though he knew all the devices for an effective sermon and knew when a preacher was applying pressure, Michael had not theorized himself out of capacity for reasonable and emotional reaction to a pastor's call to salvation. Some time after the beginning of his senior year he experienced the necessary conversion under Mitchell, convinced the members of the Cambridge church that he was sincere, made his public profession, and was admitted to full membership. Though he had thought he would be a physician, he had done well not only in foreign languages, in arithmetic and geometry, in botany, astronomy, and physics, but also in the Saturday morning "divinity catechetical" and in interpretation of the Scripture in conference with his tutors. He now decided definitely to study for the ministry. Whereas before his conversion he had been, according to his own testimony, egotistical and overweening, now he was convinced that God was the center, that seeking the praise of men was sinful.[75]

Before commencement President Dunster had his seniors follow the medieval custom of remaining in the college hall for two weeks from nine to eleven every morning and on some afternoons. The ordeal was not quite so trying for Harvard boys as for their European predecessors, for they were allowed to sit. During this period they were called "Questionists" and were required to answer interrogations from "all Commers." Scholars of the Middle Ages had been examined on the works of Aristotle. Harvard scholars were asked about anything in the curriculum. Called "the sitting of solstices," these final oral examinations were generally conducted by the ministers and magistrates of the Board of Overseers, but in their absence President Dunster kept the fire burning.[76]

In 1651 during the solstice Michael presented an oration apparently formally prepared. If so, the "questions" were not necessarily impromptu. Michael's special task was to discuss human anatomy in a two-part speech called *De Microcosmo,* copied into his notebook the next year on twenty-three very full pages. Not content with describing the nature of the body, good Puritan that he was, he went on at considerable length about the soul, for in this life the one was inconceivable without the other. Having had a career in medicine in mind, he had given special attention to this problem.

He obviously acquitted himself well, for he was graduated in August at the head of his class.[77] Later in the history of the college, commencement lists were arranged according to family and social standing. The Cottons, the Dudleys, and the Chauncys certainly would have outranked a Wigglesworth in any *Social Register* of mid-seventeenth-century New England, though Michael's father, energetic and respected, might have achieved commendable position in New Haven if he had not so early been stricken. As it was, however, driven by a fusion of pride and the ideal Puritan responsibility to work hard, Michael had risen to the top of his class and stayed there. His own bodily frailities (for he never was a strong boy) may have accounted in part for his success in the classroom as he attempted to compensate for unimpressive physique.

Commencement in 1651 was set for the second Tuesday in

August, the twelfth of the month. As usual, all alumni, magistrates, and ministers in New England were invited, for the steward, relying on the three-pound fee paid by each candidate, had laid in a large supply of provisions—a great roast of beef with sack being the main attraction at the noontime feast. The Bachelors' ceremony was in the morning. No program for 1651 is extant, but it can be reconstructed. After a salutatory address (in Latin, of course) by one of the clergymen, the seniors began their orations and disputations on the propositions listed on the thesis sheets.[78] Michael's own part, also in Latin, was a dissertation in physics grandly entitled *Omnis Natura inconstans est porosa,*[79] in which he defended the idea that without a vacuum there could be no generation, corruption, transmutation, condensation, contraction, or even locomotion. The discussion was filled with allusions to his really wide reading. At the conclusion of the candidates' parts, President Dunster proposed their names to the Overseers for their consent and then granted the degrees. After the ceremonies the entire company drew up about the tables and enjoyed the feast of the day.

Michael was not yet twenty when he was made Bachelor of Arts, but at that he was older than most of the other nine members of the class. His being out from under the direction of Ezekiel Cheever in New Haven for nearly four years had put him behind, of course. Henry Butler and John Glover were both his elders, but the others were all probably younger. What happened to him during the next several months is left to guesswork. He did satisfy the steward by paying on September 12 the balance owing the college. The chances are that he spent the winter in New Haven, where now his father, virtually helpless, was living in the cottage near the meeting-house with his wife, Esther, and his eleven-year-old daughter, Abigail.

III. Sir Wigglesworth

President Dunster was having his troubles. Money was not easy to get, for, as the migration from England diminished, indeed reversed itself, there was no hard cash income from new settlers, and the established people had to resort to wampum, beaver, cattle, grain, and other farm produce for barter. In 1652 John Hull set up a mint for the coining of silver, though it was unauthorized and the very act was treasonous.[80]

Furthermore, when the college building began going to pieces, the Corporation publicized the fact, but received very little support, let alone sympathy.[81] Purchase of a neighboring dwelling house, to be called Goffe College after its former owner, eased the space situation a little, fitted out as it was for sleeping and study, but the problem of the preservation of the original structure remained.[82]

Another difficulty was the rapid turnover of teaching Fellows, the members of the Corporation. During Michael's senior year Urian Oakes and John Collins of the class of 1649 had accepted appointments. Oakes stayed on for about three years, but Collins resigned in the summer of 1652.[83] In his place Michael returned to Harvard at a salary of two pounds a quarter.[84]

He was assigned as tutor to the freshman class. This would mean logic, rhetoric, Greek, Hebrew, history, physics, botany, and the "divinity catechetical." Undaunted, he tackled the job as he did everything else—with all his might. Two of his pupils were Eleazar and Increase Mather, sons of Richard, pastor at Dorchester and one of the Overseers. Increase was just twelve years old when he and his brother paid their admission fees the April before Wigglesworth's return.[85]

In addition to his teaching and counseling, Michael was expected to continue his own studies, as he did easily and naturally.[86] He now had free access to the college library, which for the most part had been closed to him as an undergraduate. Of the seven or eight hundred volumes in the collection, a large number concerned theology, with the exception of a good portion of the original gift of John Harvard, who had been a gentleman of comparatively broad and cultivated taste. In his library, over a quarter of the more than four hundred volumes had been published since 1630—up-to-date editions. In addition to the *Satires* of Persius and Juvenal and the comedies of Plautus and Terence were North's Plutarch, Holland's Pliny, and Chapman's Homer. Harvard's catholic selection also included Ascham's *Familiar Epistles,* Bacon's *Essays, Natural History,* and *The Advancement of Learning,* Peacham's *Garden of Eloquence,* William Alabaster's tragedy *Roxana,* and the English poets Wither, Quarles, and Niccols.[87] Though, having made up his mind to become a minister, Michael spent most of his time among the books related to his calling, he had at his disposal these other, more worldly works, which he surely did not ignore altogether. There is even evidence that Quarles may have had a little "influence" over his verse writing at one later point.

Reading for his Master of Arts degree, Michael was on his own; nothing was prescribed. This was a situation the exact opposite of the unbending undergraduate schedule he had emerged from the year before. At the end of the three-year waiting period after receiving the Bachelor's degree, he would be expected to discuss a philosophical problem or give a sample sermon, hand in a synopsis of the liberal arts, and stand up to a pre-arranged question at the commencement ceremony. To meet such a relaxed requirement, many candidates did not return to the Yard until just before the appointed time for the granting of degrees. The three-year interval and the three-pound fee were the most important conditions.[88] Michael was no doubt glad, however, for the opportunity of living at the college as a teaching Fellow, even at low pay. The position had a potential of considerable dignity. No longer listed as "Mr." in the steward's account books, he now was entitled to be called "Sir Wigglesworth." A fully accepted church member, he still was beset with pride, for it is next to impossible to shake off the sin of a lifetime in one quick conversion. One can imagine that he took at least secret pleasure in his new post.

Not only problems of finance, plant, and personnel, but other difficulties as well were besieging the President. To make a Harvard degree as meaningful as one from Oxford or Cambridge, he engineered through the Corporation and the Overseers a rule requiring four years' residence for the Bachelor's degree instead of three. Made just before commencement in August, 1652, the announcement created a furor. Seventeen students withdrew in permanent outrage. Only one man received his degree, for he had evidently been at the college the stipulated minimum of three years ten months.[89] The following summer nine young men who would, under the former rule, have been graduated in this year of 1652 received degrees on one August day, with the understanding that they need wait only two more years for the Master's degree. There must have been a great deal of friction over the new requirement, for the regular class of 1653 was allowed to graduate the next day and to take the next degree in the customary three years.[90] But the move had almost wrecked the college. In 1654 there was only one graduate, and in 1655 only two were granted degrees. It was not until 1656, with the class that Michael had brought through its first studies, that the situation began to simmer down and order began to have its way once more.[91]

In the year of his unemployment Michael may have mastered the art of shorthand, using Thomas Skelton's system, published in 1641.[92] At any rate, whenever he had learned it, in his notebook between his commencement dissertation and his 1652 copy of *De Microcosmo* are some notes on Ramus's *Dialectica,* partly in shorthand. Further, in February, 1655, he began to keep a diary much of which is in the Skelton characters. It is reasonable to assume that he would have spent his leisure in New Haven acquiring a skill as useful as this one. He would be able to make easy transcripts of sermons and lectures and now, in his diary, to entrust extremely personal observations to this generally unfamiliar written language. Because it is principally a record of Michael's daily struggles to be worthy of approaching the throne of God, the diary itself is an incomparable source of emotional history, though admittedly the constant writhings become tedious for a casual reader.

Two things bothered him a great deal: his relationship to his pupils and his duty to God. He had been a Fellow six or eight months, long enough for problems to develop; and he had been a church member two years, long enough for his conscience to become razor sharp. To achieve moderation in his attitude toward his students, in order to cultivate zeal in adoration of his Lord was his version of the ever-present Puritan dilemma.

The earliest entry in the diary sets the complex tone. It was probably written on the first Sunday in February, 1653. If, he reasoned, his recalcitrant pupils grieved him, how much the more must he himself grieve Jesus, because of "my vain thoughts, my detestable pride, my unnatural filthy lust that are so oft and even this day in some measure stirring in me. . . ." Yet he had often "comforted my self with thy love amidst my daily sins." Today, for example, sore troubled by his own problems, he tried to find God in the ordinance of the Lord's Supper, "and this gives me hope." The spiritual as well as the intellectual guide of his assigned students, he took John Haynes and another boy aside and discussed with them "what a blessed thing it was to serve and seek the Lord." (D322)[93]

[48]

Here then was the Puritan's spiritual problem. Although a man must make every effort to gain the reward of salvation, he could actually do nothing but evil and so could only hope for redemption. He could not help sinning, but he should try desperately (or rather hopefully and earnestly) not to sin. He should cultivate his talents and enhance his position on earth, but he should keep his mind on God and His heavenly kingdom.

Young Sir Wigglesworth took his obligations to heart. If at times his worrying appears picayune and even silly, he should not be condemned, for he was carrying Puritan principles to their ideal extreme. He was following the books and beliefs more closely—and more honestly—than were most of his Massachusetts brethren. His diary shows him bold and shy, aggressive and withdrawn, exultant and despondent, not in turn, but all at the same time.[94]

He refrained from scolding some students one Sunday for "profanely laughing aloud," then berated himself for his negligence. In his heart he took pleasure in contemplating how much good he could do for others, "but Lord how little of it is done for thee." He went one day to hear Jonathan Mitchell preach and found the sermon difficult to comprehend. On the subject that "he that believ's not is condemn'd already," it depended too much on logical development, needed more emotional appeal for this twenty-one-year-old auditor. (The balance between the two had presented a nice problem ever since he had started the study of rhetoric.) In spite of "vain thoughts," he worked hard at the sermon, trying to follow Mr. Mitchell's reasoning.

All of a sudden the idea beset him that, if he left the security of Harvard Yard, he would be away from strong influence for the good and would run the risk of losing his devotion to God. The thought made him shudder, for to be cast into outer darkness would be the most dreadful punishment conceivable. He was here facing the eternal predicament of a man of religion: how could he fulfill his obligation to society and remain uncontaminated by the evils of the world?

[49]

He was preparing for the ministry, but he did not have confidence that, as spiritual leader of an isolated community, he could carry on alone. (D322-323)

All these things occurred to him in the first two weeks of February. But they were not all. A further complication developed natural to young men, but to Michael burdensome evidence of mankind's sinful nature. He was so stirred by what he described as "unresistable torments of carnal lusts or provocation unto ejection of seed" that he was unable to devote himself totally to theological reading. For two or three days he fought against physical desire; he tried to pray and to concentrate on the Lord, but again and again pride and "vain thoughts" crowded out the cultivation of humility. When within about a week's time he had two lascivious dreams and "pollution escaped me in my sleep," he was terribly ashamed. After the first experience he begged God "not to make me possess the sin of my youth and give me into the hands of my abomination," but his old affliction of pride prevented his feeling repentance as deeply as he would like. After the second dream, however, a change came over him. He was able to pray; he felt an emotional affinity to the Heavenly Father when reading the Bible; he was able to find comfort in President Dunster's "exposition in the hall" on the text "Let not your hearts be troubled. . . ." (D323-326)

Here was a perfect Puritan in the making. Moderation was the best answer, but sexual urgency in an unmarried man could be only an abomination. To compensate, he was trying to fit his human self into the Procrustean bed of the uncompromisingly spiritual. He realized his tendency to melancholy and unbalanced introspection as well as his disturbing love of the "creature," and he was armed in constant battle against them in his ultimate desire and responsibility to center every thought and deed on God. This was struggle indeed for a youth of twenty-one.

Now began another affliction which was to plague him for over thirty years. He started to complain of an unaccountable bodily weakness, a lassitude which he blamed in part for his inability to fight off "pride and vain thoughts." He was suffering from flatulence and pressure in the spleen. (D325) Though as yet he was able to continue his studies and to travel considerably, his ailment gradually grew worse, until a few years later he was almost completely incapacitated. What his trouble was has remained unidentified. Some of his contemporaries thought it was psychosomatic. No doubt his tendency to the doldrums developed into hypochondria, possibly the result of deep-seated despair of ever reaching perfection, but there was also probably a real organic reason, too, for his infirmities. Now in February he prayed for speedy assistance in the relief of his suffering, but other troubles were getting in the way of a perfect union with the Almighty.

Not least, he was finding his studies dull. On his own, he was reading chiefly theology, but many of the finely argued points in his books were hard to digest and boring to follow. One of many doubts to come now assaulted his thinking: the Puritan emphasis on faith alone. He knew that, to be a good and legal member of the church at Cambridge (or anywhere else), he must swallow whole the doctrine of predestination and complete trust in the merits of Christ (sanctification), but it was next to impossible for him to discount the Arminian heresy that his parents had fled from Yorkshire to avoid, the value of good works in achieving salvation (justification): "I can believe God is willing to justify, but cannot see that he is ready to sanctify." As he thought of death, he knew he was not ready, for he had not assured himself of God's redeeming love. (D326-327) Such struggles continued to beset him for the next four years, at least—the four years of his diary. It is unthinkable that they stopped all at once. Human as he was, he must have fought doubt and heretical ideas for a good many years. For Michael, St. Thomas the Doubter was no comfort. For him doubt was not to be allowed, but smashed.

Not only his own reading, but even the church services wearied him on occasion. They were long; he was young;

there were distractions. One Sunday afternoon he realized in the middle of the sermon that he had not been listening because of his concern over one of his pupils, who was ill. This would never do. While in service, he was obligated to think only of God in heaven. He could never seem to strike the right balance between duty to God and duty to man. Over and over he complained that his involvement with the under-graduates—their successes, failures, and diffidences—would keep his mind from contemplation of the divine. If his young charges failed to do well out of indifference, he was grieved. His dilemma was all-pervasive. "When creatures fail, thy heart fails; when creatures smile, God is undervalued." (D326) Balancing of tensions was an ever-present problem. This was the situation that the Puritan point of view would logically come to.

One of the advantages of serving at Harvard as teaching Fellow was that the entire colony would recognize the tutor's availability for ordination. The pastor's task of evangelizing through sweet, or terrible, reasoning and the teacher's task of explaining doctrine and dogma in public and private session were both held in high esteem in the towns of this New English Zion.

Sir Wigglesworth was invited to be of the ministry at Salem, probably as teacher. Having been settled the year before the Winthrop migration of 1630, Salem had one of the well-established churches of the colony. But Michael had his difficulties: he had also been invited to join Mr. Mitchell in the ministry at Cambridge and had said he was "not ingaged to any others." Though he had not given a promise any-where, his needling Puritan conscience bothered him all the same. "I have sin'd I fear in the salem business, against god & man." (D328) He was constantly afraid of the little lie, the fib. He wanted nothing to blot the white garb of his sanctity. As it turned out, he accepted neither place, but stayed on in the Yard.

Once after hearing Mr. Mitchell preach two sermons on *John* 1:14 ("... the Word was made flesh, and dwelt among us . . ."), he tried very hard to catch a vision of Christ, but failed utterly. He wrote out a long prayer, the theme of which was God as his Father: ". . . thou hast found me when lost, comforted me when destressed, assisted me when unable to do thy will, thy visitations preserv my daly decaying spirits, thy right hand upholds me. Why restore to me the joy of thy salvation; caus thy face to shine upon me and I shall be saved. Put the spirit of a child into me and constantly maintain it, for I fade as a leaff and my iniquitys like the wind take me away." Here he could go no further, for thoughts of his pupils and his other entanglements interrupted. (D329)

This search for a father was going beyond the merely conventional symbol based on New Testament imagery. Michael was having a very personal struggle with his own earthly father. In mid-March, after no little difficulty in finding a horse, he set out with a friend from Cambridge for New Haven. The two of them planned to make Dedham their first stop, but became confused about directions in the wilderness. With only an hour left before nightfall, they came upon a farmhouse whence they were guided on into the settlement of Dedham. By Sunday they were in Pequot (New London), the home of the junior John Winthrop, a man of broad civic and scientific interests, who had developed skill in medicine among other accomplishments. Before reaching Pequot, the travelers had again been lost, but in spite of rugged terrain and rumors of Indian uprisings they had found their way, with, of course, the indispensable help of God. Here Wigglesworth was invited to preach. He chose as his text a verse from *Deuteronomy* 32: "For the Lord's portion is his people. . . ." Solid Puritan that he was struggling to become, he wanted to dwell on the faith of these New Englanders that they were in truth God's chosen ones. This was the young man's first sermon, no doubt long in preparation and now delivered willingly though possibly with characteristic apprehension.

Three days later he and his companion arrived in New

Haven after eight days of jolting travel that had given him extraordinary pain in "back & brest," so that he was forced to pray aloud for strength to endure the journey (and, incidentally, to distract him from self-pity). He stayed with his family about a month, attending faithfully lectures by the teacher, William Hooke, and sermons by the pastor, John Davenport, both of whom had known him as a young boy. As usual, he spent his leisure in clearing out the dark corners of his soul, in berating his "carnal heart," in alternate perplexity and concentration. He recalled how, even before he had become a member of the church at Cambridge, he had never found "substantial soul-content" except in the contemplation of God, but he was still confused: ". . . this prophane heart of mine and my proud heart, are they not my plague? Thou knowest they are a terrour to me and make me so to my self. And wilt not thou deliver from this plague when I cry?" Over and over—the same dread of pride and profane lusts.

He had come home partly to seek his father's advice on accepting a church office, possibly at Hartford. But, in privately listing his sins, he one day admitted to "want of natural affection to my father, in desiring the continuance of his life which God ranks among those sins whereto men were given up of God to a reprobate mind. Lord why hast thou caus'd me to er from thy wayes, or hardened my heart from thy fear?" (Although the Puritans disdained *The Book of Common Prayer*, they frequently echoed its phrases: "We have erred and strayed from thy ways. . . .") Pitifully crippled, his father was given to speaking sternly to his son about his "weak and silly management of every business." A devout believer, Edward was nevertheless a shrewd business man as his modestly increasing estate showed. He could not understand this vacillating son, who, because he had taken to inexorable examination of the soul, could not come to decisions often indispensable in the conduct of daily affairs. One can hardly blame Edward for feeling impatient. A Puritan knew that a man must live in the world as well as seek the Lord. The "Protestant ethic" was here developing.

Edward's constant scoldings raised the hackles of Michael's pride until the opposition was almost intolerable. The young man recorded that his father "makes my savour to stink in my owne nosethrils. This he did most eminently this week immediately after a proud fit of my owne." Michael recognized his own tendency to self-esteem; he felt humbled at his father's reprimands; yet he took offence. He suspected that there was no love in his father's reproof, "because that covers a multitude of infirmitys, but this rakes them open to the bottom." He felt that he should look upon his father's excoriation as growing from a desire to help him, but pride was always at hand to stiffen his back under chastisement. The Fifth Commandment was a hard law. He prayed to God for a cheerful spirit "for healths sake."

Not his father alone, but his mother, too, annoyed him, so much so that he would not always answer when she spoke to him. He seemed helpless in the face of sinfulness, for constant self-reproach and prayer did no good. He was in a bad situation: at college the students would get between him and God; here at home, not only his disagreements with his parents but his leisure—"my eas and slouth and pleasure are getting oft between christ and me." What a net! Whether busy or idle, he could not maintain an attitude of constant adoration.

He was like an athlete during a training period. Just as, on the one hand slackening and indulgence bring mediocre performance, so likewise, on the other, over-training brings tensions that interfere with superior achievement. This was a lesson that mature Puritans had mastered, a lesson that Michael was having to learn slowly through trial and error. Early leaders like Governor Winthrop and Ezekiel Cheever knew the virtues of the middle path. Michael himself would eventually find the mean, as middle age approached. He would even ascribe, with the support of Puritan theory, the quality to God himself:

Measure and moderation
In chastening he respecteth.
(Meat IV.10)

But not yet. For Michael the worldly and the sensual had to be trodden under foot at this stage for him to attain any feeling of spirituality. His father saw all this as one-sided, as unreasonable, as over-training, so to speak.

Michael dreaded the length of Mr. Hooke's lectures and felt that that was not right. He began to doubt his own sincerity, "for did I beleev that god were in those ordinances for my good, that would take away tediousness ingratitude, sensuality &c. . . ." Any Puritan could finish the catalogue.

At last, not willing to undergo another "perplexed and chargeable" overland trip, he set sail from New Haven on an April Sunday night and arrived on Tuesday at Martha's Vineyard and two days later in the Bay, but the boat was detained several days from landing in the home harbor by a strong northeast wind. Fortunately, it was beached near the house of some friends, and when, after the storm, Wigglesworth prayed for favorable winds, God gave "speedy passage" the rest of the way.

The return to Harvard was not a joyous one, for his students had relapsed during his absence into negligence and indifference, but, after warning them sternly of the dangers of poor academic performance, he felt much better and could look to God more intensely. (D330-338)

While on Martha's Vineyard, he must have made arrangements for a pulpit engagement, for in May he preached there —his second sermon, preserved in his notebooks, partly in shorthand. The text would have been near to his own predicament: "So I gave them up unto their hearts' lust: and they walked in their own counsels" (*Psalm* 81:12). There might have been therapeutic value in thus airing his recurring problem of self-will in the cloak of a public sermon.[95]

He was certainly not a candidate for the church on Martha's Vineyard, for the pastor, Thomas Mayhew, had been there several years and was still only thirty-three; so there would be no need for a replacement, nor for a teacher, for that matter, because of the small population on the island. This, then, was simply a guest appearance. It was good practice for an aspirant to the ministry.

All summer long perplexities continued without let-up. When his students with the natural exuberance of youth in the heat of June preferred "going agadding after vanity & mispence of time" to confinement over their textbooks and lecture notes, the tutor was distressed. The intellectual concentration required by the Harvard of those days was undeniably taxing, but over-serious Sir Wigglesworth, with his eye on the reputation of his pupils and hence of himself, would allow nothing that smelled of sloth. (D341)[96]

As was the custom among the clergy and many other Puritans, Michael would spend a great deal of time once a month on Saturdays in preparation for the Lord's Supper on Sundays, for this was one of God's ordinances, to be taken with the deepest gravity. Not as complex or joyous as the verse meditations of Edward Taylor (pastor at Westfield beginning almost twenty years later), his diary records are just as severe and penetrating. Sometimes he was successful in feeling the presence of God, other times not. One Saturday he "could find little sutable affection and mourning for the many sins and greivous [faults] that I stand guilty of before god." In fact, he was afraid that he would be committing a dreadful offense if he approached the table of the Lord unprepared. The sermon next day helped him not at all. Though he went through with the service, he thought about it for a long time afterwards, even seeking through intensive writing to come closer to the ideal: "Let christ be mine let me be his alone." (D343)

A week after the 1653 commencement, in which President Dunster had tried to effect smoothly the shift from a three- to a four-year residence requirement for the Bachelor of Arts degree, Sir Wigglesworth heard some of the students making light of a remark of his own. His conscience often led him into ridiculous corners, from which it was not easy to extricate himself. On this occasion he took to prayer to find comfort. (D358)

The disciplining of his charges was not always easy, partly because his growing habit of contemplation and prayer in an effort to find God's will made him uncertain and slow to act. (It was this outward manifestation that had displeased his father. It certainly was not a trait of the Puritan leaders.) Time and again he worried and prayed over the "contumacious & disrespective negligent carriages of my pupils."[97] Sometimes prayer would produce solution or at least solace, sometimes not. And often, when he was successful in breaking up a noisy group, his attainment would go to his head, and there he was again: ". . . pride pride, and outwandrings of heart from my resting place!" (D372)

One young man in particular gave him trouble. Son of a Governor of the colony and later himself a minister, John Haynes asked leave one summer day to go up to Ipswich. This was soon after Michael's return from New Haven, and he had been disappointed to find that John, a promising scholar, had slipped during his absence. He refused the boy permission. John went anyway—to Salem—without his tutor's leave or the knowledge of the President, and was gone three days. When he returned, he would not explain his absence. Wigglesworth talked to him at great length about his misdemeanor, about his parents' sure disappointment, if they were to know. Haynes broke out in tears and thanked his tutor for his concern. Wigglesworth pressed his advantage: "I told him also of the dangers of pleasure and how they had like to have been my ruin. . . ." But the next night tutor caught student in forbidden pastime. When Haynes "slinked home and left his game," Wigglesworth, typically, began to worry that maybe the student feared him more than God. This may well have been an accurate analysis, for on the very next day he found the culprit "playing musick" with unsavory Cambridge companions in spite of all admonition. The poor man was afraid his prayers had been in vain. He was incapable of understanding the boy's need for a change after a year of intensive study. (D345-347)

When the entire class came to him with the request that they be relieved of a second year of Hebrew, he went in tearful prayer to his Lord. He suspected that the boys were trying to get back to a three-year schedule. As a matter of fact, there was agitation among their parents for such a move, but in the end the President had his way. Right now, however, Michael had a hard time convincing the young men that they should continue in Hebrew. After argument, reasoning, and prayer, they were at last subdued, (D360) though they thought they were being abused and six months later tried once more—unsuccessfully—to have the language struck from their curriculum.

Michael was tenacious in his pursuit of the Puritan ideal. He would never let himself rest, but was always searching, searching, searching for even the tiniest shadow of sin in his soul. Inevitably, exaggeration of faults crept in. One Sunday he began to worry about a white lie he had told long before—as an undergraduate. Someone had asked him whether he knew anything about William Mildmay's sword, and he had replied that he did not, while all along he believed that Seaborn Cotton had it. He now recalled that the situation cleared itself in no time, that it had been only a trivial matter, but his present anxiety, nevertheless, was the price of a pitiless conscience. (D348, 353)[98] The cost of his education as a Puritan was proving very high indeed.

During this summer Wigglesworth was being considered by the church at Hartford, which, since the death of Thomas Hooker six years before, had been in turmoil over the qualifications of a successor. The community was large enough to need and support at least two ministers. Mr. Hooker had led his flock in the paths of orthodoxy. The present incumbent, the Reverend Samuel Stone, was inclined toward latitudinarianism.[99] The young Wigglesworth would appear to represent the principles of the Hooker partisans. While considering the offer, Michael learned that Mr. Stone was expressing unwillingness to accept him as a co-worker. (D359) Four years later, Mr. Stone was frank: "I acknowledge that I hindered the church from declaring their apprehensions by vote . . . concerning Mr. Wigglesworth's fitness for office in the church at Hartford."[100]

Meanwhile, Michael was experiencing his usual struggle. In view of "Mr. Stone's motion" and of "my father's counsel," he characteristically could come to no decision. Even prayer did not disclose God's wishes. As he analyzed the situation, he began to fear that his leaning toward the Hartford position was influenced by his need for clothing to keep him warm in the coming winter, since eight pounds a year from Harvard did not amount to much in buying power. This, he felt, would be a sinful reason for accepting the office. (D359) Step by faltering step he was coming to the conviction that would cause him to write less than ten years later:

> And what are *Riches* to be doted on?
> Uncertain, fickle, and ensnaring things;
> They draw Mens Souls into Perdition,
> And when most needed, take them to their wings.
>   (Vanity)

He even thought of throwing over life in Massachusetts altogether and returning to England in search of a living. (D363) Word had now reached New England's shores that the Puritan army had dissolved Parliament and that the new Lord Protector had chosen another Parliament which could not help being favorable to a man of Wigglesworth's persuasion, though Cromwell was somewhat disappointing to the inhabitants of the New Zion because he was tolerant of Presbyterian and Congregationalist alike. The young Fellow wanted above all things to strengthen his faith. He decided against both Hartford and England, hoped God would forgive his sins and supply his winter's needs, and remained at Harvard.

On October 15, 1653, Michael received word that his father, Edward, had died in New Haven two weeks before. "I set myself to confess before the Lord my sins against him in want of natural affections to, and sympathy with my afflicted parents, in my not prizing them and their life which

[60]

God hath graciously continued so long. [Edward was about forty-nine when he died.] My great request is for pardon of all former sins, and present deliverance from a stupid frame of spirit unsensible of gods visitation and my own loss in losing such a friend. . . ." (D369)

His inability to feel warmth towards either of his parents gnawed at him without ceasing. Early in September he had not been cordial in welcoming some of his mother's friends —just because they were his mother's. Afterwards he wanted "to mourn before God for my falseness and hypocrisy." (D361) Often-recurring passages in his diary attribute to God those qualities that he had missed in Edward. A few days before his father's death he had prayed, "Yet verily thou art my father, as thou givest me ground of incouragement," (D364) the very opposite of the gifts from Edward at home in April.

The day before he received the news of Edward's demise, he had prayed for help over the obstacles in his studies that had been troublng him for several days, and, as a result, had overcome all difficulties. *Difficilia pulchra.* That evening, at a private meeting, while he was contemplating how God had answered his prayer, he was suddenly overcome by thought of "my want of love and dutifulness to my parents, which I beg'd pardon of." (D368-369) Next day he knew he would see his father no more.

Michael had been cognizant enough of his father's pitiable physical condition. On the way to New Haven he had consulted Winthrop at Pequot. After an education at Trinity College, Dublin, and at the Inner Temple, Winthrop had traveled widely before coming to New England. His devotion to the cause of science was to bring him the favorable attention of the Royal Society.[101] Among other interests he had studied deeply the practices and superstitions which at the time were called medicine. He had agreed to go to New Haven, if possible, to examine Edward and make what recommendations he could. On the strength of this tentative promise, Edward had written a letter to Winthrop in July detailing his symptoms and the treatment he had received to date. He was virtually immobile, he had reported, except for a little freedom in his neck. He had a small but sufficient appetite. His mind and senses were still keen, but he was actually exhausted from his inability to move. The letter from goodman to gentleman concluded with dignity and pathos: "Thus having used great libertie and boldness with you, I commend you, and the guidance of you in this and all other your affaires to the good spirit of God, and Rest your poor afflicted Brother in Christ Edward Wigglesworth."[102] (Probably Esther or Abigail had served as amanuensis.) There is no record that Winthrop had been able to make the journey to New Haven during the remaining two months of Edward's life, but one can imply that Michael had cared enough to consult a well-known physician and to make report to his father.

Now, however, the son's whetted conscience would not let him alone. On the next day after hearing the news, he prayed God to make him care at all that his father had died. A day or two later, on his twenty-second birthday, he was forced to confess even more: "I found the same cause of crying earnestly to the Lord and of grace for a right spirit under God's afflicting hand that I might not be secretly glad that my father was gone." It is impossible to draw conclusion from scanty evidence, but Freudians would be interested to know that, the night before this confession, Michael had had another erotic dream with accompanying nocturnal emission, for which, he cried out, "I loathe myself and desire to abase myself before my God. O Lord deliver me from the power of that evil one." (D369) Nowhere did he detail the subject matter of his dreams. Everywhere did he try by degrading himself to repress what one must conclude were only the normalities of sexual development. The difficulty with the Puritan way, as Michael was finding it, was that it did not permit a wholesome embrace of all of life, in spite of its awareness that withdrawal from the world was not the answer.

[62]

His present indifference over the loss of his father was disturbingly persistent. In mid-November, one Saturday while preparing for the Lord's Supper, he listed ten of his chief faults, the eighth of which was "want of sence and sorrow for my Fathers death." He was puzzled as to the specific cause of his lack of feeling. On Sunday afternoon, after the ordinance of the table of the Lord, "I was assayled with fears in reference to my unsensibleness under gods visitation in my fathers death, and I fear least there should be some root of bitterness that I were not willing to part with, unsearched out. But I know none, Lord search and try me, and make me upright before Thee. . . . Lord, I believ help my unbelief." (D373) The cause of distaste for Edward must have been deep-seated indeed to escape such probing.

About ten days after the word about his father had arrived, he had a marvelous dream. He had spent several days before in preparation of a sermon which he delivered at Charlestown with great effect, though he had been unaccountably depressed the same night on his return to Cambridge. Then on the following night he had the dream: God was on His throne separating the sheep from the goats on "the great and dreadful day of judgment." So effective was the vision that Michael woke with a start and resolved "to follow god with teares and crys until he gave me some hopes of his gracious good wil toward me." Whether because of the dream or not, he could not concentrate on his studies for several days. His diagnosis, as usual, was "pride prevailing." Trying to get to the bottom of the question, he catalogued his "iniquities," among which was "negligence in not redeeming the opportunty to send a letter to Hartford according to promises." (D370) This was late October, and the Hartford church had been pursuing him since summer. No more is recorded of this transaction. The members of the harassed church now turned elsewhere in their search for a spiritual guide.

How often Wigglesworth had experienced this dream of Judgment it is not possible to surmise. As a boy he had heard his parents discussing the vivid details of the end of the world. He himself had talked about it with his parents, his friends, his pastors, whom he had heard preach sermons based on it. He had absorbed the descriptions in his assiduous reading of the Bible. For all Puritans the Day of Doom was the Great Event that gave meaning to life on earth; it was the source of anxiety and dread that colored every action and thought. That the end of time and the passing of sentence on every human being in history were a certainty dwelt firmly in the thinking of every Puritan.

Thomas Hooker had died in Hartford six years before, but his sermon on "A True Sight of Sin" was typical of the pulpit rhetoric that kept this medieval vision alive and immediate for the New England congregations. Michael as a boy might have heard Hooker deliver sermons quite like this. "Imagine thou sawest the Lord Jesus coming in the clouds, and heardest the last trump blow, *Arise ye dead, and come to judgment:* Imagine thou sawest the Judg of all the World sitting upon the Throne, thousands of Angels before him, and ten thousands ministring unto him, the Sheep standing on his right hand, and the Goats at the left: Suppose thou heardest that dreadful Sentence, and final Doom pass from the Lord of life (whose Word made Heaven and Earth, and will shake both) *Depart from me ye cursed;* How would thy heart shake and sink, and die within thee in the thought thereof, wert thou really perswaded it was thy portion? Know, that by thy dayly continuance in sin, thou dost to the utmost of thy power execute that Sentence upon thy soul: It's thy life, thy labor, the desire of thy heart, and thy dayly practice to depart away from the God of all Grace and Peace, and turn the Tomb-stone of everlasting destruction upon thine own soul."[103]

Nine years after his dream, Michael was to commit to print the details of the Judgment, in Massachusetts subject of sermons, subject of conversation, subject of nightmares. The vivid, threatening stanzas of "The Day of Doom" were to have unprecedented distribution and, incidentally, to bring their author welcome recompense.

[64]

Near the end of this fitful week Wigglesworth began thinking about another sermon, which he had been invited to preach at Concord, on the edge of the wilderness. Not until Saturday night was he able to outline the full discourse. (That awful dream must have disturbed him profoundly.) "Gods assistance was here the more remarkable." His text, from *Isaiah,* encouraged exploration of the fact of death and the wickedness of the world: ". . . merciful men are taken away, none considering that the righteous is taken away from the evil to come." This would be a congenial dish for Puritan consumption.

By nature Michael enjoyed the pleasant company of other human beings.

> Man's Nature sociable
> Delights in Company,
> Declines and dreadeth Solitude,
> And loves Society.
> Hence to be stript of Friends
> And to be left alone,
> Must needs be grievous in it self,
> A sore Affliction.
> (Sol I.1)

He was, however, unceasing in fighting off this tendency to gregariousness for the same reason that he worried about his interest in his students—that he would not be able to see God's face shining through his worldly preoccupations. More than once he had chided himself for taking delight in cordial conversation and the entertainment of guests in the college hall. Now at Concord on Tuesday after his Sunday sermon, he had stayed so late that his friends would not permit him to start back for Cambridge, and, as luck would have it, Wednesday produced such a heavy snow that he did not know when he would be able to go home. He had been concerned that in the Concord town meeting—even convened as it was in the house of the pastor, Peter Bulkeley—there was no reading of the Scriptures. Such omission would appear to him a symptom of separation of church and government, a departure from Winthrop's plan. He thought he should mention the matter, but with characteristic diffidence failed to do so and thus gave himself cause for self-torture after he had returned home. He had prayed earnestly for a change in the weather. Then on Thursday night came rain that melted the snow down from knee- to ankle-depth. Back in Cambridge on Friday he wondered, "What shal I render to the Lord for all his benefits?" (D370-371)

The next day he went down to Roxbury, where he preached from his Concord text. He thought the sermon was improved on second delivery. He was getting considerable practice in the pulpit against the day when he would be ordained permanent minister in one of the churches in the colony.

If, as these Calvinists would have it, God was involved in every slightest lift of a finger as well as in the affairs of largest import, so were men (the images of God) involved universally in the life about them. For the Puritan, Cain's insolence towards the Lord over his brother's disappearance from the land of the living was the worst kind of sloughing off of man's responsibility. Concern for one's fellows was the mark of every faithful believer.

When in December four brethren of the church in Cambridge died within "a few days," Wigglesworth could feel his own fault in the matter. He came home from the funeral of the fourth man and listed "the sins of my whole life," among which, again, was his haunting lack of "naturall affections to my father." He seemed pleased at this point that the Lord had made him sorry that he could not muster up the necessary degree of warmth. But more, he prayed for forgiveness of his personal sins, whatever they might be, that helped to bring about the death of the four men and a return of "sickness into the college." (D375-376) The intricate relationship of a single man, no matter how humble, with society at large was reason to give pause to the sensitive thinker.

Later in the winter, Wigglesworth's pupils once more balked at Hebrew and caused their tutor to recall his own stubborn resistance to both parents and teachers. Such in-

[66]

subordination in individual conflict, he reflected, could grow and grow until the whole colony could be plunged into anarchic ruin. (D385) No doubt about it, there was at every level need for the strictest discipline and the severest self-discipline if society was to maintain its equilibrium.

A short time after the four December funerals, the young theologian confessed to some doubt about the authenticity of the Scriptures. Mark and Luke had not been in the company of the Apostles. Should their accounts of the life of Jesus be taken as "devine authority?" The very thought was frightening. Though he took to prayer, the questioning persisted for several days. (D376-377)

Entertainment of doubt was not totally discouraged among the Puritans. Rather the questions were exposed, for who could tell where error lurked? Eschatological security was distasteful, even reprehensible, to the New England mind. It was possible for a whole people to be wrong. Testing, trying, examining—these were the ways of both eradicating fallacy and strengthening faith. The trial of Mistress Hutchinson had been based on this policy, but Anne had failed to prove her point.

This was not the first time "atheistic thoughts" had crept into Wigglesworth's mind. Once he had flogged them back by reminding himself that logical argument is valueless "if god do not let the beams of his glory shine into it." (D364) Once he had listened with absorption to a discussion about the infallibility of the Bible (his very present problem), about the "possibility of mistakes in the writing and because of the points in Hebrew, and the various readings in the text and margent." Afterwards he begged God's forgiveness (D368)—for what? for listening? for even considering the possibility? Just forgiveness. Loss of authority in the Bible, of total confidence in the Word would upset the whole structure of Massachusetts society. Christians were not yet ready for "the higher criticism."

Related to these doubts were the moments of inattention and the hours of actual boredom in the services of the church.

[67]

If the young man's mind wandered at a lecture, he would recall that all week he had been ruled by "such a spirit of whoardom and departure from god that I have no power against." When the annual sermon before the election of officers in the artillery company at Cambridge tried his patience, he fought back with fervent prayer: "Let iniquity never never, never have dominion over me." (D345, 366)

Once during the reading of the Bible at a lecture "an Atheistic irreverent frame seizeth upon me; . . . vile and unworthy conceptions concerning God came into my mind." He could not reconcile himself to a heaven where he would simply gaze and adore. What he wanted was action. Oh, that Arminian doctrine of the efficacy of works! He was filled with remorse and contrition. "I was conceived, bred, brought up in sin. O redeem from these devouring Lyons the hopeless shiftless soul that thou hast purchased!" (D371-372) He was in a dilemma: forced to question, he was yet forced to believe. On the one hand, he was trained in logic; on the other, he was committed to whole-hearted acceptance of the faith of his fathers. The resolution of doubt was not always to be found in the learning he had acquired at college. Emotional enthusiasm—Augustinian awareness—was entitled to its proportionate share in the growth of a man. But what proportion? That was an ever-present query: how to define balance.

And he still had not conquered his arch-enemy, pride. It was the custom at private meetings to ask one of the number to review a recent sermon or lecture. One December Sunday evening young Wigglesworth was asked to do the honors and outdid the preacher himself, so his friends said. (D378) Such praise was delightful to hear, but dangerous. The recipient again prayed for freedom from hypocrisy and falsehood.

He was making a thorough study of logic as propounded by Petrus Ramus, and here lay one source of his difficulty. Ramus supported faith in reason and based all philosophy on the observance of human nature. After Michael had bril-

[68]

liantly defended unadulterated Ramus against an opponent supporting Alexander Richardson's modifications, his student audience thought him superior, and he was consumed with pride, but he took himself to task by calling himself a "poor fool that know nothing as I ought to know." (D381)

On another occasion, after hearing a sermon by Mr. Mitchell with the text from the first chapter of *St. John* on how "grace and truth came by Christ Jesus," Michael took the lesson to heart, as usual, and asked himself, "Can God love such a proud, carnal, secure, hardhearted wretch as nothing wil mend?" He found his answer in the text and commented: "Yes for Christs merits he can and doth." (D379) These were the catchwords and could quickly lend themselves to glib repetition, but not for conscientious Wigglesworth. Every phrase he used he questioned without ceasing. For him the easy cliché did not exist. Security was death.

> Christ never flattered thee
> Nor promis'd carnal ease
> Nor Worldly Honour, Pleasure, Gain,
> Security or Peace.
> (Meat IV.5)

The life of the Puritans was a life of excitement and vigor. Not for them anything approaching an easy-going existence. Not for them indifference to responsibility for cultivating both human values and divine reverence. They were subjective, sensitive, glaringly aware of their engagement with their fellows at the same time that they were deeply conscious of their role as children of God. What the path and nature of their existence would be depended on themselves. True, God selected whom He would for eternal salvation, but He selected men who chose to follow the paths of righteousness. This was a highly sophisticated (sophistical?) point. The individual thus approved must seize the initiative and make good the contract between himself and his God.

This Michael had done as a Harvard senior early in 1651. But he recognized that the struggle must continue. To reach

[69]

a high point of conversion, profession, and acceptance in the church at Cambridge was one thing. To maintain the search, to sustain the ardor, to avoid the nominal, was quite another thing. At a sermon by little Urian Oakes, his contemporary Harvard Fellow, Michael was much moved, but candid. He reflected afterwards: "I am asham'd that I have now stood these 3 years as a shrub in thine orchard, and made so little improvement of Christ, that I may question I have him, or no." (D384-385)

Improvement was to be made in little things as well as big. He had been negligent in his social responsibility, for he had lately done little to control "lightness and mad mirth on Sabbath Evenings." (D385) Definitions of "mad mirth" would no doubt vary. And, not only involvement with others, but his personal condition needed attention. Though on one Sunday, in reading Thomas Shepard's *Sound Believer* (just off the press), he was able to overcome fear "lest my soul never rested in christ, or took up satisfaction in christ alone," (D387) two weeks later he was deep in the mire of *amour propre* again, for he had been extraordinarily perceptive in studying physics with another tutor, Nehemiah Ambrose; ". . . instead of admiring my god I found myself prone to admire my self; And so like a wretch I turn grace into wantonness." There followed the usual recriminations. (D389-390)

And another thing—a matter of college discipline. One day in late December, 1653, he forgot himself so far as to speak English, not the required Latin. (D379) He was remorseful, for as student and now as Fellow he had undertaken a contract. To fail in a promise was not the way of a follower of Christ.

His contract—or covenant—not only with the college but with God called for the highest possible development of his mind and talents. So earnestly had he been studying that he was forced to record on January 22, 1654, that "I am worn out with study wel nigh; yet God reneweth my strength." (D383) For at least a year his health had not been robust.

In the preceding summer he had listened to a lecture by the President and had "found sweet encouragement in regard to my bodily weakness." He quoted Dunster's words (derived from a passage in *Isaiah*) : "It may be thou art sickly. Why, the Lord is thy physician, who healeth thee. He can make thee strong in thy age, though thou be weakly in thy youth."[104] He was unaware, of course, of how strangely prophetic would be this passage in his own life.

His afflictions, true to pattern, he ascribed to sin and divine discipline: considering his besetting pride, he said, "No marvel then if god visits with bodily weakness to keep it downe. . . ." (D348) Fifteen years later, in *Meat Out of the Eater,* he was to examine this thesis thoroughly.

In November, though he had been ailing for some time, his participation in the "day of publick humiliation" had not been very successful: "I could not with all I could do get a melting broken heart this day. . . ." (D374) Weakness of body was not always sufficient to recall him to humility of spirit.

Though he was having "so much trouble of the spleen, as forced me to leav study," he was able to preach a successful sermon at Charlestown, so successful that the people insisted that he return to them once a month till the "March equinox." (D375) Interference from illness continued all winter, though. He began to wonder whether he should not give up his position at Harvard, for his feebleness in addition to the persistent student grumbling at having to take Hebrew was almost more than he could handle. (D388)

Insignificant though his problems may seem, they were the natural outcome of the philosophy of involvement, and his profuse language was necessary to keep the spirit whipped up to constant account. He was still troubled "with some stirrings of carnal lusts this day which I am afraid of. Notwithstanding cant get my heart so to loathe as I would. O Lord leave me not to return with the sow to her wallowing in the mire. Let me not live rather than live in my lusts." And again a few days later: "Deliver, me, O Lord, from carnal lusts. These make me afraid when I feel my spirit so prone to close with them." (D388-389)

The extravagant pressure of the language of his diary was not out of the ordinary among theologians of his century. Almost any page from the sermons of John Donne, who had died the year of Michael's birth, will give the same impression of profound earnestness. Cotton Mather, brilliant son of Michael's brilliant pupil Increase, was to continue the feverish tradition, writing in 1688 at the age of eighteen, "So filthy a Wretch as I who continually grieves the good Spirit of the Lord Jesus Christ, and grow proud and vain when Hee does exalt me with His Favors have Cause to mention His Assistances unto mee with a very trembling Soul." A few years later, almost twenty-three, Cotton recorded the melodrama of humiliation: "This Day, in Anguish of Soul, in the Sense of my Own Sinfulness and Filthiness, I cast myself prostrate, on my Study-floor with my mouth in the Dust. Here, I lamented unto the Lord, my Follies. . . ." and asked for a worthy wife.[105] The high tension of Michael's language, then, was a reflection of the age, a nervous energy shared by all thinkers who took their covenant with God seriously. In fact, in Western civilization, this was the era of the Baroque: the voluptuousness of Rubens, the ecstasies of Bernini, the magnificence of The Sun King, the exaltation of Handel. The climate invited exaltation. Even here on the isolated coast of an unexplored continent, cribbed and cabined by severe theology, the Puritan clergy were breathing the air of an exuberant age. Even within the limitations of the "plain style" they were conveying to their auditors and readers (and to themselves in their journals) highly charged emotion in a way beyond the suavity and manners of the next century to achieve.

Wigglesworth went often to towns around Cambridge— Charlestown to the north, Watertown to the west, Roxbury to the south—sometimes to preach, sometimes to listen, sometimes for other reasons. Once before his father's death he had gone to Boston to get money for his debts. It may be

[72]

assumed that his father had sent thirty-two pounds, though Michael ascribed the gift to the Lord. He had had difficulty (from unknown causes) in keeping the money, lost it, in fact, for two days, but had recovered it in time to meet his obligations honorably. (D355) Another time, he had gone to Boston to seek counsel from the ministers there about "the Salem business." But he feared his really wholesome tendency toward enjoying society. He took time off to go into Boston again for the wedding (doubtless a civil ceremony) of his classmate Henry Butler to a young widow of Dorchester, where Butler was teaching school. To appease the restless conscience for what might be frivolity, Michael attended a lecture and a private meeting at the bridegroom's quarters and felt better about the trip. (D388)

This same conscience was giving him trouble in other directions, still petty to the point of the absurd in the eyes of the twentieth-century critic. The keeping of the Sabbath was a hard point. How far should a true Christian go? One January Sunday Michael never did come to a conclusion about asking the students to check their study rooms to see whether snow had drifted in. (D381) Six weeks later a strong March wind was banging the pastor's stable door viciously. The young Fellow worried all evening about whether he should tell Mr. Mitchell. "My fear is lest my wil should blind reason." As was possibly too often the case, he ended by doing nothing at all, which amounted to not informing the minister—not making up his mind not to, just doing nothing. For three weeks that barn door was on his mind and heart. What if it had been damaged? When he mentioned the matter to one of the men in the minister's household, the reply was a very natural shrug of the shoulders. After all, no harm had been done. (D388-390)

This did not clear the matter up for Michael. In spite of recognition of the triviality of the situation, there had been a complex of duty to God and duty to man. If this principle made a man look like a busybody, was he to be governed by man's opinion, or should he continue to seek out God's will

[73]

in small as in greater issues? The answer, for the moment, was clear: God must be served at every turn. Possibly, then, just possibly he had been right in observing Sabbath holiness by not reporting the flapping door. The anguish of making choices was awful. When Michael had to decide, he felt that he was choosing to shape the image of man as he thought it ought to be: what would happen if everyone would do as he did?

Michael was still complaining of his "frail body," (D391) but in spite of this he kept at his studies, the guidance of his pupils, and his appearances as guest preacher. For one thing, in another four months, if all went well, he would be a Master of Arts and would probably be leaving Harvard. For another, he should be thinking of marriage, for all Puritans thought a man ought to marry. And he would need to support both himself and his family. So he welcomed invitations to preach at various towns, maybe hoping to come to the attention of a church in need of a pastor. The Salem, Cambridge, and Hartford offers had faded from sight for one reason or another. He must hope for a call elsewhere.

During the first week in April he began preparing a sermon to deliver at Charlestown, but he was feeling so weak that memorizing the points of his outline was almost impossible—and to use notes would have been disgraceful. The Lord was on his side, however; he delivered a successful sermon, received the praise of the congregation, and went back to the Yard full of the old "vain thoughts." He had managed, despite his indisposition, what he considered an effective "plerophory," richness of assurance, confidence in both message and style of delivery. But he knew he must balance success with humility, or at least modesty. (D391)

[74]

IV. Marriage and Malden

Toward the end of April, 1654, Michael set out by boat from the Bay to New Haven. Though there were no scheduled stops between the two ports, the voyage took twelve days, for frequent fogs were a hazard. Having arrived on a Saturday night, he went to the meeting house the next day, where he was received with "such love & respect" that he could feel inflation from self-satisfaction setting in. (D392-393)

He had gone down to New Haven for the settling of his father's estate. Made on July 12 of the year before (about the time of his letter to Winthrop), Edward's will bore the signatures of the two ministers, John Davenport and William Hooke, and of Matthew Gilbert, who with Richard Miles had now recently appraised the Wigglesworth property at something over four hundred pounds.[106] In spite of his infirmities, Edward had done very well in striking the balance toward which all true Puritans strove.

That he had maintained his religious faith and his standing is clear in the thoughtfulness of the town in building him "a litle house" near the church and in the consideration of the ministers in witnessing his will. That he had increased, on the other hand, the value of the worldly goods God had given him was recorded by his son in an autobiographical sketch several years later, apparently after Michael had transcended or forgotten his father's disapproving glares and sharp reprimands. "He lived to see & hear what God had done for my

[75]

soul in turning me from Darkness to light & from the power of Sathan unto God, which filled his heart ful of joy and thankfulness beyond what can be expressed. And for his outward estate, that was so far from being sunk by what he spent from yeer to yeer upon my education, that in 6 years time it was plainly doubled, which himself took great notice of, and spake of it to myself and others, to the praise of God with Admiration and thankfulness. . . ."[107]

Edward having left his entire property to his wife and two children, Michael and Abigail, Esther had been considered prosperous enough that the General Court of New Haven had gone to her for funds for the journey of two commissioners to Boston on colony business: ". . . they borrowed of widdow Wigglesworth five pounds in silver, which the court promised should bee repaide within three months, in the same kinde or in other paye to her satisfaction, so as neither she nor her children should suffer by it."[108] One can assume that the debt was paid, though no record of the concluding transaction is extant.

Michael stayed in New Haven probably about a month. The people of the town were glad to see him. It was for him, and a few others, that they had been willing to contribute "college corn" to Harvard. As a son of New Haven, a ministerial aspirant, and a candidate for the Master of Arts degree, he was an object of civic pride. He renewed old acquaintances and met newcomers and visitors, including a young woman "of great note and birth and piety" whose name is masked in anonymity.

During the overland return to Cambridge, he stayed two weeks at Hartford, where he preached about "the glory of the saints in heaven." In the forest journey he and his companion encountered mighty winds and unmerciful rains. The trees bent "like a bow over our heads," many of them crashing to earth. The travelers counted about forty "newly blown down." Since it was not Michael's habit—nor any Puritan's —to take such phenomena at face value, he saw at work in this tempest "the mighty power of God." He was back in

[76]

Cambridge by July 1, for on that date he signed Joshua Ambrose's diploma, along with the President, Mr. Mitchell, and Urian Oakes.[109]

Marriage was looked on as a contract neither romantic nor religious. It was a man's duty to take a wife and to have children for the continuance of the church. The Puritans could find no proof to support the Papish concept of marriage as a sacrament; so until quite late in the seventeenth century a couple would be united only in civil ceremony. Choice of partner, too, was more often than not arranged by parents or agents even outside the family. Love, they thought, was not necessary, for it would come as a matter of course after the two young people had taken up the responsibilities of a household. If romantic love never developed, probably so much the better, for there would be less danger then of distraction from the central *raison d'être,* the love of God.

In March, about a month before his voyage to New Haven, Michael had received a proposal of marriage through the mediation of a Mr. Buckley (probably of Wethersfield, near Hartford). This was on a Saturday morning, and the young bachelor's "heart was too much taken with it." He was able to put it out of his mind long enough on Sunday to preach at Charlestown and, at the Lord's Supper, "to close with Christ Jesus as prophet priest and king with some affection." On Monday, however, "I was ready to be gone awhoring after other loves and to cool my love to God." This was pretty violent language in the effort to keep God in the forefront. By night he had himself under control again: ". . . at a private meeting . . . the Lord awakened me and helped me to loath myself and so again on the lecture day." All week, in a struggle between concentrated devotion and creaturely desire, he was afraid his faith was fading and prayed that God "would not let christ Jesus be a dry christ unto me." By the following Monday, though his mind wandered from its focus on God, it was "not in the particular of marriage as before." (D390-391) Just who this young woman was must remain a secret of the past, too. It could

[77]

be that, highly sexed as he unquestionably was, Michael had been brought by this proposal to thoughts, not of regard for a specific female, but of satisfaction of the flesh in general. This could have been what was worrying him.

At any rate, safely returned to New Haven, Michael sat down to compose a letter to his mother about another proposal of marriage. (It would be strange if he had not mentioned Mr. Buckley's message while at home; so this must have been a second proposal—most likely in behalf of Mary Reyner, his mother's niece from Rowley.) Just as he was beginning the letter, he was handed a message from Esther saying that a marriage was being arranged between him and the young woman "of great note" he had met on his visit home. One can imagine the consternation with which the twenty-two-year-old bachelor received this news. Instead of pride at being in demand as huband for two, and possibly three, girls at the same time, he was thrown into desperation, fearing to hurt the feelings of one party or another. He prayed passionately for God's guidance. He wrote letters trying to undo the trouble, but could find no way of posting them during the week. At last came word in a few days that the New Haven prospect was leaving for England. How far negotiations had gone cannot be determined, but Michael was relieved: "At this news my heart was filled with joy." (D394) Without hindrance now, he could make up his mind about the previous offer.

August came, and with it the Harvard commencement. Sir Wigglesworth was unable to anticipate the occasion with much pleasure. The old flaws kept his conscience flaming: "such a carnal heart, such dead and dul affections, such distracting thoughts as posses and fill my mind, such a faint and feeble body." (D395) But he paid his "commencement charges" to the satisfaction of the college steward,[110] took part in the sitting of the solstice, handed in his synopsis of the arts, and took his place with the Master's candidates on commencement afternoon. Only one of his ten classmates—Nathaniel Pelham, son of Harvard's first treasurer—failed to

[78]

return to take the second degree after the three-year interim.

In 1657 Pelham and John Davis (who had, of course, attained the Master of Arts degree) set sail for England in a ship of which James Garrett was captain and were "never heard of more." Of the others, Michael outlived all but one. Death came in 1696 to Henry Butler and John Glover. Ichabod and Isaac Chauncy, sons of Harvard's next President, returned to England shortly after 1654, as did Jonathan Burr. (Henry Butler was also settled in Somersetshire by 1662.) Isaac Chauncy it was who died seven years after Michael. Thomas Dudley, who lived only a year after this second commencement, was well connected. His mother being the daughter of John Winthrop (and sister of the Pequot physician) and his father the son of the elder Thomas Dudley, he was the grandson of two early and distinguished governors of Massachusetts Bay and the nephew of New England's first woman poet, Anne Bradstreet. Michael's remaining classmate was Seaborn Cotton, son of that Reverend John Cotton who had been brought finally to agree, years before, to the banishment of his disciple, Anne Hutchinson. Born indeed at sea, the son had been baptized in the First Church in Boston on the first Sunday after the landing of the boat in 1633. Married to Dorothy Bradstreet, his cousin and eldest daughter of Anne, he settled as pastor at Hampton in New Hampshire, where he served till his death in 1686.

Of the class of 1651, then, three were dead by 1658 and four others returned to England. Of the other three, John Glover settled in Dorchester, and Cotton and Wigglesworth became ministers of churches north of Boston. It would appear that Goodman Edward's son had more influence on the future of New England than any other of the graduates of Harvard in 1651. His position at the head of his class was justified.

A month or so after commencement, he was invited by the church at Malden, north of Cambridge, to become their minister. With customary hesitation he went up for a trial sermon. Having listed his sins on Saturday in preparation for the Lord's Supper, he reflected, "And though Sathan cast objection into my mind because I was no member of this particular church, nor yet recommended hither by Cambridge church; yet I strive [strove] against them and said Lord I do believ help my unbelief. . . ." (D395-396)

Originally Mystic Side (on the banks of the Mystic), Malden had been incorporated as a town in 1649. As an isolated community, it had wanted a church of its own, but had had difficulty finding a minister. Within a year nine men had been invited to fill the pulpit, but there had been no acceptance until at last Marmaduke Matthews had consented to the position. The trouble was that, even before he was ordained, he had been suspected of unsound views, in spite of his unquestionably godly character. Educated in England, he had not been in the colony long. And he did not stay long. Neither the magistrates in Boston nor the members of surrounding communities approved of him, but Malden needed a minister and retained Matthews—for a while—in spite of vigorous protests. Soon after his ordination it was clear that his language in the pulpit was "weak and inconvenient," and he was fined ten pounds for "his sins." The charges were actually quite vague ("miscarriages of justice"), but the general feeling was that he was not totally convinced on every orthodox Puritan principle as accepted in Massachusetts. Except for the two men who had begun the suit, the congregation stood behind their pastor. Thirty-six women signed a petition to the General Court for leniency; so Matthews's fine was remitted, though fines imposed at the same time against the Malden church through its most substantial representatives were only reduced, and remained sizable.[111]

Matthews stayed on for a while, but had gone from Malden some time before Wigglesworth was called, and eventually returned to England. Only occasional transient preachers once more were available for sermons and the ordinances. The struggling little church was in the depths, for Matthews had left discontent and differences of opinion in his wake with the result that internecine strife of some degree was the pattern at Malden for many years.[112] One can speculate on Wigglesworth's indecision, but the Malden situation was not exactly enticing.

There were numerous changes at the college this autumn. A year before, President Dunster had refused to have his new-born son baptized—first open evidence of his departure from the accepted doctrine. Just prior to the recent August commencement he had confessed openly at Cambridge that he could not believe in the efficacy of baptism without conscious penitence. Excellent administrator that he was, he had brought the college from near ruin, through a series of drastic changes, to a position of solidarity and indeed of eminence. For nearly a year Dunster had remained comparatively quiet on the question—at the request of the Overseers, who had been shocked enough at the views of their President. When conscience would permit him no further silence, he resigned —on October 24, 1654—and agreed to live on in the President's house only to the end of the following March. A month after his resignation his successor was inaugurated, Charles Chauncy, father of Isaac and Ichabod.[113]

Meanwhile, Wigglesworth had gone from Harvard. He had left behind him a class whom he had carefully shepherded through the first two rigorous years, including the despised Hebrew. Of the eight young men in the class of 1656, seven became ministers and the eighth a physician. The most distinguished turned out to be Increase Mather, whose son Cotton was, many years later, to preach Wigglesworth's funeral sermon. Cotton had heard his father sing the tutor's praises: his faithfulness, his ingenuity in getting sometimes recalcitrant students to work hard, his influence on them as Christians, his obvious affection for them.[114] He may have been exasperating to spirited youngsters, but he had led frequently mischievous and restless pupils well along the disciplined road that ends in strong character and full capacity for leadership, as his eight charges were to demonstrate.

Michael's diary is obscure concerning his whereabouts

[81]

for the next few months. In December, wherever he was, he was perplexed by the double problem of marriage and the church at Malden, though he was quite sure that God would guide him "in the weighty business that troubles me." To these difficulties was added more than usual physical suffering: "itch and biles [boils] breaking out so as to make me lame." In spite of his misery he tried to keep his mind on God's purposes. It would be "my very happiness to do god some service before I dy. . . ." (D396-397) He had already done God some service, in his teaching and preaching, but security was unthinkable: he must continue as God's soldier.

After a hiatus of about two and a half months, he resumed his diary under the date of February 15, 1655. He may have been in troubled Hartford now. (It is almost indisputable that he was there a couple of weeks later.) The resumption of the diary shows him penitent, as analytically remorseful as usual. For example, he had been gluttonous at a recent dinner and was paying for his indulgence. The somewhat monotonous fare provided at Harvard would understandably make a young man of twenty-three take advantage of a more sumptuous menu. Michael was abject, however, assigning to all-covering "pride" the cause of "Excess in eating at a feast lately; a snare which I can hardly escape; nor know that I am beyond what is convenient for me til I feel the after inconvenience. I am ashamed and confounded that I should be so brutish. Lord forgive." (D397)

This was only the beginning. He was afraid that others would think him merely reckless in failing to discharge his duties among the congregation at Hartford, whereas he knew himself to be often simply too weak physically to perform what was required of him.

> Just when I should set forth,
> Such feebleness assails me,
> That I am like a man half dead,
> All strength and vigour fails me.
> (Strength II.2)

His most troubling problem, though, was sexual. Among his faults (he was still trying to control his sleep fantasies)

[82]

he bemoaned "dreams and self-pollution by night which my soul abhors and mourns for." He knew that the only way out was marriage. "To continue in a single estate, Is both uncomfortable many wayes and dangerous (as I conceiv) to my life, and exposeth to sin, and [is] contrary to engagement of affections, and Friends expectations, and lyable to the harsh sensure of the world that expecteth the quite contrary. . . ."[115] This dissection of the question touched on every phase of his life: himself, God, his friends, and the world at large.

The poor man thought he might have gonorrhea. What a fearful burden to sustain! That a man of most fastidious virtue should be afflicted with such an earthy disease was not only puzzling but practically unbearable. All winter long, "except the Lord almighty had supported I had been overwhelmed and even distracted with it." He had confided in no one, for he could have found no comfort in sympathy, prayer, or advice. He had even reached the point where he was afraid to pray for health and help because of an almost sure subsequent despair. His urge toward the marriage bed was ruthless; yet, by his own analysis, marriage might bring the awful disease to full development and himself to "a wretched and miserable death." Moreover, injury to his wife would completely undo him.

He decided to brave mortification and ask for advice. Carefully outlining his dilemma (tendency to sin if he did not marry; danger to the health of himself and his wife if he did), he composed frank letters to three men versed in medicine: John Alcock, a physician of Roxbury; John Rogers, the preacher at Ipswich; and John Winthrop at Pequot.

Another problem posed itself: Mary Reyner was his mother's niece. Would marriage to her constitute incest? (That others, like Seaborn Cotton, would marry their cousins did not lighten his personal moral burden.) He wrote to Mary at Rowley, putting the problem candidly and giving her opportunity to reject him.

Mail delivery being what it was, it would be several weeks before he would have answers to all his inquiries. Meanwhile, he would have to persist in his present mode of living. In spite of personal difficulties he continued to preach frequently. His ambition was to cover in his sermons all "the very main things in divinity in a little time," for he was convinced that he would not be preaching much longer, that death would take him away.

Concentration was not easy, though he still strove to center his life in God's will. Pleasant company was actually an annoyance, for it encouraged his tendency to "frothiness and love to vanity." He recognized, sensibly enough, his need of "mirth," but was afraid he would become addicted to worldliness. Sexual loneliness, too, was frustrating and confusing him. On Thursday night, February 22, he was "much overborne with carnal concupiscence nature being suppressed for I had not my afflux in 12 nights. Friday night it came again without any dream that I know of. Yet after it I am still inclined to lust." His situation was growing more and more tense. Even before he received any replies from his counselors, he had just about made up his mind: "I begin to think marriage will be necessary for me (as an ordinance of god appointed to maintain purity which my heart loveth) what ever the event may be."

Early in March he had word that his mother was coming up to Hartford from New Haven for a visit. The news added to his confusion, no doubt partly because of his guilt in not feeling any particular affection for her, partly because of boredom at the thought of her company. But come she did, appearing on a Saturday night while her son was deep in meditation, preparing for the Sabbath. She stayed about two weeks, after which time Michael hired two horses in nearby Wethersfield and arranged with a John Latimer to accompany her back to New Haven. Michael put down no impressions of his mother's visit, but one may assume that there was little pleasure in it for him.

Meanwhile, he had received an answer from Alcock assuring him that his symptoms would be cleared up by marriage. A delay in hearing from Winthrop was finally amended

[84]

when Winthrop came on business to Wethersfield. Though Michael had trouble making an appointment with his man, he was at last able to leave with him a letter he had intended to send to Pequot. The next noon he had a reply, in which Winthrop concurred with Alcock. Marriage was the solution.

Then at the end of March he had letters from Rowley. His friends there were in good health. Mary had studied his letter and still wanted to marry him. Michael resolved to "go down speedily into the Bay. . . . I hope the Lord will direct when I come there. . . . Lord increase my faith, and patience." Patience. He had all the fire and urgency of the proverbial bridegroom.

He could not make the journey at once. The following week, he spent hours on a sermon, but woke on Sunday with a sore throat so severe that he could not speak aloud and had to relinquish the pulpit to a visitor. This was the day of the Lord's Supper, however; so at noon he ventured out of the house, smothered in wraps. The following week he kept indoors. He had difficulty in swallowing, his stomach was upset, he was afflicted with fever and perspiration, and he was, as could be expected, melancholy. His medicine was "principally burnt wine, which almost set me in a swoon divers times, yet I think it did me good."

Whether from the wine or from the passing of time, improvement came so that on the next week-end, well wrapped in warm clothing, Michael could go down to Wethersfield, where, on Monday, April 15, he arranged for a horse and on the next day set out for the Bay. He was not completely recovered, but thought that maybe, provided he kept warm, the trip in the April air would do as much good as medicine. He decided to use the spring season "for marrying or taking physic, or both." By the time he reached Roxbury, he felt better though tired. A consultation with Alcock encouraged him, and he pursued his course up the Bay, reaching Rowley on Saturday. On Monday, April 25, he had dinner with Rogers in Ipswich (not far from Rowley). The two men entered into a long discussion "about the great business." Rogers

[85]

dissented from the opinion of the other two medicos. (They were not, after all, ministers.) Rogers thought it ethical to cure the body first, then consider marriage. Michael was now thoroughly in a maze. Having prayed about the matter, he returned for further conference with Rogers, who at last reversed himself to recommend an early marriage.

Michael went back to Rowley to begin the final arrangements for the "great business." The banns were published at once, and he set out for Roxbury for another conference with Alcock. In spite of Rogers's about-face Michael was worried about the pastor-physician's original caution. Should he marry first? "To run such a hazard as that of my life and health without an apparent necessity, before I had tryed the utmost that physick could doe"—this indeed might be foolhardy.

Alcock was reassuring. Whatever was wrong could certainly be cured by medicine, but "marriage and stringent cordials afterward" would be a quicker way. Alcock was convinced that the trouble was not as serious as his patient supposed and recounted various cases similar which marriage had cleared up. The "distemper . . . was *naturalis impulsis seu instinctus irresistibilis,*" natural impulse or irresistible instinct.

This was what the patient wanted to hear. With compulsion toward analysis that assimilation of the logic of Ramus had made his second nature, he listed the reasons why he should take a wife, and at once. First, he had not accepted a pulpit, was unsettled, and so could not undertake an elaborate course of medicine. Even if he could, the cost of the treatment and a specially selective diet would be prohibitive. Psychically, furthermore, it was impossible for him to remain single and still be both comfortable and honest. Finally, under present conditions his "rebellious nature" was being stirred up rather than quieted by the medicines he was taking. (Was the alcohol in the cordials having its way!)

All this would appear to amount to a self-centered attitude, but one is reminded that marriage was a business deal, a mat-

ter of property agreements between families. After the cele-
bration (if there was one) the duty of creating a family was
supposed to bring about mutual affection and perhaps love.
Michael had showed some feeling of compunction earlier
about the possibility of bringing harm to his wife, but it is
obvious that his main concern was his own relief.

Early in May, 1655, he came back to Rowley to arrange for
the marriage contract. Refreshed by the journey, in Rowley
he enjoyed the company of "my dearest friends," many of
them from his native Yorkshire. During this visit he suffered
again from a moderate attack "of the same affliction as
formerly," but he was having a comparatively good time.
Though his friends wanted the wedding postponed as long as
a month or two until the town magistrates should return from
a convention in the Bay (weddings were civil ceremonies
still), at last a date was set two weeks thence. Preparations
got under way: tailors were commissioned to make new
clothes; merchants began to lay in supplies of food. This was
to be a festive occasion, though with limitations. The Lord
Protector's leniency toward dancing was not countenanced
in Massachusetts. Three editions appeared during Cromwell's
time of John Playford's *English Dancing Master,* describing
capers with such suggestive titles as "An Old Man Is a Bed
Full of Bones," "The Friar and the Nun," "Petticoat Wag,"
and "Up Tails All."[116] New England Puritans would turn
their backs or shake their fists at such demonstrations.

With all this definite preparation going on, Michael was
still worried. As he returned to the Bay area, he was burdened
with the incest question: "the mothers sister is forbidden;
now sister in scripture language is put for a Kinswoman
sometimes." The young scholar's learning was causing him
trouble, but he finally lifted himself out of this bog.

Mary Reyner became the bride of Michael Wigglesworth
on May 18. The bridegroom's reaction would sound familiar
to men in every age. Eager though he patently was, "At the
time appointed with fear and trembling I came to Rowley to
be married." He had the assurance of his medical advisers

[87]

and Scriptural support of the "institution of marriage." He prayed earnestly "for all the blessings of a marryed estate, A heart suitable thereto, chastity especially thereby, and life and health if it be thy will."

Michael's passionate nature now had means of legitimate expression, but his worries were not over. His "former distemper" did not disappear at once, and he prayed that he and Mary would not "be a curs each to other but a blessing in this new relation." Under the circumstances he did not know "how to keep company with my dearest friend." In spite of her husband's expressed uncertainties, Mary became pregnant almost immediately.

In the early months of the marriage there were numerous trips to the Bay from Rowley, where the young couple was living. The very next week, the two of them had gone to greet Mary's father, just arrived from England, too late for the wedding. On another occasion Michael had gone down to preach at Malden, whose church people were still looking for a minister and would be willing to ordain this young man, even though he was so frail that he took a severe cold and after the return to Rowley had to keep to the house for days on end. One cold after another weakened him until he began to feel guilty, thought that his heart was becoming "light & frothy" because of his inability to "honour God with the little remaynder of strength which I have." Between mid-April, when he had left Hartford, and mid-July he had preached eight sermons, a fact that gave him some comfort in his illness.

Health somewhat restored, he was able to go with his bride to the Bay area, for a consultation with Alcock, to sell "a parcel of corn," and to discuss his situation further with the congregation at Malden. He was grateful to discover that the advice of the physicians had apparently been sound, for his "former distemper" finally disappeared. His conscience, however, would not let him take full joy in the marriage bed. Two months after his marriage he was praying for forgiveness of "my intemperance in the use of marriage for thy sons

[88]

sake," but equivocally ten days later was thanking God for "so much comfort in a married estate contrary to my fears; for this I will praise him whilest I have a being."

The Puritan attitude toward sex was that in itself sex was not wicked, except as all man's acts were evil. Rather was excessive indulgence the sinful development. Later generations of Americans distorted the Puritan view until it became infested with a prudery and pruriency that had not characterized these seventeenth-century Congregationalists. The Puritan cartoon symbol of total joylessness and abstention is drawn from misinterpretation. The men of Massachusetts Bay accepted life; they attempted only to live in balance, to keep from succumbing to excesses. In this instance the young bridegroom was trying to assign to the marriage relation its rightful proportions as he struggled against worldliness towards what he felt was the personality of a man of God. He was striving to become perfect even as his Father in heaven was perfect.

The first part of August was cold and wet. The young preacher's sore throat and cough persisting, he began to take a new medicine, but asked for his friends' prayers as supplement. Continually conscience-stricken because of his failure to develop his talents, he was, further, morbidly mystified that he should be allowed to live while death claimed two more worthy people—Theophilus Eaton of New Haven and his excommunicated wife, both dead within a few days of each other. (They were many years his senior.)

Though he preached twice one Sunday at Malden and suffered no added ill effect, he told members of the church that he felt he should not accept their offer because the sore throat seemed chronic and he was afraid that as the lone minister in the town he would not be able to carry out all the duties, that is, of both pastor and teacher. Malden was patient. The congregation was small; the work would not be heavy; would he think it over for another two weeks? Mr. Alcock in Roxbury urged him to accept; Mary's father in Rowley urged him to accept. Michael recalled that he had followed God "in the matter of marriage beyond sence" and marriage had worked out well; he hoped God would guide him likewise in the Malden matter.

September found him still undecided, staying on with his wife's family in Rowley. Winter was approaching. His colds were as bad as ever. His wife was going to have a baby. He would need to provide a house. Rather irrelevantly, at this point, Michael tried to take comfort in recalling that "Christ himself my Lord had not a hole to put his head in." The hard fact was that Michael must provide for his family. To complicate the business, his mother had finished settling the estate in New Haven and was coming with her daughter, Abigail, to live with him. He knew life had not been easy for his mother and was sorry that she was having to come into a situation just as difficult. If they all lived this way for very long, their money and goods would be gone. Furthermore, room was at a premium. Michael had not been sleeping with Mary for the odd reason that he was afraid of the recurrence of his "grievous disease." If the gossip got around, he would come in for censure. When he was constrained to tell his diary that "some night pollution escaped me notwithstanding my earnest prayer to the contrary," he was reminded of his "old sins now too much forgotten. . . . O unthankfulness unthankfulness when shall I get rid of thee."

On September 15 he drew in his notebook a strangely phallic "pillar of Ebenezer," captioned "Hitherto the Lord hath holpen me" and accompanied by statements in both English and Latin expanding the theme. He was clearly in agony, suffering from sexual frustration, from confusion about his future, from bad conscience about accomplishing nothing with his talents.

After his mother had arrived, he went down to the Bay to dispose of her goods as well as he could and to consult with the Malden dignitaries. He put them off till early October, when one of the elders, Joseph Hills, would be up at Ipswich at the general training day for the artillery company. Hills was married to a sister of Henry Dunster. It may have been through this connection that Malden had begun considering Wigglesworth in the first place.[117]

On October 4 he gave his word that he would move to Malden in two weeks. Those fourteen days were filled with wavering and indecision. Reason told him that Malden was the only sensible way out of his predicament. Certainly he could not keep his family in Rowley: the house was too drafty and too small, for he had no privacy for study, and, since there were not enough beds, he had to lie beside his wife, whose advanced state of pregnancy forbade his satisfying the highly inflamed passions her nearness aroused: ". . . we must lay together constantly which I can't bare." Among his sins he was aware of a continuing "undutifulness to my mother," which had been dogging him for years. He also was fearful that he desired "health more than Holyness," though he reasoned that good health would give him strength to sing God's "prais and honour."

It had been a miserable fortnight, but at the end he moved his womenfolk down to Malden into the parsonage that had been built for Marmaduke Matthews. Now there was more room for all of them, for himself and Mary and for Esther and Abigail and for the new baby, when it came.

The little town had been named for Maldon, England, the *o* being replaced by an *e* through clerical error, it was said. As a native of the original Maldon, Joseph Hills may have been responsible for the name. Since the population was small, twelve or fourteen families, the work, as they had explained, would not be a taxing mission for a minister of normal strength.[118] There were problems, however, for the congregation had not forgotten the unfortunate Matthews, and there were still low rumblings of disagreement among the brethren. Nevertheless, they now had a regular preacher again, though it was to be a year before he would consent to ordination.

Very early on the morning of February 22, 1656, the baby, Mercy, was born. Her father's record is vivid and pathetic: "February 20 toward night being Wednesday my wife began

[91]

to travail, and had sore paines. The nearnes of my bed to hers made me hear all the nois. Her pangs pained my heart, broke my sleep the most of that night. I lay sighing, sweating, praying, almost fainting through weariness before morning. The next day, the spleen much enfeebled me, and setting in with grief took away my strength, my heart was smitten within me and as sleep departed from myne eyes so my stomack abhorred meat. I was brought very low and knew not how to pass away another night; For so long as my love lay crying I lay sweating, and groaning. I was now apt to be hasty and impatient, but the Lord made me desirous to stoop to his wil (if He should take away her whom he had given, much more) if he should onely prolong her pains (himself supporting) and in time restore her. Being brought to this the Lord gave some support to my heart. After about midnight he sent me the glad tidings of a daughter that and the mother both living; after she had been in paines about 30 houres or more. . . ." Then, his Puritan training and conscience going to work, he began to moralize tediously on the event.

The child had a hard time getting started. For three weeks in March she suffered from fearful dysentery. Her father was deeply touched by her "pittiful" condition, but, instead of praying for recovery, he asked for strength to accept God's wisdom and will and to "maintain good thoughts of god while he afflicts." This Puritan habit of making use of every trouble for the strengthening of the moral fiber was what kept the Massachusetts settlers from developing a mature sense of tragedy.[119] God's hand was in every slightest event. Man's duty was to be grateful for every twist, no matter in what direction, and to apply the outcome towards the growth of the spirit. Michael's *Meat Out of the Eater* (1669) was to develop this concept in minute detail. Having found something of value even in little Mercy's suffering, the young father was nevertheless happy to be able to report in mid-May that the baby had not only fully recovered but was growing.

Wigglesworth was doing the best he could as minister at

Malden. He obtained from the church at Cambridge, from which he had never been separated, the "letter of dismission" required before he could be accepted elsewhere. The ruling elders and the pastor, Jonathan Mitchell, signed the letter: ". . . the good hand of Divine Providence hath so disposed that our beloved and highly esteemed brother, Mr. Wigglesworth, hath his residence and is employed in the good work of the Lord amongst you, and hath cause to desire of us Letters Dismissive to your Church in order to his joining as a member with you."[120] Such a letter transferred the subject's relation to the new congregation so as to permit that group to follow the original custom of selecting their clergyman from among their own number. The present letter was drawn up on August 25; Michael's acceptance by the church at Malden occurred on September 7.[121] But he was not actually ordained until sometime later, possibly as late as the following May.

Through the winter he wrote out prayers for humility and strength. His pleasure in sexual union still tormented his conscience. ". . . when wilt thou mortify these lusts. . . ? . . . I have desired and long begged power against the carnality of my heart, that this lust might dy, and the contrary grace be increased: but yet I find my heart as carnal as some years since for ought I can tell." (D417) Marriage had not brought abatement of passion!

Michael had become a member of the church at Malden through formal dismissal from the church at Cambridge. Mary, on the other hand, was required to give a "relation" of her experience as a child of God and to be approved as one of the elect by the congregation. Not quite a year after the birth of Mercy, as Mary stood, on February 11, 1657 (a very cold day),[122] before the sisters and brethren and testified, her husband recorded her words in shorthand. She concluded her account with the greatest seriousness: "Also hearing that in *Joshua* 'ye have backslidden from me; yet return and I will have mercy,' I thought the Lord called me to return to him, though I had backslid by my sins. Also when I considered of

[93]

God's patience and goodness to me that He continued me, yet finding an unbelieving heart much prevailing, I heard of that 'he that believes not is condemned already.' I went sadly to my heart for some time; yet the Lord was pleased by the Word to speak to me by that *Revelation*: 'Whosoever will, let him come and drink of the waters of life freely.' " After quoting the Scripture at length and applying these holy truths to her own case, she closed her plea by saying, "I desire prayer that God would give me more and more rootedness and groundedness in believing." (D443-444) This was a serious business. Not to be accepted by the church meant probable damnation in the world to come and much limitation in the world at hand. Again there is no record, but Mary was doubtless accepted into full membership after this profession, not because she was the minister's wife, for family position bore no influence (as Anne Eaton had learned in New Haven), but because of the sincerity of her story and the sturdiness of the fabric of her conviction.

Michael had not entirely given up the idea of returning to the country of his birth, first entertained more than three years before, during his quandary over the position at Hartford. Now he was in correspondence with Mary's relatives in Yorkshire. Oliver Cromwell was still Lord Protector. Many Harvard men, some with degrees, some without, were now in England, flourishing under the Puritan regime.

In a letter dated April 6, 1657 (it would have reached Massachusetts several weeks later), one M. Middlebrooke, probably related to Mary, wrote to Wigglesworth from Yorkshire after a visit from an acquaintance of Michael's. "Mr. Boyes thinks our climate would better agree with your constitution than New England doth and promises to mee or rather seems confident that you would not want a call now, a comfortable maintenance even in these parts of Yorkshire about Leeds if you would come." He ended by sending greetings to the entire Wigglesworth household: "yourself, bedfellow, Mother, . . . Sister, daughter. . . ."[123]

Finally, however, Michael made up his mind to accept the

position at Malden. On May 19 he made the last entry in the diary begun over four years before. This was the day on which his "settlement" was to be made. How much he was to be paid is left in mystery.

There had been many matters to discourage him up to this point. Joseph Hills, one of the pillars of the church, had demonstrated a tendency to non-conformity that was actually alarming. In the first place, he had had the audacity to preside at his own marriage to Dunster's sister. Though the Puritans had, it was true, taken this ceremony out of the jurisdiction of the church, Hills's act was nothing short of "ridiculous." The General Court indicted him for the offense. It can be presumed that he and his bride stood properly before a magistrate soon thereafter. Moreover, Hills still hankered after the heresies of Marmaduke Matthews. As elder-elect he had advertised an attitude unfavorable to infant baptism, and young Wigglesworth had had to intervene to prevent his ordination as elder (a post he had held in previous years) in order to preserve the true faith. Hills's influence remained strong, however, and the new minister could not ignore him.

Other difficulties presented themselves. Nightly private struggles to understand the intricacies of local autonomy in church government had induced a return of Michael's old ailment. Furthermore, the people having proved irresponsible in the keeping of promises, there had been endless and embarrassing quibbles over Michael's house. In fact, the parsonage was infested with big black bugs that were eating at the food, the clothing, even the walls. The old structure would need chimney repair, or there would have to be a new building. All these were serious considerations indeed.

Wigglesworth, however, had at last felt a "clear call" to work here. He recognized the great need of the people, whose spiritual life had sunk to desolation after the departure of Matthews. Almost everyone in town and in the churches of the surrounding settlements wanted him to stay, and Michael himself now wanted to stay, for the location near the Bay

[95]

was good, and God had given him strength enough, though he was still infirm, to carry on the work so far. (D418) In view of all this, one may—in spite of lack of authenticating documents—quite safely place Wigglesworth's ordination at about this time—toward the end of May, 1657.

His exact status is veiled in uncertainty, but because of his frailty he may have been ordained as teacher, not pastor, though he performed the rigorous office of pastor when he was able. This was not an altogether unheard-of arrangement: a teacher was sometimes the only minister a church had. The Malden records are incomplete, and Wigglesworth's diary now ceases (except for an occasional later notation). Though a few years later Michael denied that he had ever resigned as *pastor* and he is called *pastor* in various documents, he is also called *teacher* elsewhere. Since no account of his ordination exists, no definite title can be assigned him.

At the end of December, the town of Malden formally voted for the use of its ministers the house that Michael had been living in and the four acres around it. Two days later Michael himself bought six and a half acres adjoining, but he did not build on the land at that time, even though the original parsonage was proving unpleasant to the fastidious Wigglesworth family.[124]

Frankly, the newly ordained teacher was not very satisfactory. His recurring sore throat and general debility often interfered with ministerial activity. Sometimes he was too weak in both voice and body to preach the expected two sermons on Sunday. Sometimes he was confined to his home so that he could not give his people the hoped-for counsel and instruction.

> I would, but (ah!) my strength,
> When tried, proves so small. . . .
> (Reader)

Some of the congregation even went so far as to speculate that their minister was ill only in imagination, for the causes of his afflictions were not always evident.

Yet some (I know) do judge,
Mine inability,
To come abroad and do Christ's Work,
To be Melancholly;
And that I'm not so weak,
As I my self conceit, . . .

(Reader)

Things went from bad to worse.

Michael composed a long letter, which Joseph Hills of the dubious doctrine but strong influence received on June 19, 1658, to be read in church the next day. The writer admitted that he had been slow in making his decision about Malden and that even now for some weeks he had not been able to perform the normal duties of his office. But he had thought of his flock constantly during the period "of lingering weakness & long restraint." He recalled the history of the church. He asked diplomatically whether their clinging to the unsound teaching of Matthews might not be the cause of their present strife. During the short time that they had enjoyed the regular privilege of the Lord's Supper, had they made adequate preparation for receiving it? Had they sought God through "prayer, private meditation, selfe examination, dayly renewing of repentence, christian conference &c. . . ?" While the writer had been confined, they had resorted to quarreling, fighting, bickering among themselves. "Are Christs Lambs become lyons. . . ?" Repentance and love for one another were the alternatives. "I dare promise you in the name of Christ that if you turn to him he will return to you either in the restitution of him whom now you pray for (which is easy with the Lord if it be good for you) or in giving you a better. But if you still walk contrary unto God [you] shall be plagued seven times more."[125]

The letter may have had some temporary effect on the congregation. At any rate, the following November 11 they signed articles of agreement for a second, larger meeting house near the site of the first one. (What of the parsonage chimney?) This was to be "a good strong Artificial meeting-

[97]

House of Thirty-three foot Square." On completion of the structure Job Lane, the contractor, would be paid one hundred fifty pounds in food, wood, and cattle. (Money was still scarce.) For one reason or another the church was a good year and a half in the building. And even then no turret was constructed for the bell; so provision was made to place the bell on a scaffolding on a nearby rock which gave its name to the plot and later to the cemetery—the Bell Rock Burying Ground.[126]

By the end of the next July, however, Wigglesworth was despondent about his congregation. They were backsliding; his own physical weakness had increased; his wife was in bad health. He thought of going to Rowley to ask the advice of his friends there about resigning.[127] Whether he went or not, he continued at his post.

In early December, 1659, the colony held a general thanksgiving. The harvest had been plentiful; for the present there was a slackening in disease; the influence of the Quakers, "that pestilent body," had been thwarted; another great quarrel at Hartford had been settled; the churches and the colony seemed for the time to be at peace.[128]

But for Wigglesworth the thanksgiving was ironic. Joseph Hills would not be silenced. Though a leader in the community, he had been outspoken against the strict rules of selectivity in the church. He was of the belief that every baptized person was entitled to the privileges of the ordinances and the church membership whether he had made open profession and been admitted formally or not. A member of one church should be able to move freely among the other churches and enjoy all privileges everywhere. The magistrates ought to promote a reformation so that these conditions could prevail. For his opinions Hills had been indicted and censured by the General Court. The Lord's garden must be carefully weeded.[129]

Worse than this, in the early hours of December 21 Mary Wigglesworth died. Michael was crushed, but tried at once to make his sorrow a stepping-stone to greater holiness. "Oh its a heart-cutting & astonishing stroke in itself. Lord help me to bear it patiently & to profit by it, help me to honor thee now in the fier, by maintaining good thoughts of thee, & speaking good & submissive words concerning thee. And oh teach me to dy every day. Fit me for that sweet society she is gone unto, where solitariness shal no more affright or afflict me. Oh Lord make up in thyself what is gone in the creature. I beleiv thou canst & wilt do it: but oh help my unbeleif." Here was a man who sought constantly to smother honest sorrow in moralizing and "profiting." A decade later he was generalizing on this same kind of situation:

> Thy Wife, or Child, or Friend,
> They were but Blessings lent thee;
> They were the Lords both first and last;
> And doth this not content thee?
> May not the Lord require,
> When he sees fit, his own?
> Thou may'st be thankful unto him
> They were no sooner gone.
>
> (Sol II.3)

He was left with a daughter almost four years old. Presumably, his mother continued to live with him and take care of the child. (His sister, Abigail, was married now to Benjamin Sweetser.)[130] Adversity still struck out. His own health went downhill. In September, 1660, his father-in-law, Humphrey Reyner, died in Rowley.[131] Gone now was one of his most dependable advisors.

In November the colony received word of the return of liturgical worship to the churches of England.[132] Charles II had been on the throne six months and was fast undoing the work of the Puritan reformation. Surplices, candles, processions, choirs, *The Book of Common Prayer*—all would be restored. Geographically remote though it was, New England felt the tension. There was even a counter-exodus as men who had gone back to England now sought refuge again in Massachusetts. Leonard Hoar returned and a decade later became President of Harvard. Similarly, Urian Oakes came back and eventually succeeded Hoar at Harvard. There were others, including William Stoughton, who was to pass terrible judgment on the hapless victims of the Salem witch hunt.[133] The glorious years of high hope when Governor John Winthrop had painted a vivid picture of the responsibility of Massachusetts Bay as a model Zion were gone forever. Apprehension and suspicion were sprouting everywhere.

The struggling little church at Malden was no better off than it had ever been. Mysteriously afflicted, the minister was unable to serve the people. Intramural differences had developed the tendency of the people to quarrelsomeness. In December, 1661, they met to consider the feasibility of calling an assistant.[134] Though the duties could easily have been administered by one man, the man they had called was as good as nothing to his people. Where would he go? What would he do? He wanted to perform the will of God, but what was that?

He stayed on in Malden, but there is no formal record that he received any income from the church. Nor was an assistant found for two years.

V. "And read it for thy good"

In despair of ever reaching his congregation effectively through the spoken word, and yet believing wholeheartedly in the power of language, Wigglesworth decided to try his pen. Soon after Mary's death he had composed two little poems in Latin,[135] subjective, humble in tone. One of them, only two lines long, expresses no hope:

> Christe, parum doleo quia te non diligo multum;
> Quodque parum doleo, causa doloris erit.

This reads like a finely argued point in medieval disputation, in which Michael had had a deal of practice at Harvard: Christ, I suffer too little because I do not pursue Thee hard enough; and, because I suffer too little, there will be cause for grief. Doomsday was imminent: *erit,* will be.

The other poem contains eight lines, six in Latin, the concluding two in English. The Latin catalogues his afflictions and compares them to wind and wave churned by storm (*ventus et unda minax*). The closing English couplet, however, is a little more comforting:

> My sins and wants still pain my heart.
> My hope in Christ relieves my smart.
> (Ira)

Now two years later Wigglesworth was embarked on a more ambitious project—to set out in easily memorized verses the chief tenets of the kind of Calvinism supported in Massachusetts. By the end of January, 1662, he had already arranged to have his book printed at the press in Cambridge.[136] His health was bad (he thought this might be his final service to God), but he hoped to have time to finish the work.[137] Confined most of the time to his house, he could not bear the thought of pagan idleness; so he busied himself, often laboriously, writing the poems collected in *The Day of Doom.*

Verse writers were plenteous among Puritan New Englanders, whose leaders were men of culture, but creative energies were directed to setting up and keeping straight the new Zion so that elegies[138] and almanac verses were of most popular interest, probably because they were "useful." An exception was Anne Bradstreet of Andover, whose book had been taken to England for publication in 1650 under the embarrassingly grandiose title of *The Tenth Muse, Lately Sprung Up in America.*[139] Edward Taylor's meditations and sacred lyrics, begun later, were not published until over two hundred years after his death.[140]

The most widely known verses in the colony were those in *The Whole Booke of Psalmes*[141] ("The Bay Psalm Book"), the work of John Cotton and various of his colleagues. To make the lines easy to sing, their authors had cast them into unrelieved ballad meter that, for later years, precludes beauty. The *Twenty-Third Psalm,* almost positively from the pen of Cotton himself,[142] is pock-marked with sing-song accent and distortion:

> The Lord to mee a shepheard is,
>   want therefore shall not I.
> Hee in the folds of tender-grasse
>   doth cause mee downe to lie.
> To waters calme me gently leads
>   Restore my soule doth hee:
> he doth in paths of righteousnes:
>   for his names sake leade mee.

Awkward and strained though they were, these hymns were almost universally adopted throughout New England.

In line with the Puritan ethic, Michael's purpose was to

set before the common reader the truth as he and his fellow ministers saw it. The result—communication between intellectual and laboring man such as is rarely achieved in any civilization[143]—was accomplished through the "plain style" the writer had learned in college and the fourteen-syllable line everyone knew from the *Bay Psalm Book* and the ballads familiar since childhood:

> There lived a wife at Usher's Well,
>   and a wealthy wife was she;
> She had three stout and stalward sons,
>   and sent them oer the sea. . . .

And the old favorite:

> O long, long may their ladies sit,
>   with their fans into their hand,
> Or e'er they see Sir Patrick Spens
>   come sailing to the land.

Before starting on the *chef d'oeuvre,* though, Wigglesworth composed a dedication in couplets, "A Prayer unto Christ, the Judge of the World." He wanted it clear that he was not summoning the Muses to his aid. Even if his own library was strikingly barren in poetry, he had had access to the Harvard College library as a Master of Arts candidate. John Harvard had left a few volumes of contemporary verse,[144] and these Michael had doubtlessly examined. In George Wither's "Epithalamia" he would have found frequent references to Minerva, Neptune, Jove, Juno, Vulcan, Hymen, and the rest of the pagan roster. Likewise, in Richard Niccols' contribution to *The Mirror for Magistrates,* "A Winter Night's Vision," he would have read, in the introduction, of "Jove-borne Phoebus," of Ceres; he would have seen the frankly heathenish acknowledgment that "my Clio sings." On the other hand, in the third book of poems Harvard had left, he would have read Francis Quarles's "Invocation" at the beginning of the First Book of *Emblems:*

> . . . when my Urania sings,
> She sings praises of the King of Kings.

This was more to Michael's taste. Into his own work nothing pagan would be admitted, no matter how fashionable to call upon Juno or "frowning Mars" or "thundering Jove" to bless a work.

> Thou, Christ, art He to whom I pray,
> Thy glory fain would I display.

The story of the main poem was a familiar one, the subject of Michael's dream in 1653—the Last Judgment. With a flash, an explosion, and an all-revealing light, the end of the world arrives. History is over; the millenium is here. All men living and dead are summoned before the throne of Christ, no matter where they try to hide. The saved (the Sheep) are directed to the right and the damned (the Goats) to the left. The catalogue of the Sheep is soon told: martyrs for the faith; the physically afflicted who have kept their faith; the loyal able-bodied; and the spiritually weak whom God has nevertheless foreordained to salvation. This last class includes baptized infants, who have not had time to live lives of sin.

The Goats, on the contrary, are listed at greater length and, one suspects, with greater interest. All are summarily categorized as "whining hypocrites": deserters; those who have never professed the faith even when they have had the opportunity; worshipers of idols; those who have taken the name of the Lord in vain; breakers of the Sabbath blue laws; persecutors of the saints; sex offenders; the "covetous and ravenous"; grossly wicked children and their evil-minded parents who have deliberately reared them in the ways of unrighteousness; liars, murderers, witches, and drunkards; and finally the heathen, who have never heard of God.

The Sheep are invited to sit on thrones around their Lord and help to pass sentence on their less fortunate brethren. Christ announces that it has been for them (the Sheep) that He has suffered crucifixion. They are to be rewarded with the bliss of heaven.

Now the Goats must come to the bar of judgment and

plead their own cases, even though they are already doomed. First to approach are those who have preached and taught the orthodox doctrines but, as their Judge points out, whose souls have been dead all along. Also in this group are those who have dared to partake of the Lord's Supper without first clearing their hearts of fault. This amounts to blasphemy, which they must repay in perdition. The next pleaders are related to these, for they have followed the forms of the faith, at the same time recognizing their innate sinfulness and doing nothing about it. Christ dismisses them as pride-ridden and "self-vaunting."

To the "Civil honest Men" the Judge explains that all, even the saved, are sinners and that these citizens, though respected, having fallen short, must take their punishment since they have not been selected to enjoy a delightful eternity.

Now come the real whiners. Those who have had good intentions for the future are reminded that death could have snatched them away at any moment. Those who complain that they have been misled by their superiors are told that they were expected to follow the law, not human examples. Those who claim to have misinterpreted the Bible are made to see that, though the technical points may have been obscure, there was enough plain sense in the Good Book to guide the willing righteous. The cowardly, who have been afraid of persecution, draw a wrathful and contemptuous condemnation.

Claiming to have relied on God's much-publicized mercy, others are given a lecture: God's mercy is used up; the Day of Wrath has come. God has never promised to save anyone in particular. These complainers are simply out of luck. To those who say they were pre-ordained to damnation and could see no reason for keeping in line, Christ replies that they are consigned to hell, not because God has already rejected them, but because they have broken His holy laws. How were they to know in life but that they were to be saved?

Finally come those who will be granted lighter punishment than the rest. The heathen, who have not had the privilege of hearing the Word of God, should have followed the light of nature more faithfully; but, since they have never heard of Christianity, they will be let off with less painful fires. The very last group, the unbaptized babies, must be condemned because, after all, Adam's fall has made every human being a sinner. Having had no chance to get onto the right path, however, these infants will spend eternity in "the easiest room in Hell." (On Copp's Hill in Boston was a plot for the unceremonious burial of unbaptized babies.)

The trial is over. The saints are happy that their erstwhile relatives, friends, and enemies, now proved wicked, are to be tortured forever. Over the condemned the Judge pronounces the awful sentence:

> *Ye sinful wights, and cursed sprights;*
> *   that work Iniquity,*
> *Depart together from me forever*
> *   to endless Misery;*
> *You portion take in yonder Lake,*
> *   where Fire and Brimstone flameth:*
> *Suffer the smart, which your desert*
> *   as it's due wages claimeth.*
>
> (DD201)

(Final -*ed* is always a separate syllable.) Bound hand and foot, the culprits are flung into the burning lake, whence their howls make music in the ears of the saints, who ascend to heaven "with great joy and melody."

Though this was a restatement of Last Things for the culture of Wigglesworth's time and place, it was hardly different from verse accounts of preceding generations. Thomas Dekker, the English playwright (died 1641?), had written a poem on the identical subject:[145]

> Their cries, nor yelling did the Judge regard,
> For all the doores of Mercy up were bar'd:
> Justice and Wrath in wrinkles knit his forehead,
> And thus he spake: You cursed and abhorred,

You brood of Sathan, sonnes of death and hell,
In fires that still shall burne, you still shall dwell;
In hoopes of Iron: then were they bound up strong,
(Shrikes being the Burden of their doleful song).

Wigglesworth himself had drawn a picture in two hundred
twenty-four stanzas as stark and vivid as the medieval sculp-
tures around the cathedral doors of Europe, for this was a
medieval concept: *Dies Irae* had been in the hymnology of
the Church since the thirteenth century:

> (3) Wondrous sound the trumpet flingeth;
>   Through earth's sepulchres it ringeth;
>   All before the throne it bringeth.

> (4) Death is struck and nature quaking,
>   All creation is awaking,
>   To its Judge an answer making.[146]

Wigglesworth and his fellows were standing on the threshold
of the Modern Age (Newton was now less than thirty years
away); but, despite outward organization and whisperings
of democracy to come, they were still in faith undeniably in
the Middle Ages, conservatively paying no heed to the proc-
lamations of Copernicus,[147] listening only to scholastic arguments supporting a creed about to be outworn.

As poet, Wigglesworth had shown an imagination of vast
proportion, fed by the apocalyptic passages of the Bible. He
had long been preoccupied with his subject. His dream of
nine years before had been only a single manifestation. One
can believe that he wrote "The Day of Doom" not only to
bring his backsliding congregation to the paths of righteousness again but to commit to paper, to communicate to others,
to bring to form, the surging images that made his mind, his
whole being a turbulent cauldron.[148]

In shaping the poem, he made his structure more complex
than in most of his later patterns by using inner rhyme.
Built on the tension of man's false feeling of security, the
opening stanza shows the device. The scene is peaceful, but
the language portends the cataclysm:

> Still was the night, Serene and Bright,
>   when all Men sleeping lay;
> Calm was the season, and carnal reason
>   thought so 'twould last for ay.
> Soul, take thine ease; let sorrow cease,
>   much good thou hast in store:
> This was their Song, their Cups among,
>   the Evening before.

The clues lie in "carnal reason" and "their Cups among," as symbols of mankind's incompetence and frailty. The nurturing of the mind was an obligation, but to rely altogether on reason, without the leap of faith, was fatal. Likewise, beer, wine, and cordials (all food and drink) were essential, but intemperance was mortal sin. The rhyming of "night" and "Bright," of "season" and "reason," not only makes the lines more intricate, but would facilitate the reading and, as it happened, the memorizing of the poem.

For the most part Wigglesworth's college-learned logic characterizes the work, as Christ puts each class of the damned in its place. Only occasionally does the poet's burning sensitivity break through the wall of the theological treatise, and even then, the language and imagery are fenced in by Biblical phraseology. The heavily loaded words, the fast movement of the thickly rhymed lines, and the vivid realism make the narrative stanzas, as opposed to the argumentative passages, absorbing. After sentence has been passed on the unredeemed,

> They wring their hands, their caitiff-hands
>   and gnash their teeth for terrour;
> They cry, they roar for anguish sore
>   and gnaw their tongues for horrour.
>   (DD205)

On the other hand, when the "renate" (those "born again" into life eternal) reach the embracing arms of God,

> Griefs water-course, and sorrows sourse,
>   are turn'd to joyful streams.

> Their old distress and heaviness
> are vanished like dreams.
> (DD222)

Critics of early American literature have possibly paid too much attention to the uncongenial theology and not enough to the passages of power and lyricism in this poem. In 1878 Moses Coit Tyler expressed the opinion that, because of Wigglesworth's "message," it would be next to impossible to be fair to him as poet. Tyler did admit, however, to Wigglesworth's sincerity and vividness, to his unflinching vigor, but he found in the poems nothing beautiful, everything "grim, pathetic, horrible." Nevertheless, he recognized in the poet a "sensitive, firm, wide-ranging, unresting spirit."[149] If the limitations of the period prohibited full flight, notwithstanding, the intensity of the poet's feeling finds expression with rewarding frequency.

Having completed the composition of the long work, the poet re-read it and turned to address his reader in a poem less jogging, with less frequent rhyme. In the book these lines were placed as a kind of preface before the main work.

> Reader, I am a fool,
> And have adventured
> To play the fool this once for Christ,
> The more his fame to spread.

He explained that his physical infirmity had forced him to turn to writing. Preaching was too much for him; for "ten days after" he would suffer indescribable consequences. But, though he had been afflicted "more than ten years," he rejoiced to have found a way of serving God, by publishing "this little Piece" for the edification of his congregation.

> Although the thing be small,
>   . . .
> Accept it then in Love,
> And read it for thy good. . . .
> (Reader)

After Michael's mentor, pastor, and inspiration in Cambridge, Jonathan Mitchell, had read the manuscript, he wrote an introductory poem, "On the Following Work and Its Author," in which he developed an elaborate metaphor:

> Reader, fall too, and, if thy taste be good,
> Thou'lt praise the cook and say, 'tis choicest food.

Mitchell, too, explained that out of the writer's affliction had come this worthy sermon in verse to remind the reader that all things work together for good and that all men are headed for some kind of life after death:

> In those vast woods a christian poet sings
> (Where whilome heathen wild were only found)
> Of things to come, the last and greatest things,
> Which in our ears aloud should ever sound.
> Of Judgment dread, hell, heaven, eternity;
> Reader, think oft, and help thy thoughts thereby.

As a coda to his narrative of the Judgment, Wigglesworth appended "A Short Discourse on Eternity," twenty-two stanzas of the same trotting line structure in which he attempted to delineate the illimitable. No ocean, no abyss can compare with the vastness of eternity. If one were to add together the number of all natural phenomena from the stars in the heavens down to every grain of dust on earth, he still would fall boundlessly short of numbering the years of the hereafter.

> A Cockle-shell may serve as well
> to lade the Ocean dry,
> As finite things and Reckonings
> to bound Eternity.

Saints rejoice in the length of the life to come, whereas the wicked can but shudder and moan that their torment is to last forever and ever. There can be no hope. Just as Andrew Marvell—in quite another context—reminded his coy mistress that "the conversion of the Jews" will be as good as never, so Wigglesworth used an image of the impossible to drive home the everlastingness of the punishment of the doomed:

> When Gods great Power shall be brought lower,
>   by forreign Puissance;
> Or be decay'd, and weaker made
>   through Times continuance:
> When drowsiness shall him oppress,
>   and lay him fast asleep:
> Then sinful men may break their pen,
>   and out of Prison creep.

Turning from the role of fiery pulpiteer to the more intimate and gentle part of teacher, the poet in "A Postscript unto the Reader" composed over four hundred lines of rhyming couplets no less vivid in content than the long poem preceding, but more directly personal.

> And now good Reader, I return again
> To talk with thee, who hast been at great pain
> To read throughout, and heed what went before;
> And unto thee I'le speak a little more.

Repent, he advised; turn from evil before it is too late. Why kick against God, Who has done you nothing but good? His mercy will last only till Doomsday. You are not as secure as you imagine:

> Thou hangest over the Infernal Pit
> By one small threed, and car'st thou not a whit?

Here was a theme to be belatedly developed with terrifying effect in the next century by Jonathan Edwards. Reviewing the argument and situation pictured in "The Day of Doom," the teacher now pleaded with his reader to avoid everlasting punishment by turning from wickedness. The rewards of righteousness he described in conclusion with sweetly compelling power—the "plain style" adapted to the emotional purpose of conviction:

> Lift up your heads, ye upright ones in heart,
> Who in Christ's purchase have obtain'd a part.
> Behold, he rides upon a shining Cloud,

With Angels voice, and Trumpet sounding loud;
He comes to save his folk from all their foes,
And plague the men that Holiness oppose.
So come, Lord Jesus, quickly come we pray:
Yea come, and hasten our Redemption day.

Finally, Wigglesworth turned his attention to one more poem, its title familiar to all readers of *Ecclesiastes,* "Vanity of Vanities," its subtitle showing a somber wit: "A Song of Emptiness to Fill up the Empty Pages Following." The theme of the twenty-seven quatrains is, of course, that man is only "A restless Wave o'th' troubled Ocean." The descriptive catalogue is familiar and inevitable: beauty, pleasure, friends, riches, honor, sovereignty, strength, valor. Though "mean Mechanick" and "Country-Clown" can sleep without fear, "greatest Princes" frequently toss in troubled insomnia. History's great figures have come to nought:

Where are the *Scipio's* Thunderbolts of War?
Renowned *Pompey, Caesars* Enemie?
Stout *Hannibal, Romes* Terrour known so far?
Great *Alexander,* what's become of thee?

After demonstrating at length how ultimately pointless is the pursuit of the worldly, the poet dared mankind, with a mockery born of hard-won faith in God, to cultivate material security:

Go boast thy self of what thy heart enjoyes,
Vain Man! triumph in all thy worldly Bliss:
Thy best enjoyments are but Trash and Toyes:
Delight thy self in that which worthless is.

The tone of this poem depends heavily on Wigglesworth's wide reading—not just on Biblical allusions familiar to every fireside reader. Here the poet departed from the obvious effort of popular appeal he had made in "The Day of Doom." A concluding truth, couched in Latin, would reach only readers of education and comparative sophistication, a line again of somewhat scholastic involvement in its diction:

Omnia praetereunt praeter amare Deum: All things fade into insignificance before the act of loving God.

When he had completed the manuscript, Michael took it or sent it to Cambridge to the only press in the colony, in operation since 1639.[150] It may have been at this time that Jonathan Mitchell read the major poem and wrote his introductory verses. Though of extant copies none contains his lines until the edition of 1701, nevertheless, since he died in 1668, he would have written the piece soon after the completion of the original version of the poem.

While printers Samuel Green and Marmaduke Johnson were setting up the book, its author, now in the swing of composition, went to work on another poem, not so long, not destined to be so widely read, but historically important. The summer of 1662 was marked by a tremendous drought.[151] Moreover, now that the first splendid enthusiasm for the new Zion had passed with the passing of most of its founders, backsliding was common, mutterings of discontent were frequent. Frankly, the Bible state was in difficulty. The breadth of the Atlantic was no safeguard against the Anglican opposition of the restored throne. On August 24, by the Act of Uniformity, about two thousand dissenters in England had been removed from their pulpits. And on New England's own shores the lure of commerce and riches was gaining a power unpredicted by the zealots of the Great Migration. In matters of belief there were growing indifferences, especially in the matter of baptism.

Periodically over half the year 1662, from March to October, the Synod of Massachusetts Bay met to work out a solution for the continuance of the church. Were the children of baptized but unprofessed parents eligible for baptism? Having argued in all directions all summer long, the Synod concluded that, provided the parents in presenting their children testified to loyalty to the church, even though not with the intention of receiving the ordinance of the Lord's Supper, the children could be accepted for baptism with, then, the privilege of profession and full church membership later on.

This settlement became popularly and somewhat derisively known as the "Halfway Covenant," a necessary concession if the church was to prosper.[152]

Furthermore, in the little towns there was an increasing demand for more space. In June, Malden petitioned the General Court to permit expansion at Pennycook (now Concord, New Hampshire). Among other causes, the citizens claimed "That hitherto we have had no inlargment from the countrie, nor can we have any neere adjoining, being surrounded by sundry townships. That our charges to the countrie and ministry much exceedeth sundry others who have many times our accomodations. . . ." How much their "charges to the . . . ministry" amounted to is unrevealed. Exactly what the final item had to do with expansion is not clear: "Our teacher, Mr. Wigglesworth, also hath been long visited with verie great weakness from which it is feared he will not be recovered." Joseph Hills, Job Lane, and a few others signed the paper "In the name of the rest."[153] They wanted to be sure that the General Court recognized the incompetence of their present minister ("teacher"). Nothing was done about him, however. In refusing to grant the petition the Court felt that the church would lose its influence if the members—some of them, like Joseph Hills, unorthodox at best—were scattered over the countryside.

Sickness had increased throughout the colony, especially strength-sapping respiratory infections and chills and fever. Probably more serious yet, the early summer had been blighted by canker worms and by lack of rain, serious enough, reported John Hull, "that the grass and corn was so scorched, there was little likelihood of any harvest, and so as God seemed to shut out their prayers." Incidentally, he went on to record that the ministers, meeting for another purpose (no doubt the formulation of the Halfway Covenant), devoted one day to "fasting and prayer; and the Lord gave a speedy answer, and a full supply of rain, and a pretty comfortable harvest."[154] But this came later in the summer.

The Puritans were now finding in adverse phenomena not

so much a cause of trouble as a manifestation of God's wrath against the colony. For ten years the emphasis in sermons and pamphlets had been shifting to sins like sloth, hypocrisy, and sensuality as reasons for storms, dry spells, and bad crops. The first generation of the Massachusetts Bay Company was being gathered to its fathers. Because the ministers and magistrates were having unforeseen difficulties in maintaining enthusiasm for the original positive purposes of the settlement, they were stressing the restraining, negative doctrine of punishment to try to bring the colonists back into line.

Wigglesworth, then, used the "great drought" as point of departure for a poem blasting out full strength at the people for their negligent habits. Called "God's Controversy with New-England," it was written "by a Lover of New England's Prosperity." The first stanzas are in the ballad meter of "The Day of Doom," but without the inner rhyme.[155] "The Authors Request unto the Reader" makes clear that the poet knew that he was limning his own faults when he listed the sins of the reader and that it was God, not he, that was warning the wrongdoer. After two opening stanzas in English, Wigglesworth composed a Latin quatrain in which he begged the *Lector Amice,* Reader Friend, to take the poem seriously, for God, the prophets, and finally he himself were speaking.

In the next section, labeled "New-England Planted, Prospered, Declining, Threatned, Punished," the poet detailed the history of the colony's fortunes, reminding his reader that God had seen fit to drive the Indians out to make way for the Englishmen and drawing a parallel with the Biblical heathen:

> Those curst Amalekites, that first
>   Lift up their hand on high
> To fight against Gods Israel,
>   Were ruin'd fearfully.

He rather minimized the facts of the early years:

> Amidst the solitary woods
> Poor travelers might sleep
> As free from danger as at home,
> Though no man watch did keep.

He romanticized the spiritual life of that first generation:

> Our morning starrs shone all day long: . . .

Then came clouds and the thundering voice of the Almighty. At this point the poet shifted from the ballad meter to a more dignified stanza structure: five decasyllabic lines and a concluding hexameter. God asks, in a series of grandly rhetorical questions, whether these can be the same people He has sent on His errand into the wilderness. Those first settlers had sacrificed their inheritances in England and, prizing liberty more than riches, had been carried to these shores and protected from savages so that they could establish their New Jerusalem. They had been saved from the bloodshed of the English Civil Wars, they had been blessed here with "a fruitfull paradeis," they had been nourished on "finest spirituall food most finely drest," they had entered into "a Covenant of peace" with God to guide them in grace and love. It is incredible to Him that these descendants of the first settlers have now succumbed to all the "grosser sins." For the sake of the righteous remnant He has refrained from general punishment, but, unless the backsliders repent immediately, there will be trouble.

> What should I do with such a stiff-neckt race?
> How shall I ease me of such Foes as they?
> What shall befall despizers of my Grace?
> I'le surely beare their candle-stick away,
> And Lamps put out. Their glorious noon-day light
> I'le quickly turn into a dark Egyptian night.

As God's dreadful threats cease, the ballad form returns to describe dramatically the awful groans of earth and the blackening of the welkin. The details of the illnesses and the "great & parching drought" are tabulated.

> This O New-England, hast thou got
> By riot, & excess: . . .

In the final four stanzas the form is yet again changed, this time to quatrains in iambic pentameter. With great dignity and overflowing love Wigglesworth himself had entered the poem again and was admonishing his readers to obey the will of God that the colony's prosperity both material and spiritual might be once more restored.

> Cheer on, sweet souls, my heart is with you all,
>   And shall be with you, maugre Sathan's might:
> And whereso'ere this body be a Thrall,
>   Still in New-England shall be my delight.

On such a tender note had the poet returned to the reader earlier in the year in the "Postscript" after the lurid pictures of "The Day of Doom." One can only conclude that he was a gentle man, loving and affectionate by nature, that he had moreover become a rooted American, but was being driven to castigation both by the fierceness of his medieval theology and by his genuine concern for the salvation of his flock. Wigglesworth being an introvert, contemplative and quiet (partly by physical necessity), for him the state of his mind and particularly his soul was of more importance than the state of his surroundings. Puritan ministers as a whole tried by example continually to keep this concept before their congregations. God's gifts should be nurtured, but the soul was the most precious instrument of salvation.

"God's Controversy" was the first full-scale denunciation that now became a stylized form in New England culture.[156] Increasingly the clergy assigned entire days to fasting and self-examination for their congregations. More and more, their sermons took to the structure and content of the diatribe. No longer was the city upon a hill an ideal achieved. No longer could God be regarded as a loving Father of a special people, a new Israel, but now most emphatically was a God of wrath, thoroughly disappointed in the paths his erstwhile followers were taking. In Wigglesworth's opinion a false prosperity, the growing materialism, was outranking regard for spirituality. At the instigation of their pastors, the colonists sought expiation through observing formalized days of self-denial and repentance and through listening to sermons full of the punishments of the Almighty. There was no call, be it noted, for acts of charity, for community good deeds, as a means of bringing the soul closer to God. Repentance was all.

Notably the topical sermons at the time of the general elections held in Boston every spring began to follow this pattern. In 1668 William Stoughton—severely orthodox—told his holiday crowd what their sins had become: ". . . O New England, thy God did expect better things from thee and thy children; not worldliness and an insatiable desire after perishing things; not whoredoms and fornications; not revellings and drunkenness; not oaths and false swearings; not exactions and oppressions; not slanderings and back bitings; not rudeness and incivility, a degeneracy of the good manners of the Christian world; not formality and profaneness, to loath manna, to despise holy things, to grow sermon-proof and ordinance-proof; not contentions and disorders; not an itching after new things and ways; not a rigid pharisaical spirit; not a contempt of superiors; not unthankfulness and disrespect to the instruments of choice service; not a growing weary of government and a drawing loose in the yoke of God: not these things, but better things, O New England, hath thy God expected from thee."[157] Such a list would indicate that the second generation had wandered far from the highways their fathers had thought to build in "those vast woods."

Four years later the junior Thomas Shepard's election sermon was given the title *Eye-Salve, or a Watchword from Our Lord Jesus Christ unto His Churches: Especially Those Within the Colony of Massachusetts in New England, to Take Heed of Apostasy; or, A Treatise of Remembrance of What God Hath Been to Us, as Also What We Ought and What We Ought Not to Be to Him as We Desire the Pro-*

longing of Our Prosperous Days in the Land Which the Lord Hath Given Us.[158] The sermon was considerably longer than the title! A not uncommon figure, the "eye-salve," was derived from *Revelation* 3:18: ". . . anoint thine eyes with eye-salve, that thou mayst see." Wigglesworth himself transcribed the reference a few years before Shepard's sermon in a poem of 1669, "Poor Men's Wealth":

> I counsel thee to buy
> Eye-salve, that thou mayst see, . . .[159]

On went the scorching indictments. In 1685, nearly a quarter century following Wigglesworth's poem, after lashing out with a cat-o'-nine-tails of accusations, William Adams reminded his congregation of God's mercy: "It is indeed wonderful condescension in the infinite God to vouchsafe His regard to such low worms as the best of the children of men are. That the great God should look upon such nothings is a great stoop."[160] Wigglesworth's "God's Controversy" had set in motion such swirls of scalding rhetoric as had not been dreamed of in the first years of the colony. The Malden minister and the other clergy were members of "the Party" (to borrow from present-day jargon) and by persuasion, argument, excommunication, banishment, yes, and even torture and execution were trying to make everyone else conform to the truth as they saw it, to force everyone into total participation in the company of the saints.

Wigglesworth was dedicated to the cause of community (as he showed in "God's Controversy"), for he knew that man is a social being. He recommended that those who were under a cloak of guilt should seek counsel. Only in prayer, he said, should a man cultivate solitude, which otherwise was not only unnatural but actually harmful. Man could not depend entirely on private worship, but must come together with his fellows in a "gathered" church.

Wigglesworth could see man's total powerlessness before infinity. When many of his fellow New Englanders were beginning to experience the sweet deceptions of worldly power and distraction, he blasted out against them in the theological terms of the day. The inevitable encroachments of science and secularism were destroying the values of the city upon a hill. They were leading to eventual technology and to bureaucracy, to mass art, mass media, to comic books and tabloids—a long distance from the widely distributed *The Day of Doom*.

The jeremiad was beating futilely against the exciting and adventurous future. If its hysteria had been tempered, if its searing threats had been controlled, if its Baroque-related excesses had been more controlled, the next century might have retained some perception of man's final impotence and a responsibility to neighbor and to God, instead of relaxing into a man-centered, pastel-colored deism. America has now come through the rule of reason to a point of crisis, to a virtual return in many ways to the position of Wigglesworth's New England. There is now an awareness of wrath impending. Evil cannot be destroyed; it only rises again in new quarters and new guises. What is needed, as was needed then, is a recognition of the inevitability of love as the only healer (love not as sentimentality but as concern). Despite the fact that Wigglesworth's graphic sureties of the supranatural have now become imagery, human attitudes are stunningly similar. One frightening difference is that craftsmanship has become automation, the uniqueness of the individual has become absorbed in the facelessness of the mass. Community has become confused with mere joining.[161]

The summer of 1662 over, the little volume containing "The Day of Doom" and its companion poems was published. Green and Johnston had printed almost eighteen hundred copies. The success of the venture was immediate and astonishing, for within a year the entire edition was virtually exhausted. Though no account of the gross income is extant, a comparison with the sale of *The Bay Psalm Book* would give some idea of how Wigglesworth fared. Printing and paper for seventeen hundred copies of the hymnal had come to sixty-two pounds. Sales at twenty pence a copy had brought in better than one hundred forty-one pounds, leaving a profit of over seventy-nine pounds[162]—more than many a minister's annual "settlement."

The Day of Doom, then, within a year had enjoyed a distribution of one to every thirty-five people in the colony. The new book was devoured metaphorically and actually, for no whole copy of the first edition is known to exist today. Children memorized it; it was given as a gift; preachers used it in their sermons. The chief poem itself is said to have been printed even on broadsides and sold throughout New England. The book became America's second best-seller (after *The Bay Psalm Book*), outclassing every other book for a hundred years, until the appearance of Benjamin Franklin's *The Way to Wealth,* a work of a different color as befitted the eighteenth century.[163] It went through four more editions in America, and several in England, before its author's death.[164] The next two hundred years produced many more editions, the last in 1929.[165]

Its contents, vivid and horrible, were accepted as a matter of course. There is no way to measure its influence. In an era of growing dependence on reason and of exploitation of natural resources for profit and, candidly, for wealth, it no doubt had a restraining effect, at least on the sensitive. Its tremendous popularity most assuredly produced widespread clarification as to the meaning of the theology of the Massachusetts Puritans. Its lines were used to support many a fireside argument, for the problems of divinity and the cosmos were not confined to the conversation of the college-bred.

Whatever his income, Wigglesworth did not improve in health. The winter was hard; his chronic sore throat kept him weak. When he discovered that the money from the book would pay for a voyage to a more genial climate, he consulted his physician friends, who all, with the exception of the too-distant Winthrop, advised him to try, as he proposed, a trip to Bermuda,[166] with which island, by 1663, a brisk trade had developed.[167]

Bermuda had had a varied history since the spring of 1610, when it had been claimed for England by Sir George Somers, for whom it was first named. It had entered English literature almost at once in the poetry of Shakespeare and Marvell ("the still vexed Bermoothes," "the remote Bermudas"). In 1652 to avoid trouble, its inhabitants had at least outwardly agreed to submit to Cromwell's Commonwealth. The discipline of the church there was strong. In 1662 a man was sentenced to a whipping for fishing on the Sabbath. To the credit of the magistrates, the sentence was later commuted to exposure in the stocks on lecture day. Drunkenness was considered a crime.[168] The moral climate as well as the temperature seemed suitable to the young Malden minister.

In September, 1663, an acquaintance, John Younglove, sent a Mr. Barr, master of a ship from Bermuda, to talk over the advantages of the reputedly balmy place with Michael— its healthfulness, its moderate weather, its inexpensive food. Though the situation looked promising, the trip would be costly at best. Moreover, Michael's daughter, Mercy, now past her seventh birthday, would have to stay behind, probably under the care of her grandmother.

Nevertheless, toward the end of the month, Wigglesworth and Younglove set sail with Barr. In a few notes on his journey,[169] Michael recorded that he had "a pretty competent estate to take with me," including several barrels of flours, from the sale of which he would hope to acquire further funds. The voyage, which took about a month, was a tedious experience. Unfortunately, toward the end of the journey, the ship encountered severe storms in which Michael caught a serious cold that weakened him considerably. It was true that the temperature was much milder during the winter than in New England, but his health did not improve in the way he had hoped. He succumbed to "a generall faint cold that few escaped," and this, added to his chronic infection, kept his resistance low.

The relation between the churches around Boston and of Bermuda was a close one. In 1650 New England had shipped out eight hundred pounds worth of supplies. On the boat had sailed Nathaniel White, Jr., whose father, a pastor on the island, had sent his son to Harvard seven years before.[170] Now thirteen years after that voyage the son, settled permanently in New England, had no doubt asked Wigglesworth to visit his father, for Michael appears to have become a very close friend of the elder White, from whom on his return he received a lengthy and deeply concerned letter.[171]

The visitor discovered that Bermuda had its troubles, too. In bad weather the outlying islands were virtually isolated so that ministers had difficulty in reaching the inhabitants to administer the ordinances. The clergy were few; money was scarce; the widows of ministers must be cared for. Quakers had invaded the settlements.

In the matter of economics and trade there were vexing problems. The ships from New England often brought wine and other commodities which the sailors would then sell to the inhabitants. Orders had to be passed restricting the privileges of retail trade to the islanders in order for them to make a living. There were attempts to control whale fishing, and the market was glutted with tobacco. New Englanders were causing trouble in another way: they had to be restrained from chopping up valuable cedar trees as ship's firewood.

By May, 1664, the "sickness and distemper of body" that had been plaguing the people was beginning to clear up. The governor declared a day of public humiliation (not thanksgiving). The people had obviously sinned; otherwise, God would not have sent this heavy burden upon them. (Such censure was not limited to Massachusetts Bay.)

Michael was discouraged that his body had not been greatly strengthened. As he meditated on the situation, he came to the realization again that he probably desired health more than holiness. "I find my heart very subject to this vanity." For the Puritan, God's ways were always steady and uniform. What seemed to man an irregularity was really God's manner of punishing wickedness and vice. Man's responsibility was to seek out God's wishes, to follow constantly and carefully God's moral law. If this course was sometimes hidden or ambiguous, the fault was man's, not God's. So Michael blamed himself.

The flour he had taken with him in eight barrels was not selling well, for the islanders had discovered that they simply could not make decent bread with it. The visitor's money was dwindling fast, the cost of living in Bermuda being higher than expected. Moreover, the housing was makeshift —"very mean and unfit to keep out either cold or heat." Michael's companion, Mr. Younglove, was unwilling to stay away from New England longer than a year. So, when Wigglesworth discovered that a Mr. Willoughby was master of a ship returning to home shores, he engaged passage. Though the voyage took only twelve days in June, it was not a pleasant one for Michael, who, suffering most of the trip from constipation, could eat only "sparingly."

In thinking over the implications of his sojourn, he concluded that God had brought him to this expensive trip to show him that vanity was one of the sins from which he suffered most, for a restless change of scene had not produced much change in his bodily condition. Another reason for God's removing him temporarily from New England was to permit the church at Malden to make an unhampered choice of "a more painful labourer" in the vineyard of the Lord. He had gone away partly with this reason in mind and had returned to find a second minister ordained for service in the local church—Benjamin Bunker (whose father, incidentally, owned the property in Charlestown known as Bunker Hill). Bunker's views were more liberal than his own.[172] Possibly Joseph Hills, who lived in Malden till 1665,[173] had had more than a little to do with the ordination of this young man. In spite of differences, Wigglesworth found Bunker to be good and lovable and was delighted to take him to his heart.

He discovered now, however, that the people of Malden, both town and church, were more willing than before to cooperate with him. Their attitude was not so acid; their feelings had softened. He was able to work quietly among them to secure a more solid bank of faith. The physical exertion required in going from house to house, from meeting to meeting, and in preaching the necessary lengthy sermons and delivering the weekly lectures he could now leave to the new minister, who with his family had moved into the parsonage. (It is not recorded where the Wigglesworths lived until their own house was built on the six and a half acres Michael had bought seven years before.) In general, the situation was more tolerable, and Michael was thankful. "What shall I render to the Lord for all his benefits! how mysterious are his dealings, & his wayes unsearchable! He brings meat out of the eater. O blessed be thy gracious & holy name most dear Father."[174]

During his stay in Bermuda Michael had improved the hours by taking up seriously the study of medicine. In his undergraduate days, before his conversion, he had thought he might become a physician. His formal discourse at the sitting of solstices had been on human anatomy, and his commencement part had developed a concept in physics. Scientific study was not a new venture for him, though medicine could hardly by present-day standards be called a science. It required an acquaintance with the "simples" popular with the ancient crones sought out by townsmen in time of illness: elecampane, elder, wormwood, anise. Minerals included nitre (a favorite of the junior Winthrop), antimony, and occasionally iron, sulphur, and calomel. Now and then doctors would try rhubarb, jalap, and horseradish, powdered coral, and amber. It was not unheard of to prescribe "electuary of millipedes," honey or syrup mixed in a paste of thousand-legged bugs![175] Michael acquired several Latin textbooks and applied himself to the study of remedies, not only to serve his community but to find relief for himself.

A week or so after he had arrived home, he wrote a letter to Nathaniel White, Sr., in which he disclosed that some of the islanders still owed him money, that he was here without a house, that his health was just about as bad as ever. White's reply assured him that prayers would ascend from Bermuda for his general betterment, that, if Michael would name names, the money would be collected, that both in lacking a house and in suffering from ailments Michael was experiencing the ordeal of Christ Himself and should take comfort and find profit in his plight. Though God's purpose might be obscure, the Bible was full of the promises of the Lord: "Hee never never will faile nor forsake the righteous. . . ." In addressing the letter "To the Reverend & much Loved in the Lord Mr. Michael Wigglesworth," White called him "sometimes pastor of a Church of Christ at Maldon in New-England."[176] Was he using *pastor* as a term of respect? Had Michael announced in Bermuda that he was pastor at Malden? Had he actually been ordained pastor in the first place? These questions cannot be answered.

It is certain that he took very little active part in the ministry after his return. He supported his mother and daughter no doubt in various little ways. The income from his father's estate, if invested at all, could not have been more than negligible. Though his book had sold well and eventually went through a large number of editions, it could not have brought in enough to depend on wholly. The people of the community must have paid him something for his services as physician. As an ordained minister he may have continued to receive donations from some of the members of the church, even though most of the work was now being done by Bunker. There is some slender evidence that he may have tutored a few boys in preparation for Harvard. But he had to live very modestly.[177]

Now that Charles II had been on the restored throne four years, church and civil government were on uncertain footing in New England. Michael's letter to White expressed deep concern that great changes were imminent through interference from London. White had advised mending local fences to make strength for defending autonomy against hierarchy. And there were many fences to mend. Forty-four of the colony's ministers and officers of Harvard now signed a letter written in Latin to the Reverend John Durie in England saying that, though they "refused subscription to the hierarchy, they claimed fellowship with such as profess the Gospel."[178] Durie had expressed himself as favoring making peace with those branches of the church that were governed by other methods than the congregational. For years he had supported the principle of "a national synod." Since Massachusetts Bay had been established on the basis of local government, the ministers were forced to write this letter to protect the very stones of their foundation. But there was a note of tolerance creeping in: they were willing to recognize as within the "fellowship" any who believed in the Word of God as revealed in the New Testament. Michael Wigglesworth's signature appeared with the rest, with the designation of "pastor" of Malden. (It is hard to think that a man of Michael's integrity and scrupulosity would have named himself "pastor" if he had not been so ordained.)

The uneasiness continued. On March 22, 1665, John Hull reported "a solemn fast throughout this Colony for ourselves, in all our public concernments; and for England, their peace, and freedom of the ministry of God's word."[179] These days of humiliation were frequent, hours of repentance for past error, not only to attract favorable attention from God and Charles, but to keep the people acting together—mending their fences—so that New England would survive. The clergy, frankly, were losing their influence. Congregations and the deputies to the General Court were itching for a change: more power invested in the people, if not more tolerance permitted in religious beliefs. (Trouble had broken out again in the Hartford church, for example.) In order to suppress the colonists' desire for popular reform (what had Robert Child wrought?), sermons dwelt more and more on the dread hierarchy of bishops and on the possibility of tyranny from the throne. Though limited franchise permitted the people to elect their leaders, ministers felt that those leaders should be unquestionably obeyed once in office.[180]

Again, November 8 was "a day of solemn thanksgiving that

the Lord was pleased to spare so much of the fruits of the earth; that we had not want, but were able to supply other countries; and likewise the continuance of our health and present peace." It was followed, typically, on November 22 by a day of "solemn humiliation."

That winter was a hard one for England. She was again at war with Holland. The plague was killing thousands. In an effort to break off his dependence on Parliament, the King was adding to his standing army and was willingly receiving monies from the King of France. Incidentally, he was leaving New England alone, for the nonce. Thus Hull's reference to "present peace."[181]

Even though Wigglesworth was aware of all this, his infirmities would not permit him to take a very enterprising part in the life of the church, either at home or in the colony at large. He spent a great deal of time in his study tinkering with "The Day of Doom," adding notes and scriptural citations in the margins. When one group of the damned try to defend themselves before Christ, they confess:

> Our true intent was to repent
> and make our peace with thee;
> But sudden death, stopping our breath,
> left us no liberty.
>
> (DD107)

In the margin the author now affixed a note: "Those that pretend want of opportunity to repent." For Biblical "proofs" he cited two passages, one from the Old Testament and one from the New. *Proverbs* 27:1 reads: "Boast not thyself of tomorrow; for thou knowest not what a day may bring forth." The citation from *James* 4:13 might more appropriately have been verse 14, but the poet would expect his readers to study entire passages and not be content with single verses as proofs. *James* 4:14 begins: "Whereas ye know not what shall be on the morrow. . . ." In 1666 Wigglesworth turned over to Green and Johnson in Cambridge these additional notations for the entire poem and authorized a second edition. In this year also the book was reprinted in London, anonymously.

Michael in these years was composing other verses, some of which remained in manuscript for two centuries, others of which surely are lost. Following his own pattern of tirade set first by "God's Controversy," he now wrote in the ballad meter another poem to which he gave no title.

> When as the wayes of Jesus Christ
>   Are counted too precise,
> Not onely by some Babes or ffooles,
>   But also by the wise:
>   . . .
> When some within, and some without,
>   Kick down the Churches wall
> Because the doore is found to be
>   Too strait to let in all:
>   . . .
> When Godly men cannot agree
>   But differing mindes bewray
> And by their fell dissensions
>   Shall make themselves a prey.
> Then O, New England is the time
>   Of thy sad visitation,
> And that is like to be the year
>   Of God's fierce indignation.

After this climax in the fourth stanza, the poet continued to describe the problems of the church and its people, resorting to the familiar figure of the shepherds and their sheep. The poem closes with a prayer for God's grace in tempering the reactions of the "uncharitable."[182] Recognizing the importance to the New Jerusalem of maintaining the civil *status quo,* Michael was joining the chorus of perplexed clergy who through plea and threat were working overtime against intractable and, in the end, insurmountable odds to keep the church select, to protect the government from encroaching secular influences.

The ministers formed a tight and warm fraternity as they struggled together to keep their people in "the wayes of Jesus Christ," according to their lights. When the Reverend John

Wilson died in Boston in the late summer of 1667, it was learned that in his will he had bequeathed ten shillings apiece to a number of his "reverend and beloved Brethren and fellow labourers in the work of the Ministery," including Jonathan Mitchell, Thomas Shepard (the younger), Richard Mather, and Michael Wigglesworth.[183] Michael might not have physical strength to carry out the duties of a pastor, but he had gained the respect and love of his brethren by his poetry. Mitchell did not live long to enjoy his ten shillings, for he died the following summer, "the chief remaining pillar of our ministry," according to Hull.[184]

Further complication developed when, through a confusion of circumstances, the Second Church in Boston brought Michael's old New Haven pastor, John Davenport, up to fill the vacancy created by the death of John Cotton, whose opinions had leaned away from the straight and narrow orthodox in late years. Davenport's own conservatism created a schism and brought about the organization of the Third Church. Davenport did not approve of the synodical form of church organization; every congregation should act for itself, in the original way. The old man died within a few months after his election sermon in May, 1669, in which he nearly split New England asunder by earnestly advocating that the General Court follow the ways of Jesus Christ and pay no attention to "men's opinions" as developed in a colonial synod.[185] Reactionary, he was pleading for a return to the very structures which Robert Child had valiantly fought against—government by the whims of men and not by law, for despite his terminology he was supporting as a basis of rule, not a codified system of regulations, but the interpretation of the Bible by the clergy.

Within two years, three of the most influential ministers of the colony had died—John Davenport, Jonathan Mitchell, and John Wilson. Wilson's last sermon had been printed soon after his funeral. In the mainstream of clerical warnings of the day, it had borne the title of *A Seasonable Watchword unto Christians Against the Dreams & Dreamers of This Generation.*[186]

[130]

Through the death of his colleagues and his own pertinacity, Wigglesworth was becoming one of the last of the old-guard party (though he was just thirty-seven). What he had written up to this time would testify to his partiality for the conservative point of view. "The Day of Doom" was orthodox Puritan Calvinism. "God's Controversy" interpreted drought as a judgment of God against a people leaning toward tolerance and secularism. "When as the wayes of Jesus Christ" threatened the wrath of the Lord on New England if it opened the doors of the church to all comers. Michael's pen was proving a welcome weapon in the arsenal of the orthodox.

Dread was the reality that impelled the vigor of New England's ministers. For Wigglesworth dread was grounded in the indestructibility of the soul, which at Judgment Day would meet its reward for right choices or punishment for wrong choices. The limits of human existence, man's finitude, also mattered to Wigglesworth, for his sure knowledge of everlasting life after the Great Resurrection did not relieve his anxiety. Mortal life was only too short a period to prove one's worthiness of a heavenly crown.

In spite of his literary activity Wigglesworth found it hard to be reconciled to chronic illness. He was faithful in the study of books on medicine. Years later, at his death, his library contained volumes on bleeding, on the scurvy, on drugs, fevers, stomach disorders, and other such subjects. He was no half-way scholar. In the early spring of 1669 he consulted with other physicians in an effort to discover a remedy for whatever ailed him. John Alcock, whose plasters had given some relief, had been dead many months. Far away in Pequot, Winthrop refused to prescribe. Michael's dead wife's cousin by chance came across a book by an English Dr. Lockyer and some of Lockyer's pills, which had been good for Cousin Reyner's acquaintances. Hopefully Michael began to take the new medicine, but he still was almost altogether housebound.[187]

VI. *Meat Out of the Eater*

"I have been long imployed in a great work composing poems about the cross."[188] So wrote Wigglesworth on September 17, 1669. For the three weeks preceding, he had been laboring hard enough that he had been able to fill three sheets of sermon paper with fair copy and had written over a hundred stanzas besides. When he was feeling comparatively well, he could in a single day put together as many as twenty stanzas. If he had been fairly constant in composition and copying, he probably had been working at this manuscript since at least late spring.

The book was to be called by the title of the first part— *Meat Out of the Eater,* a phrase in common use from the story of Samson: from tribulation could come blessing; from weakness strength. In his introductory poem to *The Day of Doom,* writing of his former pupil's ailments, Jonathan Mitchell had commented: "But from this eater comes some meat." Michael himself had used the phrase in his Bermuda account.[189] The subtitle of the book would show more plainly the nature of the contents: *Meditations Concerning the Necessity, End, and Usefulness of Afflictions unto God's Children. All tending to Prepare them For, and Comfort them Under the Cross.*

For the next four and a half weeks in the autumn of 1669 Michael applied himself with great diligence to the task before him. It was not easy. On September 29 the air was chilly and the words came hard, but he was able to copy out "5 sides

fair" and to compose about a dozen more stanzas. Daily he prayed for the re-charging of his energies. The language of his petitions grew from his earnest compulsion. On October 4 he wrote: "And now do I seriously & honestly begg thy help & assistance for I am deeply sensible that without thee I can do nothing, & for thee I desire to do all. Oh guide my head, heart, hand, & all my might this day for the sake & for the honor of thy name Amen." The nervous drive in this prayer, if it could have been translated into physical activity, would have made the thirty-eight-year-old minister an irresistible leader in Malden and all of Massachusetts Bay.

The second—and longer—part of the book, devoted to "particular ails," he entitled "Riddles Unriddled or, Christian Paradoxes Broke Open, smelling like sweet Spice New taken out of Boxes." Once he had got into the habit of rhyming, he could not forego making even this title a rough couplet. The "Riddles" illustrate specifically the general principles laid down in the first part. By means of nine major paradoxes and a variety of images and examples, the poet was returning to his primary precept, that only those who suffer some kind of cross would gain a reward in heaven. To borrow a phrase from music, the book is structured like a theme and variations.

On October 15 he could see the end of the work: " I am now upon the last Head (Heav'ly Crowns &c)." Three days later he was rejoicing: "And now through thy grace & daily assistance, I have done composing. *Laus Deo.*" Praise be to God. This was his birthday and "the birthday of this Book it being finished this morning." In another three days he had completed the entire fair copy.

The manuscript was much bulkier than that of *The Day of Doom,* four thousand lines, for the most part in eight-line stanzas or "staves," the third and seventh lines being eight syllables long, the others six, thus escaping the "fourteeners" of balladry of the earlier best seller. Though the rhyming words come less often, the accents are as monotonously regu-

lar as ever, the inverted sentence order as frequent. The poet had little control over his form.

Though the poems in this work do not have the advantage of the physical movement and dramatic situation of "The Day of Doom," occasionally they can rise to an intensity growing out of the author's convictions. Occasionally, too, they are lifted from mere sermonizing and Scriptural paraphrase by an unexpected image. But generally they are limited to an account of how a conscientious sinner's troubles, his disappointments, deprivations, and bereavements, can be turned to profit, can make him more humble and eventually more content with the providences of God. Michael's own weaknesses and the loss of his beloved wife, Mary, had made him an expert in these matters, for he remained true Puritan to the end, believing that the finger of the Lord directed every disaster and searching his conscience and conduct for the cause of every trial.

The title work is made up of ten "Meditations" and "A Conclusion Hortatory." Each meditation is prefaced by a rhyme setting out the content of the section. The argument proceeds with assured logic from the premise that it is necessary to suffer in order to be worthy of Christ. Saints should remember that worldly goods are but a snare and a delusion, that God chastises his own to give them opportunity for humility and preparation for the ineffable joys of "heavenly rest."

Meditation X would appear to be an early plea for racial tolerance and an understanding that all human beings are God's children. At the time of this poem there were some Negroes in the colony, most of them slaves, all of them in subservient position. They were not always treated justly and were sometimes driven to such desperate retaliation as setting fire to dwelling houses. John Hull's diary records several instances of this sort in which Negroes were at least suspected as the instigators. Starting with a transcription of a verse from *Psalm* 45, Wigglesworth pleaded the cause of the Negro:

The Daughter of the King,
All glorious is within,
How Black soever and Sun-Burnt,
May seem her outward Skin.

Because I Blackish am,
Upon me—look not ye
Because that with his Beams the Sun
Hath looked down on me.

A patient suffering Saint
Is a right comely one:
Though black as Kedar's tents, and as
Curtains of *Solomon.*

. . .

(Meat X.4)

He concluded the Meditation by saying that, on the other hand, many a fair body is foul within. The poet had borrowed heavily from the Bible:

The king's daughter is all glorious within: her clothing is of wrought gold.

(*Psalm* 45:13)

I am black, but comely, O ye daughter of Jerusalem, *as the tents of Kedar, as the curtains of Solomon. Look not upon me, because I am black, because the sun hath looked upon me:* my mother's children were angry with me; they made me the keeper of the vineyards; but mine own vineyard have I not kept.

(*The Song of Solomon* 1:5,6)

The "Conclusion Hortatory," addressed "To those that are, or hereafter may be in Affliction," becomes more informal than "The Day of Doom" could have possibly been because of its dramatic subject. In these final fifteen stanzas the poet used the personal approach, confessing that, though for a long time he had been "A Scholar in this School," he had made "little progress" toward purifying his soul of sin, but he would continue to work at the task. He urged his "Dear Brother, Christian Friend" to do likewise. Not only did he speak to the solitary reader, but

Oh! let *New-England* turn,
When gentler Warning's given:

[135]

Lest by our sins the Lord to use
Severity be driven.
(Concl. Hort.13)

God and New England were still in controversy. His clergy were still trying to ward off the threats of leniency and liberalism in church and state.

Come let's return to God,
He hath us torn, he'll heal:
He hath us smitten with his Rod,
And bind us up he will.
(Concl. Hort.15)

Though the language for the most part was in the "plain style" Wigglesworth had learned as a student at Harvard, he now and then produced an allowable metaphor that related this otherwise fairly abstract subject to the everyday life of the colonists.

We must not on the knee
Be always dandled,
Nor must we think to ride to heaven
Upon a featherbed.
(Meat I.3)

He said the journey to heaven requires rowing upstream, sailing against wind and tide, climbing an arduous hill. God's laws he compared to a "Fining Pot" in which dross is consumed and gold made purer and to "Fullers sope" which will "wash our spots away." (Though Biblical, these were homely metaphors.) In fact, Meditation III is built principally on a series of figures. As frost clears the air, so afflictions "Correct the Rankness of our hearts." Just as an excess of honey makes one bilious, so "too too much Prosperity" makes one proud and wanton, to be returned to wholesomeness only through the "bitter Aloe" of afflictions. He depicted other concrete situations—too much food and drink—and prescribed again the *"Catholicum"* of suffering. Adversity he compared to ballast "I'th' Bottom of a Ship" and to a plow that prepares a weedy field.

[136]

In this same vein, the seventh stanza bears a phrase which
thirty-five years later appeared on his tombstone:

> Full Diet, dainty Fare,
> With Idleness and Ease,
> Heap up bad Humours and Contract
> Many a foul Disease
> To Soul and Body too.

His epitaph was to name him "Mauldens Physician For Soul
And Body Two," evidence that this book was well known, as
indeed it must have been at the rate of four editions in less
than twenty years.

The second part of the book, "Riddles Unriddled," in the
main continues the stanzaic pattern of the first, though a
variation is introduced occasionally. Furthermore, the author could not by this time resist a rhyme: in addition to the
rhyming in the title of "Paradoxes" with "out of Boxes," the
image is expanded in a six-line stave:

> Each Paradox is like a Box,
> That Cordials rare incloseth:
> This Key unlocks, op'neth the Box
> And what's within discloseth;
> That whoso will may take his fill,
> And gain where no man loseth.

Was Wigglesworth, like Jonathan Mitchell, familiar with the
poetry of George Herbert?

> Sweet spring, full of sweet days and roses,
> A box where sweets compacted lie; ...
> ("Virtue")

Even the table of contents is in rhyme, the nine Paradoxes
arranged in a stave on the second page:

> Light in Darkness
> Sick mens Health,
> Strength in Weakness,
> Poor mens Wealth,
> In Confinement,
> Liberty,

```
              In Solitude,
                 Good Company,
              Joy in Sorrow,
                 Life in Deaths,
              Heavenly Crowns for
                 Thorny Wreaths.
```

These division subjects are in apposition with "Christian
Paradoxes," which

```
              Are presented to thy view,
                 In the Poems that ensue.
```

At the bottom of the page Wigglesworth introduced himself
into the work, for his songs and meditations, not just objective commentary on Puritan doctrine, had burgeoned from his
own troubles:

```
              If my Trials had been thine,
                 These would cheer thee more than Wine.
```

Wigglesworth was never very far from contact with another being, whether man or God. Sometimes he would use a
plural vocative ("readers" or "New-England"), but he had
a profound sense of the dialogistic situation, for he often
would refute objections and answer arguments as if in conversation; also he made use of dialogue as a form: God
speaks to man; Flesh and Spirit address each other. Wigglesworth's pervading feeling of responsibility for men and his
unceasing observance of the two Great Commandments constituted his dialogue.

The first paradox, "Light in Darkness," consists of ten
"Songs," several of which are in the form of the medieval
"debate." Anne Bradstreet's *Tenth Muse,* in 1650, had made
use of this frame, in a conversation between the Flesh and the
Spirit, but whether Michael had read her book is unknown.
At any rate, here, when Flesh says he had hoped his sins
were pardoned, Spirit reminds him that God chastises out of
love. But, says Flesh, God's punishments are so severe that
he surely does not love me. Spirit in reply cites the cases of
Biblical heroes as being much, much worse and goes so far as
to suggest that Flesh may laugh at his present troubles when

he gets to heaven. In another debate, to the worrying of Distressed Conscience that, because his heart will not be softened, he fears damnation, Rectified Judgment is reassuring: it pays to keep trying, for God's sunshine can melt rock. Flesh and Spirit again take the stage, Flesh complaining that even after prayers God sends more affliction, Spirit maintaining that God often delays answering prayer in order to build up satisfaction in His gift of ultimate salvation. Spirit becomes impatient and tells Flesh to hold his peace, for his false reasoning is the work of Satan. When Flesh suggests that even Spirit's faith may not last, undermined by unbelief, Spirit testily blames his doubts on the statements of Flesh, but announces his determination to hang on doggedly. The following Song then develops the idea that, though the history of the saints shows "Blasphemous hellish thoughts" to be inescapable, Christ inflicts no more than man is capable of bearing. Then comes the admonition to keep on praying, for, if one concentrates on the good, current evil will disintegrate (only, of course, to re-form and return).

At the end of Song VIII the poet announced:

> Reader, I give thee here
> Two Songs in other Meetre:
> I hope they will not make a jarre
> But close up all the sweeter.

The effect is of rising to a climax. Song IX, in the familiar "fourteeners" of ballad structure, is a variation on the *De Profundis* of *Psalm* 130:

> Lord, from the deeps I cry'd to thee,
> My voice Lord do Thou hear.

The inversions and distortions are almost as wrenched as the lines in the *Bay Psalm Book*. Wrote Wigglesworth:

> But such as walk by their own fire,
> Lie down in sorrow must.

This song is a somber preparation for the conclusion of "Light in Darkness," Song X, which, cast in quatrains, six-syllable lines in couplet rhyme, is another dialogue, this time between

"the Believing Soul and her Saviour." The first stanza, opening Soul's address, is a translation of the poet's Latin verses
written shortly after Mary's death (a decade before):
Christe, parum doleo. . . .

> Oh Christ my grief is such,
> Because I love not much;
> As addeth to my sore,
> Because I grieve no more.

Soul begs for power to love God more and more. The Savior
answers that, if Soul will believe with all his heart,

> Light, pardon, joy and peace,
> Eternal life and ease,
> With full Redemption,
> Shall be thy portion.

Soul is elated. Can such generosity actually be?

> O Gracious Grace indeed!
> Shown in a time of need,
> O God of Grace, *All Grace!*
> How pleasant is thy face!

The entire passage is joyous, a light-tripping hymn of thankfulness and praise rising in metric contrast to the longer
lines and grave themes of the first nine Songs. The box has
been, as the author promised, "Broke open, smelling like
sweet Spice":

> Let no sin interpose
> To hide, or make me lose
> Thy Countenances light,
> Which on me shines so bright.

Carefully pursuing the image of the paradox, the poet had
demonstrated, in both development of subject and in choice
of forms and diction, a control over the relation between subject and meaning that, given other environment, creed, and
purpose, might have yielded a poetry of high quality.

The other boxes are "Broke open" successively. "Sick
Men's Health" presents the paradox of a man's physical ail-

ments turning him into a spiritual giant. As in all the poems of this book, Wigglesworth here ranged widely in the Bible for sources both of ideas and of diction. In the tenth stanza of Meditation IV, for example, he moved about freely in *Jeremiah* 33 and in *Romans* 8: "Who shall separate us from the love of Christ?"

Song I of "Strength in Weakness" paints man's own powers as very fragile:

> Man's Strength meer Weakness is,
> As frail as *Venice* Glass:
> And all his Excellency like
> The flower upon the grass.

When one is weakest, he leans the most heavily on Christ, at which point he becomes invincible, for Christ's strength is in him. Song II is a personal one: the poet himself had been frail. When in answer to prayer he had had strength to do God's public work, he had collapsed immediately afterwards. But he could not complain:

> Hath not the Potter power
> To frame out of the clay
> One vessel for to serve him thus,
> Others another way.

Following the pattern, "Poor Men's Wealth" is of course God's love and promise. "Earth's Treasures are but dung" compared to the riches of the celestial kingdom.

Where, in a secular situation, Richard Lovelace could sing to his love:

> Stone walls do not a prison make,
> Nor iron bars a cage. . . .[190]

Wigglesworth showed that this was true in his religion too. "In Confinement Liberty" concedes that

> Most men love Liberty
> And covet Elbow-room
> To have their Wills, to serve their Lusts,
> And up and down to rome.
>
> (Con I.1)

[141]

But, if that is the only use to which they put their freedom, they are slaves to sin:

> And, being under no Restraint
> They run to Hell more free.
> (Con I.3)

Physical liberty is desirable; yet the Lord can give freedom in captivity by subduing the captive's will to his own. The saints have often found more freedom "To meet with God" in prison and banishment than not—for example, John on Patmos, Paul and Silas in stocks.

Song I of "In Solitude Good Company," the sixth paradox, states the theme: Man delights in companionship, but God is able to take away "The bitterness of Solitude" of all "true Believers." In this Song Michael recalled the shock of his bereavement in 1659:

> I can remember still
> That dismal Solitude,
> The horrour of that Lonesomeness,
> (And state of Widowhood)
> Wherein my Soul was once,
> From God estranged far:
> That was a wilderness indeed,
> Such only Lonesome are.

In his diary, from time to time, Michael had confessed to his natural desire for companionship, had feared lest it prevent his total focus on the Lord. For him the loss of Mary had been a "horrour," coupled with alienation from the Creator. Only those who are thus deprived, he said, can know what lonesomeness is. Through persistent searching, prayer, and meditation, however, the believing man—whether sick, feeble, sitting alone, wandering "in the Woods," lying down in sleep, or endangered—will find that God is near and companionable. The key is to think of the dead relative or friend as on loan from God, Who remains one's friend even closer than the one he has lost.

The Third Song of this group Michael identified as one he had written at least "Eight years agone," soon after the death of Mary, about the time, then, of the Latin poems. Cast in the useful form of debate between Flesh and Spirit, it formalizes and hence dignifies the author's obviously genuine grief at the loss of his wife. When Flesh says he will bear any cross but parting from "one Whom I esteem so dear," Spirit speaks sharply, demanding whether mere mortal can dare to instruct God. Flesh whines that he has thought he was suffering enough and receives the familiar response that God inflicts no more than man can bear. One is not to compare himself to others, for every man's sins need punishment—to what extent is God's concern. Finally, when Flesh complains that surely no one has suffered as he has, Spirit snaps back that Flesh is deceived there—but what if the suffering is of a new and more intensive sort? Someone must lead. Besides, great suffering will bring on greater admiration of the Lord. "Love ordereth all for good." An early exercise in Christian discipline after Michael's first great loss, this Song had set the pattern for the ensuing decade in which he had become accustomed to "Widowhood," had in fact turned it to good account in his relation with his Heavenly Father.

In "Joy in Sorrow" the poet resorted to figurative speech again. It should be understood that the "plain style" was not primitive and unsophisticated, but had developed out of the kind of training in the Trivium (grammar, rhetoric, and logic) that Michael had received at Harvard. Within the framework, cautiously built, he was free to use images for illumination, so long as they did not shine with the distracting brightness he had described in his second Harvard undergraduate oration on eloquence as "periphrastic circumlocutions" and "catechrestical" excesses. On the other hand, communication must not become so formalized as to lose all emotional appeal.

In this poem, for example, he said that when one honestly works at repentance, the "Spring Tides of Joy" make deeper the channel begun by grief. Just as bleeding (that medieval practice) will ease a man's disease, so a bleeding heart will lessen grief and God's "Cordials" will revive him. The

[143]

deeper the plowing of repentance, the richer the yield of spiritual joy and holiness.

> If drops of heav'nly Pleasure
> Be sweet unto thy taste:
> How sweet will streams and rivers be,
> Where drink thy fill thou mayst?
> (Joy III.6)

Song IV of this group is introduced by a Latin phrase: *Solamen miseris socios habuisse doloris Christum cum sanctis:* What solace for the afflicted to have had as companions in sorrow Christ and the saints. This Song is built on St. Paul's image of the saints as the body of Christ: when one suffers, all suffer. (This notion of engagement was often in Wigglesworth's mind.)

In "Life in Deaths" comes the tenet that death is only the bridge to a larger life. Daily a man dies as he leads a life of sin. The Puritan would understand that the demonic forces of evil are never destroyed. If through prayer and hard work one temporarily conquered a current fault, his sinful soul would nevertheless be guilty of something else and even of a repetition of the same fault. His faith was a religion of crisis from which there could be no escape. Repentance must be constant. But for the Christian there could be comfort in the knowledge of bliss to come. "O Death where is thy sting, ...?" (Life III.8)

The last paradox climaxes the book: "Heavenly Crowns for Thorny Wreaths." The author could not understand why sinners resist God's grace. Whereas in "A Song of Emptiness" in *The Day of Doom* he had challenged the unregenerate to continue enjoying their worldly "Toyes" and to suffer the consequences, here in an even more vigorous burst of violence he went further in daring them to show preference for everlasting damnation:

> Which is the better choice?
> With Christ in Bliss to dwell,
> Or for to roar eternally
> Amidst the Flames of Hell?

> What! Are you in a doubt
> Which of the twain to chuse?
> Well, chuse to burn, if that be best;
> Chuse Hell, and Heaven refuse.
> (Heaven III.9)

He hoped that this horrible prospect would turn all his readers to Christ and subsequent "Crowns of Glory." To the argument that being good in order to gain a heavenly crown is mercenary, Wigglesworth replied that, if Christ lists rewards to make men work harder at being good, are they not being negligent in ignoring them?

Of the nine "Riddles" the first is based on the image of darkness—separation from the Lord. The ninth is based on the image of thorns—suffering in general. The intervening seven are developed from concrete situations—sickness, weakness, poverty, confinement, solitude, sorrow, and death —arranged in an order that could conceivably have been climactic for the poet, whose training and experience had taught him the power of organization in presenting ideas.

After a familiar ascription to God of "Glory, Honour, Power," a kind of postscript heartens the afflicted:

> Be cheerful, Suffering Saint,
> Let Nothing cast thee down;
> Our Saviour Christ ere long will turn
> Thy Cross into a Crown.

These were the words of expectation Michael had penned on the morning of his thirty-eighth birthday. This was the position he had won in the almost twenty years since his conversion in Cambridge. As his diary and the poems themselves show, the victory had been hard. And there is no reason to believe the battle was over. For the true Puritan, giving up the struggle against his proclivity to sin was sinking into a false complacency. Without doubt Michael fought manfully, and with greater and greater assurance, against the Adversary to his last breath.

Meat Out of the Eater was published in 1670, with some marginal references to the Scriptures, of which its lines were often only a paraphrase. An advertisement at the end of Thomas Walley's 1669 election sermon, the second printing (1670), announced that Wigglesworth's book was "now going to press."[191] This second book, like *The Day of Doom,* was widely purchased. Within nineteen years it enjoyed four editions, a match, up to 1700 in America, for its predecessor, which, however, outstripped it eventually with English editions and many more printings at home. The income from these two books was surely welcome during the years of their author's physical incapacity, for most of the available funds in Malden would have to be appropriated to the support of the assistant ministers, who did most of the church work.

While *Meat Out of the Eater* was being printed in Cambridge, Benjamin Bunker died. He had served the church well for six years. In spite of any difference in point of view on doctrine, the two ministers had got on well together. Bunker's death occurred on February 3, 1670. A few days later Wigglesworth composed an elegy "Upon the much lamented Death of that Precious servant of Christ, Mr. Benjamin Buncker, pastor of the Church at Maldon. . . ." (There would not have been two pastors for this little congregation!) The elegy was a common form of poetic expression among the educated American Puritans.[192] Peter Bulkeley, pastor at Concord; Jonathan Mitchell; the junior Thomas Shepard; the Mathers, Richard, Nathaniel, Increase, Cotton —all commemorated the demise of their friends in verse.

Wigglesworth's poem[193] is divided into two parts, the first of which concerns "Mr. Buncker's Character." According to his eulogist, the young man had grown through the years until

> He was most sound and Orthodox,
> A down-right honest Teacher,
> And of soul-searching, needfull Truths
> A zealous, painful Preacher.

(Incidentally, the title of both *teacher* and *pastor* would hardly have been given to one man.) Benjamin had followed

Michael's pattern in constantly seeking out his own sins and recognizing his own inadequacies.

> His constant self-denying frame
>   To all true saints his love,
> His meekness, sweetness, Innocence
>   And spirit of a Dove,
> Let there be graven on our hearts
>   And never be forgot,
> The name of precious saints shall live,
>   When wicked mens shall rot.

At this point the poem changes direction. Instead of dwelling on the sense of loss, on the inexplicable ways of God, on the cutting short of a life full of promise, the author, true to form, made use of Bunker's death to preach repentance to the citizenry and thus deflected any potential awareness of tragedy that the situation might have elicited. Malden had been deprived of a beloved leader because of its transgressions.

> Good Lord awaken all our hearts
>   By this most solemn stroke
> To search for, find oute, and forsake
>   Our sins that thee provoke.

If Malden should refuse to profit by Bunker's death,

> Doubtless the Gospel will ere long
>   Be wholly from us taken,
> If we repent, return to God,
>   Esteem his Gospel more,
> Improve it better: then the Lord
>   Hath mercies yet in store.

So ends the elegy. Not just a sorrowful fact to be borne, death was a punishment, a deprivation, for the wrongdoing of the living. If the cause of affliction were rooted out, life would be improved—if not on earth, at least later, in eternity. God's controversy with New England, and specifically Malden, was a continuing struggle. Thus through warning and castigation was Wigglesworth using the method adopted by his fellow clergymen throughout the colony in trying to

[147]

maintain his hold on errant townsmen.[194] The concept of "meat out of the eater" was applicable to anything. The purpose of every happening, no matter how slight, was to aid New Englanders to "close with God." Technically, of course, for the Christian, and especially the New England kind of Puritan, there could be no tragedy, for, if God willed, all would end in heavenly glory. To call Wigglesworth and his brethren optimists in relation to the cosmos would be near exaggeration;[195] nevertheless, for those church members who had made a covenant with the Lord, the shining and singing privilege of beholding the sublime throne of God was a certainty, making of existence a divine comedy. Because of the "scandal of the Cross," God's grace would bring glowing reward to the predestined few, at least.

For five years after the death of Bunker, Michael was Malden's only minister again. Since his health continued poor, he probably was no more satisfactory than he had ever been. Furthermore, the fact that the clergy all over the colony did not have the authority of the first generation did not help his case. Though they could still bring their congregations together in formal acts of humiliation and repentance, nearly every church was in truth at the mercy of a "tribe of pragmaticals" who gave lip service to pastoral authority but ran their churches to suit themselves. Joseph Hills had been a case in point. Wigglesworth's careful orthodoxy had met opposition in Hills's reasoning that baptism should be delayed until public profession. Hills had never forgotten his sympathy with the views of Marmaduke Matthews, and many in the town had sided with him. Even if their attitude toward Michael had softened and Hills had moved away several years before, nevertheless there was continuing discontent in some quarters.

All the churches for the next several years followed a routine of days of humiliation and then of thanksgiving—for drought and storms on the one hand, for rich harvest and rescues on the other.[196] The clergy lost no time in capitalizing

on natural phenomena and affairs of government to keep
their people coming to church. If in August, 1673, there was
a public fast because the Dutch were threatening New England, yet on November 26 a public thanksgiving celebrated
heavy crops.[197] The balance of regret and rejoicing was a
tenuous but calculated technique.

In 1672 Wigglesworth's daughter, Mercy, was married to
Samuel Brackenbury (Harvard, 1664). Brackenbury had
preached for two years at Rowley, but had settled on a career
in medicine. The couple's first child, Samuel, Junior, was
born in Malden in February, 1673—Michael's first grand-
child. Shortly after, the Brackenburys moved to Boston,
where the demands for a physician were more challenging.
There they had two more children, Mary and William.
Samuel the father did not live long. He died in 1678, leaving
Mercy a widow with three children all under six years of
age.[198] What she did then is not a matter of record, but it is
known that she remained unmarried for ten or twelve
years.[199]

Michael now had a new loneliness to combat. Though
again there is no account, one can assume that his mother
was dead by this time. Bunker was dead. Mary was dead.
And Mercy had married and moved out of town.

He maintained interest in his writings and prepared a
third American edition of *The Day of Doom*, which appeared
anonymously also in London in 1673. The dates of the second
and third editions of *Meat Out of the Eater* are lost; if the
fourth edition came out in 1689, however, he must have been
busy in the meantime working over copy for the earlier ones,
changing a word here, adding a marginal citation there.

In the 1673 London edition of *The Day of Doom* was a
poem which was printed nowhere else, not even in later editions. In the London book it was placed immediately after the
title poem, before "A Short Discourse on Eternity." More
lively than certain other of the author's works, it shows a close
observation of nature that colors none of the other poems.

> I walk'd and did a little Mole-hill view,
> Full peopled with a most industrious crew
> Of busie Ants, where each one labour'd more
> Than if he were to bring home Indian Ore;
> Here wrought the Pioneers, there march'd the Bands,
> Here Colonies went forth to plant new Lands:
> These hasted out, and those supplies brought in,
> As if they had some sudden seige foreseen:
> Until there came an angry Spade, and cast
> Country and People to a Pit at last.

The next lines describe a beehive, busy with division of labor

> Until the greedy Gardner brought his smoke,
> And, for the work, did all the workmen choke.

As clergyman, Michael now felt constrained to put these word pictures to use:

> Lo here, frail Mortals may fit Emblems see
> Of their great toil, and greater vanity.

(Quarles's *Emblems* had been in the library at Harvard.) All is vanity; all ends in death.

> Leave off your circles, Archimede, away,
> The King of Terrour calls, and will not stay.
> Miser, kiss all your Bags, and then ly down;
> Scholar, your Books; Monarch, yield up your Crown:
> Give way Wealth, Honour, Arts, Thrones; back, make
>   room,
> That these pale Souls may come unto their doom.

There follows a listing of worldly accomplishments, their winner

> Adorn'd with Titles, but defil'd with sin.

And now, his reward:

> My greedy Heir now hovers o're my pelf,
> I purchase Land for him, Hell for my self.

Then, in a tone he had used before, the poet challenged those who aspire to success to write brilliant books, gain "Diadems and Thrones," heap up treasures. But he warned that the Day of Judgment was coming.

> Then there will be (and the time is not far)
> Fire on the Bench, and Stubble at the Bar.

He begged his sinful readers to take these thoughts seriously.

> Christ yet intreats, but if you will not turn,
> Where grace will not convert, there fire will burn.

Granted the illiberal Calvinism on which the piece is based, this is, nevertheless, much better poetry than almost anything else Wigglesworth left behind. The rhyming pentameter couplets with occasional run-on lines and varied caesuras escape the singsong quality of his version of the ballad structure. Distorted sentence order is rare. There is also a fairly wide range of graphic pictures both of the world of nature and the sophisticated world of man such as Michael was able to give his readers in no other poem. "The Day of Doom" had been dramatic and vivid, but most passages in the present poem are more concrete in remarking details of daily life. It seems odd that it was excluded from all editions save one and has never been printed elsewhere. (These facts might help to make plausible an argument that the poem was included in the London edition by error and is apocryphal, but there is no other reason to think so.)

In November, 1673, William Foster, master of a small ship and citizen of Charlestown, related to Mercy by marriage, was returned with his son from two years' captivity under Turkish corsairs. Their deliverance came about through the death of their captor, a man of princely rank.[200] Shortly after their reappearance in Massachusetts Bay, Wigglesworth composed a song of thanksgiving, a poem circulated in manuscript but not printed for two hundred years. Written in the familiar "fourteeners," it bears the lengthy title: "Upon the return of my dear friend Mr. Foster with his son out of captivity under the Moors. A Song of Praise to keep in remembrance the loving kindness of the Lord."[201]

Making use of the sentiment of many of the Psalms, the poem, in sixty-four lines, moves from the *De Profundis* theme through a catalogue of God's deliverances to a concluding *Benedicite:*

> Because the Lord the poor doth hear
> Nor's prisoners doth despise
> Let Heaven, earth, sea, him praise, and all
> That moves therein likewise.

Borrowing heavily as it does from the Bible, the language is bookish, howsoever sincere the concept. The poem lacks both the vigor of Wigglesworth's outbursts in the "Chuse Hell" passages and the sweet invitation of "Be cheerful, Suffering Saint" and "So come, Lord Jesus, quickly come we pray." The structure is logical, nevertheless, and, despite the jerking out of line of various syntactical elements, the tone is both joyous and dignified. For all the awkwardness of paraphrase, the poem is patently in a great tradition.

Between the beginning of 1662 and the end of 1673, Michael had composed all the poetry that is today extant except three pieces dating from the time of Mary's death (December, 1659) and two short poems on death written probably in his last year (1705).

He had written in a wide variety of poetic forms: lyric ("Mr. Foster," "Light in Darkness" IX); dramatic, both monologue and dialogue or "debate" ("God's Controversy," "Light in Darkness" X, "Sick Men's Health" IV, "In Solitude Good Company" III); narrative ("The Day of Doom," which is of course expository and even hortatory in purpose); descriptive (of place in "New England Planted" from "God's Controversy" and of person in "Mr. Benjamin Buncker"); didactic and hortatory ("A Postcript to the Reader," "When as the wayes of Jesus Christ," "Poor Men's Wealth" I, "Heavenly Crowns for Thorny Wreaths" V); and autobiographical ("To the Christian Reader," "Strength in Weakness" II).

His stanzaic structures and line lengths show considerable range. For the most part his foot was iambic, but his rhymes were sometimes masculine, sometimes feminine ("season"

—"reason"). The lines varied from dimeter (table of contents for "Riddles Unriddled") to hexameter (the last line of the six-line stanzas of God's reproaches in "God's Controversy"). The stanzaic forms ranged from the couplet (trimeter, tetrameter, pentameter) through tercet, quatrain, six-line stanza, eight-line ballad (sometimes inner rhyme, sometimes not), another eight-line stanza (all lines trimeter except 3 and 7—tetrameter), to a fourteen-line stanza (the table of contents of "Riddles Unriddled"). The rhyme schemes were correspondingly varied.

Granted his time, his place, his Calvinist orientation, Wigglesworth nevertheless was something of a conscious craftsman in the building of his poems.

His subject matter was man's spiritual life. He tried to show what one's attitude should be towards earthly existence, but gave little concrete description of or advice about the conduct of daily life: dealings with one's customers, rearing of adolescents, contributions to a harmonious marriage. If one obeyed the two Great Commandments in all things, it could be assumed that these problems would be solved satisfactorily.

The imagery was in fact quite bookish. References in "Mole-hill" to ants, bees, smoke, and spade, and to a feather-bed in "Meat Out of the Eater" are from daily life, but these are the exceptions. On the other hand, the personification of Truth, Mercy, Peace, and Righteousness, the metaphors of the rod of the Lord, "Gods Fining Pot," and "His Fullers Sope," and the simile of "wicked men like Grass" are Biblical. Allusions to myth (Pelion and Ossa, Croesus, Midas), to intellectual history (Archimedes), and to ancient heroes (Julius Caesar, the Scipios, Pompey, Hannibal, Alexander) he recalled from his college assignments in classical literature. In "The Day of Doom" he appears to have limited himself to the Biblical and to have avoided learned references deliberately in a prodigious effort to appeal to the ordinary reader, but elsewhere his scholarship (including the Latin language) was allowed free play, in addition to the

[153]

direct borrowings of single words and entire phrases from the Bible.

The core of meaning running through the whole of Wigglesworth's work was the central structure of New England Puritan theology. Nowhere had he mentioned or even implied belief in those clauses of the two statements of creed of the Established Church of England, the Apostles' and the Nicene, which he would have said were links with Popery:

> And was incarnate by the Holy Ghost of the Virgin Mary . . .
> And I believe one Catholic and Apostolic Church. . . .
> (Nicene Creed)
> Who was conceived by the Holy Ghost, Born of the Virgin Mary. . . .
> He descended into hell. . . .
> The holy Catholic Church. . . .
> (Apostles' Creed)

Christmas was pagan; Mariolatry was Romish; the harrowing of hell was unbiblical; a universal church was inconceivable since only the predestined could "gather" a congregation —in the manner of the first Christians.

For him death and judgment were inevitable, and, in preparation, God required lives of rectitude on earth. The Lord's infliction of adversity was not to be taken amiss, but, though it might be interpreted as punishment for sin, to transcend it was to emerge a stronger soul. The two books as well as the shorter occasional pieces had rung the changes on these two themes. For the Puritan who did his utmost to keep from backsliding, there was always hope of a joyous reward.

> O set wide open unto mee
> The gates of righteousness.
> I will go into them, & will
> The praise of Jah confess.
> (Foster)

Of the three major poets in Puritan New England, Edward Taylor (1645?-1729) was the most private, so private, in fact, that he left instructions that his poems never be printed.[202] Religious in nature, most of his stanzas were a secret aid for articulating his faith, for glorifying his God, and for preparing him for the Lord's Supper. In style they were in the vein of the "metaphysical" poets of England, oddly enough, since the only verse in his library was a copy of Anne Bradstreet's *Tenth Muse*.[203]

The poems of Mistress Bradstreet (1612-1672) were more public in intent and showed the influence of Du Bartas, Spenser, and Sidney. Her quaternions—*The Four Elements, The Foure Humours in Man's Constitution, The Four Ages of Man,* and *The Four Seasons of the Year*—formed one long poem, in which the sixteen characters each boast of their qualities and powers. Another quaternion, *The Four Monarchies of the World,* followed. And the book concluded with minor poems: "A dialogue between Old-England and New," elegies for Sidney and Queen Elizabeth (both dead several years before Anne's birth), a poem honoring Du Bartas, a version of a passage from the second book of Samuel (in iambic pentameter couplets), and "The Vanity of all worldly things." Six years after her death a second edition was published—in 1678.[204] This book now included some more personal and less dependent pieces, "Contemplations," a poem in memory of her father, an epitaph for her mother, and "Several other Poems made by the Author upon Diverse Occasions . . . which she never meant should come to publick view," including lines written about an illness, during a pregnancy, in the absence of her husband, and on similar domestic subjects. These additions would be classified as "private" in a way that Taylor's were not, being more homely and womanly.

This may be explained partly by recognizing the masculine nature of the Puritan faith. Taylor was more energetic in preparing himself for the Lord's Supper; Mistress Bradstreet's role was a more receptive one. Whereas Taylor may have had to *prove* himself, Mistress Bradstreet had just to *be* herself. Taylor's literary passion was spent upon his Lord, Anne Bradstreet's often on her husband and family.

Nothing so imaginative as Taylor's conceits ("Heavens Sugar Cake"), nothing so dully competent as Anne Bradstreet's quaternions is to be found in the verse of Wigglesworth, who wrote only a very few "private" poems, such as the Latin verses at the death of Mary and a poem on death in his final year—and these served to formalize emotion rather than to express it in realistic simplicity. In spite of his allusions, nothing in his verse, moreover, parallels Anne Bradstreet's liberal learning and general culture—partly, of course, because of differences in purpose.

Michael's intent—in contrast with that of Mistress Bradstreet and Taylor—was always to bring sinners to repentance, to encourage the saints, as well as to praise God. Wigglesworth felt the masculine compulsion toward taking the initiative. His religious concern was more public than that of either of the other poets. Taylor would write a personal entreaty:

> Lord, blow the Coal: Thy Love Enflame in mee.
> (Meditation I)

Anne Bradstreet would write with feminine receptivity:

> Lord make me ready for that day
> then Come deare bridegrome Come away.
> (As weary pilgrim)

But Wigglesworth, expressing pastoral care about others, would often use first person plural:

> So come, Lord Jesus, quickly come we pray:
> Yea come, and hasten our Redemption day.
> (Mole-hill)

Or he would address his readers in direct second person:

> Christ yet intreats, but if you will not turn,
> Where grace will not convert, there fire will burn.
> (PS)

In his more personal poems he was inclined to apology and defense, guilty as he probably felt because of his enforced inactivity in the battlefields of the Lord.

> Yet have I stood some shocks that might
> Make stronger Men to reel.
> (Reader)

[156]

This tendency toward a romantic wearing of the heart on the sleeve was held in fair check, however, by utter sincerity in his vocation of healing souls and bodies. The inwardness of soul-searching balanced by the natural outgoing qualities of his duties gave to his verse tensions and variety of emotion that deepened its significance and usefulness for its readers.

To convey the unplumbed fact of being, existence, writers have no recourse but to imagery, to paradox and irony. Even while keeping a steady eye on the object itself (existence), they are forced into metaphorical language to communicate ideas about it. In this sense, then, their efforts are "non-objective." In the twelve years of his greatest poetic activity, Wigglesworth had used paradox and metaphor, not for decoration or for mere joy in the language, but in the "plain style" attempt to delineate God for some sort of human understanding and to describe, suggest, drive home man's finitude and his dependence on his Lord.

His term "renate" is the Christian metaphor for a new lease on life, springing from submission, forgiveness, and love. Wigglesworth, his wife Mary, and their Congregational colleagues said "yes" when they made public acknowledgment of their sins and of their new-born feeling of relation to the Creator, and so became "renate."[205] For them religion was not a thing apart, but as everyday as the blinking of an eye or the eating of a bit of bread.[206]

For all his assurance as one of the elect, Wigglesworth had a sense of inadequacy, not however in space but in time, for history would end and judgment would occur at a definite date, though humanly unknown. The vastness of eternity did give him pause, of course, for he could not measure it in terms of time:

> And that they are from rest as far
>   when fifty thousand year,
> Twice told, are spent in punishment,
>   as when they first came there.
>   (Eternity)

He had rather to resort to figures of speech, and even then
he was forced to give up the attempt to communicate the
concept:

A Cockle-shell may serve as well
to lade the Ocean dry. . . .
(Eternity)

Nevertheless, souls would go to a definite place, either the
mansions of heaven or the lakes and rooms of hell. In this
respect the immensity of the universe did not trouble him,
for the world was still the center of operation. He did not
have that awareness of the infinite spaces that frightened
Pascal or of the homelessness of man today in finding himself on a mere spot of dust in one of countless universes.
To the concern of the Puritan, science has now added the
dimension of space, so that contemporary despair is increased
by a sense of the tremendum, the great unknowable, both
outwardly in nature itself (the macrocosm) and inwardly
within the human psyche (the microcosm).

The Age of Enlightment produced much that man would
not want to give up—a new freedom of thought. Before that,
however, Wigglesworth and his colleagues had possessed a
profound sense of the power of evil, coupled with a realization
of the mystery of God's ways to man. Modern science and
technology have, in attending to daily details, not thought
about man's link with this underlying mystery. It must be
boldly said that insofar as they protect themselves from
and evade acknowledgment of the ultimately unknowable,
scientists are not fully realizing their human potential (and
limitation).[207] They have lost the Puritan feeling of eternity
through their concentration on the near at hand, though it
is only fair to say that many scientists, if not technologists,
are returning to this fundamental fact, that there must always be an impenetrable. If one substitutes for the seventeenth-century fear of an unprepared-for explosive end of
the world the twentieth-century fear of extermination by
explosion of hydrogen bombs, he may have discovered one

reason for the return to an awareness of man's confinement, of legitimate, though far from stultifying, dread, despair, guilt, anxiety—all the traits that urged New England thinkers on three hundred years ago, the traits that mortal man finds intrinsic to himself, that give added depth and meaning to his decisions in a way that reasoned humanism cannot, because it stops short of the ultimate.

As Puritan responsibility for increasing God's material gifts developed into Yankee shrewdness, as Puritan reliance on logic and the world developed into acceptance of the reasoning of science and technology, the American people lost the Puritan sense of evil, the feeling of awe, the realization of ultimate human helplessness. At the contemporary possibility that the material may get completely out of hand, many American thinkers are now recognizing the necessity of returning to the checks and balances of faith and logic. Now America's unfortunately misplaced blind confidence in technocracy and bureaucracy is breaking a little as some of her subtlest scientists again are becoming profoundly aware of the tremendum.

Granted, Wigglesworth did not have to meet the Newtonian mechanical laws for atoms and planets. There was no need for him to return to an acknowledgment of primal mysteries from which he had never departed. He had simply to deal with the unknowable by describing the eschatological cataclysm and by using paradox and metaphor.

Furthermore, his generation had no open argument yet with Descartes, who rejected everything which carried for him the least doubt. Especially in the years immediately after his Cambridge conversion, Wigglesworth beat down doubt, ran over it straight into the arms of God. Whereas the Cartesian anguish over initial nothingness (total doubt) was alleviated by the light of reason (God's gift), Wigglesworth's anguish was related to the soul's salvation and was alleviated by repentance and honest striving for high ethical behavior and foursquare faith in divine forgiveness of failure —with the privilege of beginning again.

[159]

VII. Right Hand, Left Hand, Center

M ichael Wigglesworth's view of life and the cosmos was conservative and orthodox in the New England theocratic vein. He had the friendship and support of such staunch hewers to the line as the Mathers, Increase and Cotton—both ordained, both powerful, both prolific—and the devoutly Puritan layman Samuel Sewall. Since the leading preachers of Massachusetts Bay all held much the same views,[208] a survey of Wigglesworth's thought would be an examination of concepts and beliefs received throughout the colony as the basis of life in this world and hope for the world to come.

When on that night of October 24, 1653, Wigglesworth had dreamed vividly of Judgment Day, he had not been experiencing a fantastic nightmare, but had been envisioning the eschatological event—the end of history—which Puritans believed literally was man's fate. Everything man did, everything he said, could be held against him in this last court of justice. A devout Puritan had a thorough sense of dread, lightened somewhat by the hope of undeserved forgiveness. Accompanying this anxiety was the realization of his mortality, his finitude—the brevity of life on earth. Much had to be done in this short time, all directed toward proving himself worthy of heaven. Hence, the smallest decision—even the decision to do nothing at all—weighed on him heavily, freighted as it was inevitably with ultimate concern.

Even while he may have been fairly well assured that he had been elected to salvation, the Puritan was conscious of himself as unworthy, as guilty no matter what he might do. He struggled constantly against separation from his God, being cast into outer darkness, a situation so dreadful as to be intolerable to the imagination. From time to time he was overcome with despair, for no mere mortal could deign to approach perfection, and anything short of perfection was an insult to God's glory. All a Puritan could do was to throw himself on the mercy of the Lord, to keep forever at the attempt at reunion with the Creator.

The American Puritans were an articulate group, for they believed in the efficacy of the word—in tracts, pamphlets, broadsides, and books. Even the most humble farmer would spend his evenings in argument and discussion of theological matters. The situation, however, did not limit itself to conversation and writing: every idea must be translated into action to be of any value. Theirs was a living, constantly tested philosophy, immediate, personal, inescapable, practical. Even the most apparently insignificant tenet of a stated view was related to the ultimate establishment of union with the Almighty, to the return from man's inevitable alienation toward the mansions of the Father.

Wigglesworth's poems, then, supplied his readers with ammunition for storming the gates of heaven. Not only did they show forth the unreasonableness of sinful indulgence in the prospect of hellish reward, but they also mapped out the path to be pursued by the seekers after righteousness. Though in one place the poet would write of the fearfulness of estrangement from God, nowhere does the reader get the impression of nihilism, of vacuum, of nothingness. If the joys of heaven were ineffable but certain for the elect, likewise the fires of hell were positive and inescapable for the damned.

In explaining the glories and vexations of life, the Puritan would ask several questions. Wigglesworth faced some of them squarely and discovered sound answers. Why were the worldly and wicked often patently happy and prosperous? In the course of his devotion what attributes would a man find as belonging to the Holy One (God, Christ, and the Holy Ghost) ? What were the reasons for suffering, the uses of adversity? What was the nature of the road the devout ("the saints") must follow? What would be the reward of the conscientious pilgrim?

Wigglesworth wrote because of a malady which prevented his preaching and conversing. He realized that the function of a pastor included carefully constructed and persuasively delivered sermons, but, since he himself was too frail to occupy his pulpit effectively, he wielded his pen, instead, in the service of the Lord. During his first ten years of physical disability and confinement his persistence in seeking strength in his Christian faith had yielded several conclusions obviously concurred in by his more vigorous New England colleagues.

What, then, were the saints like? The few contemporaries who had evaded the coils of wickedness through repentance would belong chiefly to the Congregational churches of New England. Altogether, the Sheep on the right hand of the Throne would be in four classes on the Last Day. There would be the martyrs, those who had undergone humiliation, sorrow, and disaster for the sake of their faith. Standing "like champions," they would already have testified with their blood and would now need no more defense or further appeal. The second class, the "afflicted ones" (was Wigglesworth here hopeful for himself?), would never have complained while suffering nor have allowed their faith to grow dim, but would have increased in their love of God. Next would be the ordinary folk, believers who had not been called on to suffer through sacrifice or ailment, but had been happy as figurative bearers of the Cross. Finally in the company of the saints would stand the Lambs, those selected for redemption who had been weak in their faith, doubters sometimes, but who had on the whole remained loyal and had accepted the Gospel as the statement of truth. Though feeble part of the time, they would have waxed stronger with experience. This group would include the babies who had been fortunate enough to be baptized before death had taken them away from their families, Christ in his mysterious way having died for them even though they had not had time on earth to accomplish any good (DD 22-25).

But what of the wicked man, the man who had no interest in the salvation of his soul, the man who had not been preordained for celestial joy? What was he like? Why did he prosper? What would be his penalties?

"The Day of Doom" listed vividly the types of the damned. Before the Throne of Judgment they were reduced to whimpering shams—all of them. Gone was any tone of bravado or rebellion. Tears and quivering remorse had replaced the false sense of security that had marked the world's men, the men who had fastened their attention on pleasure and material comfort. Wigglesworth supplied the reader with two catalogues: the first as the sinners stood trembling on the left hand of the Throne; the second as they approached group by group to plead their cases compulsively but futilely.

In the first listing, transgressors of all the Ten Commandments were represented (with the possible unexplained exception of the Fifth): those who worshiped other gods and thus were disobedient to the first two Commandments, those who were guilty of taking the Lord's name in vain, those who had profaned the Sabbath, those who had used fraud, force, rascality, and sly dealings, those who had borne false witness, and those who had cultivated covetousness and greed. The Fifth Commandment, concerning the honor due to parents, was not altogether unnoticed: two groups included those so proud and presumptous as to despise their correctors and those whose parents had been responsible for reprehensible upbringing and who were now scandalous in every way— including by implication disrespect for those guilty parents. The reader wonders if Michael was gingerly in his consideration of this Commandment because of his own collegiate diffidence towards his own parents.

In spelling out the particularities of transgression, Wigglesworth named more specific offenders: deserters from the faith; thorough sinners who had maliciously done wrong in spite of sure knowledge of what was right (these being consigned to the worst punishment of all); those who had declined to profess faith in the efficacy of redemption through Christ in spite of their opportunities; those who, hating the Lord, had refused to shelter any anxiety about their doom; persecutors of the saints; men who had acquired wealth too rapidly for their own good; innumerable "Witches, Inchanters, and Ale-house-haunters"; and those heathen who had not lived by the saving laws of natural goodness, available to them if they had cared (DD 27-35). One other aggregation the poet named only at the close of the pleading scene, a position one would be inclined to think he had chosen as climatic, as the setting for his trump card. These were the babies who, whether still-born or for whatever reason, had died unbaptized (DD 166).

The habits and attitudes of these sinners could be defined fairly well from their classifications. In various poems, however, Wigglesworth chose to describe in vivid terms the activities of these evil ones.

They all had in common an indifference to their fate, an unconcern for the ultimate, a superficiality on the brink of the depths of outer darkness. For the poet, to look for the good in *things* was futile. Anxiety, care, and cost were lost on worldly honor. Scholars learned everything possible, wrote brilliantly successful books, but without knowledge of God's grace. Conquerors gained the whole world, but without assurance of reward in heaven. Rich men added wealth to wealth, but without acknowledging Christ as Savior. All this activity was useless, for death put a stop to everything. "The King of Terrour calls, and will not stay" (Mole-hill).

In "The Day of Doom" the various defendants explained how they had lived and what their attitudes had been, and then learned from Christ what had gone wrong. One group of ministers had used the name of Christ to cast out devils, to raise the dead, to help the afflicted. By careful teaching and by moving sermons they had converted many sunken sinners. Christ saw through their hypocrisy, however, and asked them why they had not made the effort in themselves to stop sinning and to grow in the faith they preached.

In participating in the Lord's Supper, a second group had been guilty of murdering Christ because they had approached the Table without admitting their vileness and disgrace and honestly vowing to forego the world and its evil desires. A third group had admitted to being sinners but had counted, now they saw, too heavily on God's forgiveness. Christ pointed out that their show of ultimate concern had been impelled by a negative fear of eternal punishment rather than a positive love of heaven. They had looked for the praise of men in their pious activity. Such self-love as the source of energy could end only in itself, for absence of affirmative relation with God could bring nothing but sterility.

A crowd of "Civil honest Men" pleaded that they had never done wrong to other human beings: they had not been guilty of sexual malpractice, murder, bickering, idolatry, robbery, cheating, craftiness, lewd conversation. Where had the trouble lain? Christ's answer: no man could achieve "perfect Obedience"; hence all men deserved damnation. Their small accomplishment had led them to boast of righteous living, but their defense had given them away: they had thought by their own deeds to gain the reward of heaven. In other words, they had failed to put utter trust in Christ as the sole source of salvation. What they had desired, mostly, had been mortal reputation.

The Judge had only contempt for the group that pleaded that they had intended to repent but had been cut short by death. They had had time to repent. What if it had been short? They had seen and been taught that death could strike at any moment, but they had failed to seize the day. Obviously, their intentions had been merely pretty deceits, actually concealing evil.

For those who claimed they had been led astray by men they had considered their betters, Christ pointed out that

[165]

they had been in error to follow human example. In spite of the Biblical laws, they had chosen to imitate men, who at best could be only sinners. Even if they had followed those mortals who had been foreordained for salvation, all they had managed to do had been to copy the inevitably bad habits and to neglect to do good.

That even the intellectuals had not been able to agree on what the Bible meant was the argument of some of the condemned, to whom Christ replied that there had been enough plain truth in the Scriptures to guide any man in the right paths. Their trouble had been that they had not wanted to know the meaning of the difficult passages and so had not studied them; the obvious precepts they had clearly ignored.

Other damned ones included the cowards who, living among scoffers, had not dared to confess piety for fear of loss of friends and contempt of the wicked with possible torture and loss of property. Christ reminded them that they had forgotten that such suffering would not have lasted forever, that winning everlasting pleasure should have been their true end, that saving their human skins had been only superficial salvation in time.

Some pleaders appealed to the principle of fair play. If pardon made God's glory shine brighter, why should He not have chosen to release them from their doom? To these, also, Christ said that they had had their chance. Again He said that even the slightest misdemeanor deserved suffering forever. The wonder was that, knowing the final price of sin, they had continued in evil.

One impudent crowd declared that they had not been able to help sinning since they had been foreordained all along to destruction. Christ laid the blame, however, not on God but on the men themselves, who were now rejected not from predestination but from their breaking of the immutable laws. To the argument that men condemned before birth had no power to repent, to break their hearts, or to divert their wills, Christ made what must seem to most twentieth-century thinkers an equivocal reply: It was not man's potentiality ("his *Can*") that condemned him, but his determination (that is, his own decision) to do evil, not good. Being naturally base, these men had deliberately chosen death and decay, had willed to destroy their souls' well-being. It would have paid them to seek mercy during life. Had anyone ever been refused? (This would seem to argue that any man of acumen and desire could have made open confession and so gained admittance to church membership, a fairly reliable measure of salvation. Earlier pleaders, however, had been damned in spite of churchly activity.)

The last two groups of Goats were let off with lighter sentences than the others. The heathen, who had not heard the Word of God, had nevertheless not lived up to the best that had been in them, had not followed "Natures Light." Finally, babies who had been still-born or had died before baptism would be consigned to "the easiest room in Hell," for they had not had time to commit wickedness on earth, but had unfortunately been caught in original sin through the fall of Adam, which, since Adam represented all men, was their fall, too (DD 69-181).

"The Day of Doom" was essentially narrative. In other poems Wigglesworth traced in considerable detail the patterns of conduct of the unregenerate. He made it clear that in his theology they followed their own wills (Meat II, 6.) and longed, whether secretly or overtly, for the reign of lust, for satisfaction of the senses, for wealth, for power. What man mistook as strength was ultimately only the cause of ruin. Human vigor was after all as frail as a flower or a piece of Venetian glass (Strength I.1). Though man might exercise his will, he paradoxically had no power to choose anything but evil, but evil he nevertheless did choose. (For more liberal thinkers, this is very thin logic from Wigglesworth and his colleagues.) Those who slaughtered and enslaved others for the sake of an earthly kingdom might lose their prize overnight and certainly would have to give it up at life's end (Heaven V. 10). The Turkish Empire, for example, vast in lands and riches, was but a bone tossed out to dogs by the Master (Poor V.6). Its potentates could not take it with them when they approached the Throne on Judgment Day.

Even if the poet could pity sinners, he could offer them no comfort, for no peace was promised to the wicked (Joy V. 3). Furthermore, important as it was for the attainment of humility and insight, suffering itself was no guarantee of salvation, for what made martyrs was not suffering, but the cause they suffered for (Heaven I. 8). Thus a man could be tortured pitiably, but, if the faith he was agonizing for was in error, he would be afflicted futilely. In Wigglesworth's view most men were doomed. Though they seemed free, they were really free only to run easily along the road to hell (Con I.3; Meat I.6). What most men wanted was liberty to go where they pleased and to act as they pleased, not to abide by the restraining laws of God (Con I.1). If he would only understand it, a wicked man was Satan's prisoner, no matter how much physical freedom he might have (Con I.10).

Wigglesworth gave a great deal of attention to the rich and prosperous. It was true that occasionally a good man got wealth and a wicked man was brought low, but often— far too often, perhaps—it was the evil man who did well in worldly affairs (Meat VII.2). The world took men at face value, not considering how they had acquired their property, whether honestly or not, but counting up and paying honor to their "yearly Rents" and "Possessions" (Poor II.1). God did not, on the other hand, take into account the degree of poverty or prosperity (Meat VII.1).

Nevertheless, it was easy to grumble when the faithless appeared to suffer very little, in spite of arguments that the flesh was "silly" and "sinful." The non-believers were often healthy, rich, and secure when others, theologically more conscientious, were not; they feasted, sang, and slept soundly while others worried about sin; in their success and surface happiness they thought God loved them, though in truth they themselves loved amusement and distraction more than they did God (Meat VII.4-6, 8).

The world indeed was generally very good to them. They

grew fat and excessively wealthy, blessed with honey, milk, butter, oil. What God gave them they wasted on sensual satisfaction, though, making daily sacrifice to Mammon. They made the world their idol, the more covetous they became. In spite of the truth that both belonged to God, heart and head concentrated on the world. With wealth came pride; with plenty came surfeit and blindness to the Gospel and the grace it revealed. With prosperity came rebellion against God and alignment, rather, on the side of Satan. Insolence, intemperance, drunkenness, pampering, the services of the Devil—all sprang from worldly well-being. The wicked had no sense of fundamental dread because they felt no pain; God being deliberate, they were unafraid to indulge their senses (Meat II.5; VII.10-15; VIII.7,9). Though they dressed in finery, they were dead within; though they had clean houses, their hearts were filthy; though their bodies were clean-limbed and lithe, their souls were foul (Meat X.6).

Occasionally the Almighty would warn them that they were on the wrong road. He might destroy some as an admonition to the others, but the unwholesome remnant paid no attention. Even when God visited affliction on their very selves, either they did not sense the reason for the suffering, they stubbornly refused to repent, or they made empty promises to do better, but they would return to their worldly ways when the suffering stopped ("wallowing in the mire" like hogs, eating vomit like dogs). Their sin, though, was on their own heads: they *chose* ultimate ruin. God in his wisdom would let matters run their course, then would call the sinners at last to awful judgment and consign them to the lake of everlasting fire (Meat VII.16-19).

What they refused to realize was the transitoriness of material wealth, the true poverty of an intransigent soul. They did not take to heart the example of the ulcerous beggar Lazarus, carried to heaven by the angels, and of the poor rich man Epicure, condemned to hell because he had laid up no riches in the realms above. So it was with every man who provided for his outward comfort but neglected the husbanding of inner riches (Poor I.3-6). Earthly treasures, carnal delights, ostentatious clothes—all were base compared to the rewards of the honestly righteous (Poor V.8). Moreover, a rich man's grasp on his wealth could weaken in a single day's time. Then, without the inner resources of faith, he would be very poor indeed (Poor III. 4).

When the wicked thus prospered and ignored the condition of their souls, they were in a state of separation from the Creator, a "fearful" state (Meat II.7). Wigglesworth himself expressed the devout wish that sinners would awake, look about them, and become genuinely grieved for their sins and for their loss of God (Joy V.4).

Of course, not sinners alone, but even the faithful experienced this dreadful separation. The law of sin within men made them rebel against God's law, which they knew (intellectually) was good, but which they could not absorb (emotionally). What they wanted to do they could not because of their natural perversion. In fact, the faithful might exert every possible effort but be frustrated by the Devil's subtleties. They knew that this meant spiritual death, and, though they made complaint about the ruggedness of the perpetual Christian battle (Life I.4,5), they should remember that Satan never relaxed in his efforts to allure and seduce the unwary—and the wary, for that matter, because it was his nature to ruin any man's soul whenever he could (Life II.4,5).

Wigglesworth felt genuine pity for those who had never felt the presence of God and a sense of His mercy. If creature comforts were taken away, they had absolutely nothing to depend on for assurance and happiness. Their loneliness was indescribable. The poet's sympathy sprang from experience. He recollected the period after Mary's death when, estranged from God, he too had been the victim of sheer loneliness (Sol. I.8, 9). But now, ten years later, he had discovered the profound truth that, for those who persisted in the pursuit of faith, whenever God withdrew, it was for a divine purpose. He would return, and the reunion would be all the richer for the temporary division (Sick IV.9).

Actually, in the Puritan cosmology, the power of Satan to annihilate the human spirit was only figurative, for the soul was indestructable (PS 7). Alienation from God on earth was as nothing compared to the last terrible separation—the condemnation to eternal burning. Even if a man gained the whole world, a misspent inner life would bring everlasting suffering in "the Infernal Pit." When at the Last Day a sinner had to confront the flame of hell, he would then understand—and only then—how horrible the punishment was to be, so horrible as to be at present indescribable: "an hundred fold More terrible than ever you were told" (PS 135 ff.).

Wigglesworth begged the sinful to end the separation before it was too late, for God had not promised long life to rebels. How was it possible to say that sin was sweet and at the same time agree that "it ends in bitterness?" The longer a man sinned, the harder it would be to break away. Furthermore, late repentance, as on a deathbed, might be only the hypocrisy of a frightened soul, a Satanic trick for gaining more fuel for the flames (PS 225 ff.). Eternal life was worth every effort: the repentant sinner would not regret giving up his evil ways and attitudes. It paid to keep knocking at the door of redemption. If the Lord chose to induct a man into a realization of salvation (though He was not in the least obligated to do so), that man would have new riches, new cleanliness, new protection (PS 361 ff.).

Doubt and fear, natural even in the devout, came from one direction. Bickering and quarrels, however, came from another, for difference of opinion needed at least one other person to breed. Whereas doubt was based on the individual's faith, quarrels were more than likely to be based on doctrine, church government, the definition of orthodoxy— the more or less open and public considerations.

Wigglesworth always wrote from the point of view of the conservative. Any change in the carefully wrought original structure was heresy pure and simple, unless it had been thought through to some agreement by the ministers of the area. Uncertainty and anxiety were to be expected among the faithful, but quibbling over the teachings of the leaders, over the control of the local organizations, or over the centering concepts of Puritanism could not be tolerated. Such irregularity would be treated as the symptom of a festering disease in the body of the church.

Probably a short time after his return from Bermuda in the summer of 1664, in spite of feeling a comparative willingness among his people to cooperate, Wigglesworth wrote "When as the wayes of Jesus Christ,"[209] which warned its readers of God's displeasure with just such pettiness. He singled out the principle of selectivity of church membership as the object of the quarreling he abhorred. He had found that this one of Christ's laws was proving too confining for everyone in his community, be he baby, fool, or savant. Both members and non-members were complaining about the stringent requirements for belonging to the church, and hence the limitation of the vote in the community. He defended this political principle on the grounds that without the limitation good people would be replaced by an "unruly rout" and that, if the innocent consorted thus intimately with the unholy, they would lose their guilelessness. Moreover, if bickerings continued, serious trouble would develop. Dissent should therefore be routed out. More personally, a congregation that was growing more and more suspicious of its minister and was not treating him with proper reverence was courting disaster. On the other hand, to be quite fair, if a minister was insinuating into his sermons some irregular ideas, he was breeding calamity. (Wigglesworth's predecessor, Matthews, had thus not been good for the church at Malden.) If a minister was suspected, even by his "best friends," of cherishing heresy, whether to please the men in power or otherwise to insure his position and income, he should act very carefully in order not to destroy the fabric of the church, for after all a minister was as much subject to sin as any member of his congregation. In an intellectual community like New England, discussion, whether among pastors or among people, would inevitably give rise to opinions that could be interpreted as heretical. Here was the danger.

The only answer to these problems was repentance and its accompanying humility (Meat concl. 14). God would have plenty of cause for punishment if his people did not return to him. Everywhere in Wigglesworth's verse was the call to repentance—sometimes a sharply-worded warning, sometimes a gentle plea, always urgent (Joy V.5-8). The Christian had before him the promise of an "Incorruptible Crown." It seemed unreasonable that he would be unwilling to change his ways, to be cheerful and affirmative in following the good, with such a goal in store (Heaven V.8). If burdened by wicked thoughts, a man could help himself by a genuine turning to God, Who would always be at hand, though He might seem to be far off. Sorrow over sins (frequent burning of dross) would eventually make the soul approach worthiness (purify the gold) (Light VII.11, 12).

Genuinely concerned about this process of returning, Wigglesworth wrote of it not altogether in hypothetical cases, Biblical examples, or third-person instances, but in first-person plural, so that he himself was identified with his people in wrong-doing and in requiring the about-face (Meat 15 ff.). He specifically named New England, which he had grown to love, as needing to repent, before the Lord, in retribution, making physical matters worse (Meat concl. 13).

He had been urging Massachusetts Bay to repent for a decade. In "God's Controversy with New-England" (1662) he had listed the flaws that God had discovered in the Puritan community: carnality, worldliness, indifference, dead-heartedness, excess, pride, luxury, debate, deceit, contention, strife, false-dealing, covetousness, hypocrisy, sensuality, presumption, conceit, stubbornness, perversity. He admitted that not everyone was guilty in the same degree of all these foul errors, but they were rampant nevertheless. Though, because of the zeal and earnestness of the faithful, God had so far restrained His terrifying hand, still dreadful punishment was inevitable if New England did not mend her ways. True, after the judgeship of Joshua the Israelites had fallen from the way, but after all they had not had the advantages of the men of Massachusetts: for them the rules and precepts as set up in the Gospels had been lacking altogether. New England could have no legitimate alibi. Even among the heretofore "best" people there was the ever-hateful security and its accompanying sloth. As for the populace, the gross sins had developed beyond enumeration, for not only had they paid no attention to the teachers and pastors who had issued warning after warning, but they had ridiculed the few who had dared to follow the Lord's direction. All they could expect in consequence was harsh judgment, "an All-Consuming stroke," if they did not totally repent. (All this was spoken by the Almighty in the poem.) At the conclusion, Wigglesworth himself made a plea for his "dear New England" to turn wholeheartedly to righteousness. He could be severe, even violent, in his warnings, but his gentle nature ever and again would break through in his poetry as he sought to bring the people of the colony—not just his own congregation—to the necessary submissive attitude.

When in early 1670 his assistant Benjamin Bunker died, Wigglesworth indicated to the congregation at Malden that God had taken this holy man away from them as punishment for their sins. He pressed them, "secure hard hearts," to wake up and busy themselves with grief. They were to apply dust, ashes, gall to their spirits, for it was later than they knew. The harvest was nearly past, the summer was over. The bellows were burnt out, the lusts remained. If they did not repent as a result of Bunker's death, God would take away his benefits. If, on the other hand, they did show true sorrow for their misconduct, if they began to seek earnestly after religious growth, then they could expect more kindness from God.

One of the most potent arguments for immediate repentance was the brevity of human life, for God could wipe out a man's existence at any moment. Indeed, the whole world could come to its cataclysmic end at any moment. Sinners unprepared for the Judgment could expect no mercy at the last.

In the volume with "The Day of Doom" were several shorter works, including twenty-seven stanzas at the end called "Vanity of Vanities: A Song of Emptiness to Fill up the Empty Pages Following," owing an obvious debt to *Ecclesiastes*. Here, life at best was a wave, a dream, a lifeless picture: like wind, flower, vapor, bubble, wheel, reed, stone, dust, chaff, stubble, shadow, it was nothing. The world could provide only trinkets, "no true Contentment," only vanity. Beauty was a fading flower; pleasure, the bait of the Devil. Friends could be lost through estrangement or death. Riches were undependable; far from being the source of redemption, they could draw men to perdition. It would be foolish to desire all these things above all else, for they would disappear quickly, having meanwhile increased man's natural tendency to sin. The more of the world's pleasures and funds one had, the more he would want. The happy man would be spiritual, directed toward the eternal; the wretched man would be economic, directed toward the present, deceptive world.

Honor and sovereignty could never be wholly sufficient; the ears, eyes, and stomach could never be satisfied. Even if a man owned, as he might wish, the whole world, he would still want something. One had but to recall the case of Alexander the Great. Who could envy a man that owned everything and yet was beset more and more by the demonic drive of greed? Most men in power were like that, though there were a few exceptions of God-centered leaders. Generally speaking, however, rulers were contemptuous of the men they controlled and were forgetful of God—unless "great grace" intervened. (Wigglesworth could have been thinking of Charles II.) Honor could blind even the wise, as the sun blinds insistent gazers.

Paralleling increase in power and responsibility would cause worry, which would produce insomnia! Craftsmen and farmers slept better than such rulers. Attendant honors were so transient that one hour could bring them to nothing, to misery or sudden death. Whether suddenly or not, everyone had to die, fair and foul alike. All the wealth and power in the world could not make the great men of legend and history immortal in the true sense. Everything must succumb to death: gifts, bribes, power, force, threats would come to nought. This realization should bring everyone to lead more devout lives. Let men of vanity take pleasure in the world; the best thing to do was to love God.

What was God like? Who was this all-powerful Being to whom prayers were to ascend? He was tri-partite, of course, in the Christian tradition. Promised by Christ, the Holy Spirit lived in the faithful, though not in the worldly (Joy II.6). This Spirit was the Comforter, the strength-bringer. By Its indwelling It was able to be persistent in renewing the will of the soul, to conquer lusts, gradually, and to overcome everything that would oppose the soul's potential holiness. If It made the heart humble, paradoxically It would contribute greater strength and lead to ultimate victory over the world (Light X.14-16).

Not only the Holy Spirit, but Christ and God Himself were always with the faithful. Dependable, They would never withdraw Their love, in spite of the necessity of punishment (Sick IV.10; Light II.5). Love implied support, which the believer could always count on. The weaker he became, the more surely would God and Christ bear him up (Strength I.11). No matter how sympathetic, earthly friends could not always help, but Christ was always at hand, would never leave His own like orphans "sad and comfortless" (Joy II.5). God would always appear in time of trouble, to take up His child in His "Everlasting Arms." Whatever the difficulty, He would be present, whatever elements were interfering with man's well-being: let water, let fire, let any affliction strike (Meat VIII.6, 8). The world, the Devil, one's own wickedness—these were the foes against which God in His three parts would protect man. If occasionally the Almighty seemed to neglect man, it was because man himself had been neglectful and needed to stumble and fall in order to realize his weakness (Strength I.6).

To Christ could be attributed the qualities of teacher and

[176]

example. His life had showed the earnest searcher how to turn tribulation, suffering, and calamity into glory and actual rejoicing (Joy II.7). Though, according to the Bible, He had never been sick, He had suffered enough to take away any taint of that evil mortal natures might have (Sick III.1). He could pity man because He Himself had had man's experience. Since He had gone through man's afflictions, it was as if man had none at all. Though He was above grief, He could feel profoundly the sorrows of men. In fact, He would not count His own glory as perfect until all members of the church had become as glorious as He (Joy IV.10, 11, 13). To this end He had supplied "wondrous food" in the Lord's Supper, much better provision than anything God had given the infidels (Turks and other pagans) (Poor V.3, 4).

The Trinity had the power to bring cheer—to the sick, the solitary, the downcast (Sol. I.10, 11). Whether man was asleep or awake, God was by his side. When other friends forsook, the members of the Trinity were immediately available for companionship (Sol I.2, 3, 7; Joy IV.9).

God was also a Father. The faithful were His heirs, would come into the kingdom of heaven (Poor II.6). Rich, wise, and kind, He lacked neither the will, power, or knowledge to understand what was best. He knew man's need before man asked, and He often bestowed what was needed before the request was made (Poor IV.6).

As Physician, Christ could bring spiritual health from bodily sickness, could actually make pain seem less severe (Sick III.2), through sharing, through example, through teaching concentration on things heavenly, through understanding that affliction was for a positive purpose. He could cure the ailments of the soul by encouragement of faith in the cleansing power of His blood and by the "Sovereign Balm" of His presence and support (Meat IX.5). He could administer such cordials as would revive the sufferer (Joy IV.12). As Surgeon He could perform such operation as to remove what was a hindrance to the growth and health of the soul (Light X.7, 8).

Having tried to describe divinity in terms of kindly, helpful men—companion, father, teacher, example, physician, and surgeon, the poet attempted in still another way to show God as source of being, the way of natural imagery. He called God an ocean from which all streams came and to which they returned, a never-failing spring, from which man's pitcher could always be refilled. As with the sun, man enjoyed the privilege of God's light and warmth even when denied man's fires and candles. As the sun supplied its beams and the spring or fountain gave origin to the brook or river, so God was the source—and the sole source—of the grace man needed to live the upright life (Strength I.3-5; Poor III.9, 10). God measured man by his virtues (developed through grace) and not by his worldly possessions. With all Babylon as his treasury, Belshazzar still had been of no ultimate account (Poor II.2). Without God's gift of mercy, no man could have hope.

These pictures of God, Christ, and the Holy Spirit as gentle and generous came after years of suffering had brought Wigglesworth through the trials of the soul—successfully, from the Christian point of view. Earlier, his picture of God and Christ had not been so benign. In the poems in *The Day of Doom* wrath had predominated, not the brooding, compassionate spirit, but the fire-wielding, threatening God. After the exposure of the sinners, God's ire had been said to be so hot that tears of repentance could not quench it (DD 189). The days of His mercy were over; man had had his chance. Through Christ He condemned evil doers to depart from Him to eternal suffering (DD 201). Christ blasted out the word *Depart* with such force that they rushed from His presence "as if in haste," albeit unwillingly (DD 206-207). In exercising His justice, God smote them unceasingly and forevermore (DD 215). Even in these early poems, however, for the saved, God was loving and merciful, His face bright as sunshine, no longer covered with a veil (DD 221, 223). "God's Controversy" pictured the Lord in time—before the Last Judgment. Dissatisfied with the recent history of New England, He threatened harsh sentence if the people failed to turn at once from "Pride, and Wantonness." He was shown as willing to have given them what they had asked for, but only if they had continued to obey His holy laws. In 1670, at the death of Bunker, God was again a threatening ruler, whose benefits would cease unless Malden repented.

When in 1673 Wigglesworth's friend Mr. Foster was returned from captivity as if by miracle, God was portrayed as a saving God, Whose punishment was reserved for princes, tyrants, and cruel masters, but Who gave freedom of body and soul to His faithful. The beauty of His holiness deserved the praise of all creation.

Finally, like a fierce echo, in Wigglesworth's valedictory "A Farewell to the World" (ca. 1705), God was again the "King of terrors" whose grace New England had ignored and who was sure to visit all except the godly few with a bitter judgment. For the most part, though, this last poem (with its companion, "Death Expected and Welcomed") showed forth Christ (as representative of the Godhead) as man's only permanent friend, in Whose company the conscientious could at least hope for everlasting happiness, though no one could be absolutely "secure," the only recourse being "trust." The poet himself, however, was leaving the world on a note of high expectation: at the Great Resurrection he was reasonably (rather, *un*reasonably—that is, by faith) certain that he would emerge from his grave marvelously hale—and as glorious as Christ.

VIII. The Uses of Adversity and a Pattern for Living

After years of doubt and growth in the faith, Wigglesworth arrived at full acceptance of the Puritan tenet that the Lord inflicted all suffering in mercy and for the Christian's good (Meat IV.3). God's temporary frown would turn into a smile in due time as grace and kindness touched man in their eternal flow (Joy III.2). If a man was forced to taste the bitterness of affliction and was sad for it, how much sadder was God, Who found no pleasure in punishment, but was forced to it when provoked (Joy I.7), just as earthly fathers were full of pity for the very children whom they must chastise, but whom they would never turn out of the house, however angry they might become (Light II.7). Since God had no desire to afflict, why should a man defiantly anger and grieve Him (Meat concl. 10)?

In fact, it was possible through the right point of view to turn affliction itself into a source of spiritual health, so that paradoxically one could be sick and well at the same time (Sick intro. 1). Admittedly, long-extended bodily ailment could be both vexatious and anguishing, but, if one realized that God thus harrowed man only out of ultimate love, the burden might be easier to bear. Wigglesworth gave a graphic description of Job's ailments and cited Hezekiah and the two Lazaruses (Christ's friend and the sick beggar) as Biblical support of this idea. Out of all their grievances had come the saving health of God's grace (Sick I.1-9).

In a like way, the curse of imprisonment or banishment, if the cursed one continued to think of God as finally merciful, could bring him a freedom of soul and conscience he had never known before (Con II.2; III.1). Though banished, Jacob, Moses, and John on Patmos had heard the voice of God more clearly than ever before. Imprisoned though they were, Daniel, Shadrach, Meshach, Abednego, Paul, and Silas —all had been guarded by angels or even by God Himself (Con III).

The Puritan God, then, was a God of justice, but His justice was lightened with mercy, if the sufferer would only seek it out. Though God was a God of thunder and lightning, the end result of retribution was the merciful flowering of salvation. Little enough attention has been paid to this aspect of Puritan theology. New England's God was severe, but His severity, however black, was purposed for kindness, a seeming paradox that mere man was often not far-sighted enough to see.

Furthermore, heavy though infliction might seem to the recipient, God would not punish to the point of total destruction, for this would mean a loss of souls rather than their salvation. The load, then, would never be more than the sufferer could bear, for God would not be capable of deserting his own (Meat IV.10,11). God's tests would never exceed man's endurance, for with an increase in pain would come an increase in spiritual joy and the strength to endure —provided the tormented one maintained the right attitude (Sick IV.2,5). The Devil was not entirely a free agent, for Christ kept a continuing hold on him and would not permit him to trouble a man longer than was fitting (Light VII.13).

Soon after Mary's death, Michael wrote a poem in which he tried in all humility to put this principle to work. Later included among "Riddles Unriddled," the poem was in the form of a dialogue between Flesh and Spirit. Wondering that God should punish him with this bereavement, Flesh was answered by Spirit that God would give only what man could bear. He should be thankful that the affliction was no

[181]

worse. On the other hand, God would no doubt have been milder if Flesh (*i. e.,* Wigglesworth) had deserved less grievance (Sol III.1-3).

In this point the Puritan took some little comfort. He always reminded himself that he deserved more punishment than he was receiving (Joy I.6; Sick II.4,6). By virtue of Adam's fall and his own consequent innate and ineradicable sinfulness, he had every reason to expect God to strike out at him eternally (Sol III.8); so he should be thankful that the scourge cut no deeper (Sick II.6).

In a way this reflected a strong position with relation to sickness, poverty, and other inescapable misfortune. Signifying much more than mere abject acceptance, it demanded applying the trouble to affirmative use. Assured of the final love of God, man was now put on his mettle to make the most of his predicament, to receive his humanity, and to work positively with what he was toward what he could become. Such an attitude toward affliction, not as adverse circumstance to be borne courageously, but as outright punishment for sin committed, had come to dominate the thinking of Massachusetts Bay in the early 1660's. In spite of admonitions to submit meekly to the yoke of Christ, the images of struggle and aggressive fighting pointed to a responsibility to create a vigorous life out of the very mortifications that weakened the body and the spirit.

In fact, a man should not only accept affliction as a matter of God's course, but he should realize that he needed adversity on which to strengthen his spiritual muscles (Sol III.4). God's blows were intended to save souls—to prevent man's loping easily along the path to damnation and, on the other hand, by their purgatorial influence to make man spell out a program for a righteous life (Meat III.1). To help him see the error of his current ways, chastisement was indispensable. Just as medicine stirred up the body, so chastisement aroused sinful corruptions, not to increase them, but to make man aware that he was harboring them at all (Light IV.5). Then he could map the road to improvement.

Such purposefulness in hardship was not always easy to

comprehend. Even the best of men would object, as the saints had proved. That God intended calamity to be productive had to be embraced by the ideal Puritan both intellectually and emotionally (Light IV.6). In other words, merely to make suffering plausible to the understanding was insufficient. The point of its productivity must go beyond theory, must also be felt, be fervently absorbed so that from suffering would come great strength (Meat IV.12). For those who thus knew and responded, chastening could perform a number of desirable offices through grace (God's mercy): it could serve as a test of a man's loyalty to God; it could encourage growth as a child of God; it could effect in a man the substitution of humility for pride; it could cleanse a man of his besetting sin, make him more nearly holy, and lead him to a hitherto unachieved spiritual robustness that would equip him for more strategic battle against the forces of Satan (Meat III.11). For life was a two-way struggle: one had to combat evil, but he must also cultivate good. Through broken fortune he learned not only how to avoid the old ways but to perform his newly discovered duties with zeal, a lesson David had learned at great cost (Meat III.2,3).

The affliction nearest Wigglesworth's own heart was bodily ailment, since he himself had been thus burdened for a decade before writing *Meat Out of the Eater*. From his suffering he had apparently derived wisdom. It was far better, he had discovered, to have a sick body and a hale soul than the other way around, for spiritual sickness dishonored God, whereas in physical illness one could find means of glorifying Him. Just as bodies sometimes needed medicine more than food, so souls required sickness and pain for their edification. Human nature tended toward spiritual ills—original sin. Through physical affliction a man's will was subdued to God's will, his soul was cleansed of pride, self-love, impatience, worldliness, and like cankers. Instead, he was sent in pursuit of peace with holiness and the recompense that heaven would provide (Sick III.4-8).

So by physical irregularity a proper man was made eager

to do his duty, he ceased to find anything attractive in sin, he reflected more and more on his ultimate destiny—the necessity of leaving this world behind. He saw his inadequacy and patent sinfulness clearly and longed more and more for the esteem of the Father. In feeling the griefs of earthly existence, he desired release into heaven, he counted less on earthly possessions as means of genuine comfort, he leaned more heavily on Christ as the source of redemption. And in this weakening of the material would come the strengthening and daily invigoration of the spiritual. Wigglesworth could not imagine anyone's not desiring such reward (Sick III.9-11).

His two chief instances of affliction were sickness and incarceration, in both of which conditions the man who sought would find "More Liberty" than he had ever known before (Con I.5), happy in the knowledge that sweet joy and bitter sorrow could join hands to find mutual strength (Joy intro. 1). In contrast, some physically sound men had sick souls, blind eyes, hard hearts, and stiff wills which prevented richness of experience for the spirit (Sick III.3). There was no way out but that the soul bear a great deal for its health's sake (Meat IV.4), as well as to insure heaven at last (Heaven II.9).

Whether vexation or severe torture, affliction in any degree, then, could be put to creative use. For Wigglesworth sickness apparently was inevitable. His Puritanism had helped him, not toward mere stoic bearing up, but to an aggressive use of adversity (what some might call making the best of a bad bargain) to improve his inner life and his relation with the Creator.

God's way of testing and correcting man assumed various forms. One thing was certain: everyone, even the best of men, must be chastened in some way or other before he could learn to enjoy the pleasures of heaven (Meat II.2,3). In *Meat Out of the Eater* Wigglesworth intended to present the case for affliction in rather general terms. He did, however, contrive in the first section of the book to pile up an impressive list of specifics. His recurring advice was never to be downhearted, since difficulty was natural for "our frail Condition" on the road to paradise (Meat II.1). In the second part of the book, the paradoxical "Riddles Unriddled," he attempted deliberately to picture the variety of griefs, temptations, and distresses (the Devil's instruments) that God permitted man to experience in his campaign for spiritual strength (Light I.1,2).

To get at the nature of affliction, Wigglesworth mingled fact with metaphor, literal with figurative. He indicated at intervals the absurdity of finding strength in weakness or freedom in confinement, but it was nevertheless not unusual to see the weak *become* strong and the imprisoned *become* free. The incredible paradox was how ailment and bondage could at the same time *be* health and liberty (Strength intro.; Con intro.). Cited as archetypical of this seeming contradiction were the situations of Jacob, Joseph, Moses, the three youths in the fiery furnace, Daniel in the lions' den, and the shipwrecked Paul (Meat VIII.7).

Among the real obstacles to physical comfort he listed enforced change, danger to life, fire, flood, even bad roads (Meat V.8). Elsewhere he added sickness, deprivation of material possessions, the death of friends, a multiplication of wants with accompanying piling up of woes. Another burden would be conspiracy of men and devils to make one's present suffering worse (Meat IV.13). This would be especially hard on man since he was by nature gregarious and would feel the profoundest depression at being deserted by other men—not only deserted, but seriously put upon (Sol I.1).

Two kinds of death engaged Wigglesworth's interest. One, physical death, took away friends and relatives. It was impossible to know who would be next, so uncertain was the length of man's life—the only certainty being the necessity of its end. The daily death-knells were witness to human finitude. New Englanders were "in the midst of Deaths." But the other kind of death was even worse: the succumbing to temptation, the yielding to sin, which meant spiritual decay and separation from God. Since man was subject to this kind of death every day of his earthly existence, only physical death could liberate him from these daily deaths (Life III.1-3).

In order to make clear the nature, strength, and universality of these unavoidable, inconvenient, but requisite grievances, Wigglesworth resorted to figurative language, an appeal to the imagination that a literal catalogue of troubles could not satisfy. The general description of life as a rugged course to be run (Meat V.4) was at least as old as St. Paul. With persuasive rhetorical interrogation the poet invited his readers to undertake obstacles with an understanding that at their end they would have all the more reason to be grateful to God and to adore Him (Sol III.7). Or, if one thought of life as a battle against the forces of Satan, who could hope to win by running away (Meat V.4)?

Afflictions were the water God mingled with His wine, a figure from the Lord's Supper—a necessary modification since strong wine induced drunkenness and since intemperance in every direction often accompanied peace and prosperity (Meat III.8), which must for salvation's sake be reduced periodically in headiness to remind man that he was not master of his fate.

Wigglesworth's figures were hardly ever original, but were derived, sometimes copied almost word for word, from the *Psalms,* the Gospels, the Prophets, or the *Book of Revelation.* Only occasionally was an image taken from daily life. The *Psalms,* for example, provided the image of affliction as a refining vessel which, God willing, would consume "the Dross" of sin and leave the pure gold of essential being and as fuller's soap that washed out stains left by evil thoughts, intentions, and deeds. Like frost, he said, affliction cleared the air and the blood to increase one's spiritual health. Frost also eventually softened the earth for the reception of seed with the outlook of greater fruitfulness (Meat III. 4,5). Thus, in suffering the frost of estrangement from health, friends, and God Himself, man could be after the thaw a more fertile field for the flowering of righteousness and deeds dedicated to the adoration of the Lord.

If prosperity yielded pride and wantonness (as too much honey stirred up "Gall/and Cholerick Excess"), so on the other hand, like the unpleasant but wholesome aloe, did adversity cleanse man of these evils. Any rich diet would induce a diseased soul and body and would invite, for the zealous man, a purgative (Meat III.6,7), which was precisely what God's medicine was; the problem was to get the patient to believe in its effectiveness. The method was to expose the sin, make the patient realize that he wanted relief and that he needed help, and bring him to grieving for that sin. This humbling of the self was the point at which God could enter (Light IV.8,9) and begin the building up of strength both to fight the offense and to cultivate its opposing virtue. If men would only recognize it, God was probably with them all the time (like unconsuming fire) (Sol I.5), working at the healing process (Light IV.9).

If life were all roses, man would tire of the fragrance. Like a ship's ballast, afflictions were necessary for balance (Meat III.9). Otherwise, pride and the moral and physical decay of constant comforts would make a man list dangerously, just as wine undiminished by water would make him drunk.

As frost was nature's way of breaking up the ground for more productive sowing, so was affliction like a plow, which broke the ground, killed the weeds of lust, and prepared man for God's use (Meat III.10). No farmer would expect a crop, bumper or otherwise, without plowing and sowing. No Christian could expect salvation without suffering and the implanting of the seeds of righteousness.

Affliction, then, took many forms, more than could be thoroughly described. The afflicted one had to understand that, whatever the kind, it was bestowed from the depths of God's mercy and that it would never exceed his capacity to bear it. The ultimate purpose in suffering was to bring spiritual

[187]

strength to the victim and make him a more worthy citizen of the heavenly kingdom.

The honest seeker after the soul's health would encounter many impediments, however. In addition to the enticements of sinful, sensual behavior would be the problems of intellectual doubt and inexplicable emotional fear.

Often a man would feel dejected because he knew he was continuing to sin, was constantly reminded of his shortcomings. He had thought that his sins had been cancelled by the sacrifice of Christ and the subsequent reconcilement of God (Light II.2-4). Furthermore, he often experienced the feeling that suffering, instead of indicating mercy and opportunity, was the result of God's hatred towards him, that if God were really a Father He would be gentler, at least sometimes, instead of sending more and more trouble (Light III.1,2). The man could understand that it was sin itself that created these questions and inspired this fear, but he could not help himself. Try as he might, he could not feel sorrow for his misdoings (Light IV.3,10). The more he prayed, the more he suffered (Light V.1). He grieved because he could not do all he knew he should (Light X.1; Strength III.1; Christe).

What he did not see was that he possessed a hidden tenderness; grieving at all was a sign of humiliation (Light IV. 10, 11). Not infrequently, believers were so blind as to decide that they were damned, but even so, God still remained on their side. In actual truth they had not lost their fear of the Lord (Light I.5). It was rather the fleshly part of man, the sensual and pleasure-loving, that encouraged these doubts in the spirit, normally strong in faith if temptations did not interfere (Light VI.2), but the problem was that Satan stood ready to traduce at every turning (Life I.2).

In prospect of temptation, in extreme pain, or in dire poverty, mortal man would naturally ask how he was to resist succumbing, to cultivate the virtue of patience, or to keep from blasphemy (Strength I.9; Sick IV.1; Poor III.1). He would fear that God would desert him in his greatest need

(Sick IV.8). He had to understand that the world was a wilderness—dangerous, fearful, inimical, woeful, destitute. Since sin was predominant, he inevitably would have to lead a "dying Life." Sin was the common lot. Instead of discouragement after constant cries for deliverance, he would have to learn to shoulder his griefs and be patient (Life I.1,3).

At Mary's death, Michael had had this very experience; so he was not writing purely from theory. As an educated Puritan, believing in the effectiveness of the word, the value of articulation, he had written a Latin poem describing his condition: the wrath of the Lord was oppressive; though he knew that his sins were weighty, the compensating affliction of losing his wife was breaking his back. He felt deserted by the world, too. Sick, poor, bereft, exhausted by the weight of his sorrows so that his body itself was languishing, he was undergoing a debilitating deficiency in spirit. Adversity was getting the best of him. Storms of grief were following storms; wind and threatening wave of sorrow were both at the same time bearing down in him. He had concluded with an English couplet:

> My sins and wants still pain my heart.
> My hope in Christ relieves my heart.
>   (Ira)

In that lone last line he was trying to find comfort and strength, those riches he had been teaching his congregation about for several years.

He was praying at this time that he be given courage to continue to hold God in esteem despite bereavement. Another poem, two Latin lines, showed his anguish in the knowledge that he was being tempted to limit his adoration because of the hardships visited upon him. Addressing Christ, he said that he was suffering too little because he was not pursuing his Lord hard enough; and, because he was not suffering enough, he would find cause to grieve. He had realized logically the value in endurance of bereavement, but, while it was still fresh in his experience, he was finding it hard to take profit from. This was the weakness that bothered him (Christe).

Two things were involved here: the sinner doubted God's love because God did not answer his prayers for relief as soon as he thought He should; and the sinner doubted his own sincerity when he found himself impatient or tempted to blasphemy. The resolution of these doubts constituted the maturing process for the Christian—moving towards complete trust in God and toward indomitable earnestness on his own part.

Now and then God permitted some saints to fail in order to arouse all to a realization of the imminence of evil. Those that were weak would find the answer to their problem in greater dependence on the mercy of God through Christ (Strength I.10). Even the strong would stumble occasionally in the strait way, but on their recovery would be more vigorous than ever, like Peter after his triple denial of his Lord (Meat IX.17).

Physical restraint, too, would often nurture humility which would lead to repentance. In captivity, Manasseh had become apprehensive of his former way of life and gained a new submissiveness. "Jonah's stubborn Will" had eventually been broken. The whole Jewish nation had finally returned home from Babylon, having learned humility in bondage (Con I.6-9). From all these Biblical examples, the individual could learn the importance to his soul's health of honest begging for grace, the recognition of God as forgiving Father in spite of His chastisements (Sol III.11; Joy I.4; Light II.6).

Indeed, departure and eventual return would help any mortal's state, though departure was not encouraged in the first place. If alienation did occur, the subsequent grief over sins would be as good for the state of the soul as bleeding for the feverish body. To change the figure, the deeper the plow of repentance, the richer the "crop of spiritual joy/And holiness." This worked both ways, for the more spiritual joy one experienced, the more humility he would cultivate (Joy I.9-11). One should therefore bewail his manifold wickedness, but he should not stop there: he should try to do better, amend his life (Strength III.9,10).

Those who strove constantly to kill the sin within them would eventually find permanent joy in heaven (Joy II.1). To seek out and destroy all stubbornness (Meat concl. 8,11) would be to know God's cheer (Joy II.2). Then, after this life, one would no longer be troubled with worldly sorrow (Life intro.3), the presence of misery in sins such as pride, sloth, and wantonness, or the slippery sophistries of the intellect. No longer would he be plagued by the passions, by ignorance and unbelief, by the rebelling will, by the insistent senses. Passing through the Red Sea (death), he would escape Pharaoh-Satan, who would be drowned and lost to rejoicing man forever and ever (Life II.1,2,6,7).

It was clear, then, that repentance was not a one-time event. The man who had made public profession and had become a bona-fide member of the church was not immune to sin. He would need to turn constantly from his misdeeds, to regret, and to try anew to follow the rough path towards righteousness. Repentance was never done.

After the initial turning of the face to God, what then? What attitude should the true believer cultivate? What should be his affirmative program of action?

First, he should resort frequently to prayer. For the Protestant Puritan there was no intermediary: the path between a believer and his God was direct. In seeking forgiveness and progress in the good life, the responsibility of mortal man was heavy, constant, and inevitable. He would need to look for help and power through the medium of unceasing supplication.

Secret prayer was essential to rooting out evil. (In virtually every other circumstance solitude would be undesirable for the ordinary Christian.) To wrestle with one's problems alone was, of course, not being strictly alone, but face to face with an inexorable though loving God (Light VII.1,2; Sol *passim*). It was certain, indeed, that, if one took advantage of the privilege of being often alone with God, he would not miss and need human companionship as much as before (Sol I.15). Though talking over temptations (and yieldings) with one's pastor was an effective way of overcoming them, even of preventing them (Light VIII.6,7), in the last analysis the situation lay between the sinner and God Himself.

With full recognition of his depravity and deep despair the petitioner could still possess utter faith in God's power of forgiveness and so have nothing to fear if he cast himself altogether on God's mercy (Light IX.1, 4). He must, however, be persistent—and patient. Even though his prayers were weak, though he might sense an inadequacy in his seeking, a lack of fervor and profound honesty, he must not give up, for to stop praying would be to make a positive decision in favor of the Devil, who would be incessantly attempting to pry the Christian away from God's door (Light VIII.3, 4). The Christian would have to pray continually that nothing—no blandishment, no sin—should come between him and his Lord, that the Lord's light be always in view (Light X.29). For that light was a source of comfort in the face of perplexity and temptation (Light, epigraph). In prayer the petitioner should be forever in pursuit of total identification as God's child, of total union with Christ, for prayer was to be addressed now to God, now to Christ, since Both were Members of the Godhead (Light X.5).

As for the response, sometimes it would come in a different form from what the petitioner might expect. He would have to depend on God to know best (Light V.7). Sometimes indeed the desired result would be withheld altogether, following the good judgment of the Lord (Poor IV.7). Storming God's door, keeping forever at it, was necessary, even though God might seem deaf and slow to answer (Meat IX.13). Delay was God's way of causing the petitioner to examine his life minutely to clear out any deterring sin, His way of making the suppliant more persistent, of testing his willingness to deny himself, of trying, and strengthening, his trust, affection, and patience. It was His way, too, of increasing the brilliance of His power when at last He would answer, of glorifying the fact of salvation all the more (Light V.3-6).

When a man prayed, he was to ask for an increase in faith, in belief in ultimate heavenly reward, in ability to submit to God's purposes, in willingness to admit God's possession of the soul (Heaven V.12). He should acknowledge his guilt, which he knew should by all rights send him to hell; he should admit that he was amazed that God had permitted him to live so long. He should remind his Father of the gift of forgiveness, through the purchase Christ had made. He should recall that God could add glory to Himself in covering the sinner's shame, by exercising grace, which Christ had paid for with His crucifixion. He should petition for a surrender of his "stubborn Will" so that Christ could subdue his carnal obsessions. He should listen for the call of Christ, Who actually was more generous than the petitioner was inclined to believe. Above all, he should pray constantly, especially if he felt that there was a delay in the answer, for thus would the Lord help him recognize his ultimate unworthiness of salvation (PS 305-360) and would help him cultivate the necessary virtue of quiet perseverance (Light IX.3).

Not all asking, prayer should also contain a goodly amount of praise and thanksgiving. One should express his gratitude for the saving power of God and for His determination to punish tyrants, cruel masters, and unregenerate sinners of all conditions, and he should be thankful for the beauty of God and for His love, which was beyond all accounting (Foster; Light X.26).

Though a Christian might live in the promise of heavenly reward, he must always understand that he could never be worthy of that reward. Only because Christ had been munificent in sacrificing Himself could he hope that his own salvation had been purchased (Meat V.3) and that any punishment he might receive on earth would not necessarily mean contempt or rejection (Meat IX.6). He lived a life of humble gratitude because Christ's gifts to the soul were free:

[193]

light, pardon, joy, peace, full redemption, eternal life and rest. If in return for this tremendous promise he embraced the mercy of Chirst, was content to be ruled as well as saved, then he need never fear that Christ would discard him (Light X.9-13). The fierce testing, the "serious Self-Denial" required on earth was only a mite of the debt a man owed to Christ after He had borne the ire of God for man's eternal good (Meat IV.6). Though no one deserved anything but vengeance, the faithful would at the last wear "Royal Robes" and crowns of glory (Heaven III.8).

To the skeptics' argument that this promise of reward cultivated in man "an Hireling Spirit," Wigglesworth replied that, if Christ had set out these rewards, was man to ignore them? Man's realization of the love of Christ for mankind should help him do his duties, bear his cross, suffer his afflictions. Did it not seem reasonable that man should take the trouble to win the crown promised him through grace (Heaven V.3-11)?

In consideration of the reward, then, man's grief was short, his adversity easy to endure (Meat V.1). Man should bear always in mind that it was only one brief step into eternity and everlasting felicity (Life III.5-8). Thus armed, no soldier ought to fail his Captain (Meat V.7). Though no punishment was pleasant, man would do well to concentrate on the future, since the rewards were sweet, and let the present take care of itself (Light IV.7). Surely a God Who would give man eternal life would provide now for his good. If He granted riches to "bloody bruitish men," how much more would He give to His own children. Indeed, no mere mortal could begin to picture what Christ had in store for His believers. The stateliest palaces were hog-sties compared to the "Caelestial Mansions." Staunch total faith in Christ's efficacy would bring a sure guerdon (Poor V.2-10). It was better to mourn now than to "wail eternally," for the pleasures of sin were short, their result, everlasting pain. In return for comparatively light suffering, on the other hand, a man would gain eternal joy and profit (Joy III.5).

The pleasures of heaven, then, were beyond adequate recounting. If the present drops seemed sweet, man should think of the future streams and rivers. God's joys were like an ocean. Man must enter into *them* (himself make the effort); they could not enter *him*, because of their immensity. The whole concept was so large that not only could the intellect not express it but even the emotions could not begin to realize it. Sorrow having been drowned in heaven's ocean, man would recall how sad he had been on earth and rejoice all the more (Joy III.6-8).

Just as some stars outshone others, but all were full of light, so in eternity every vessel would be full of glory, though some would be larger than others. Christ would recall every least kindness, even a cup of water. Both great and small would be rewarded. What was to be remembered was that, if the saints, whether weak or powerful, did not come to glory, Christ Himself would lose His own glory. The mortal could have faith that Christ would not forfeit the purpose for which He had died (Heaven II.4-8). Every saint, a diamond in Christ's crown, would have to be ineffable to be worthy, would have to "shine like suns" so that "Christ's own Beams" might be so much the clearer and brighter (Heaven III.4).

The change would be transcendent. The natural body would become spiritual. If now it needed meat, drink, and sleep, then it would have no such mundane needs. If now it was marked by weakness, then it would be marked by power; if now by dishonor, then by glory; if now by infirmities, then by health, strength, and activity. If now, "subject to reproach," it had to be quickly buried, then it would rise at Christ's command, beautiful and lovely. What sin had marred would be restored in the image of God. When reflecting light and praise like mirrors, when moving in a "Sea of Bliss," men would be ecstatic forever in "The sweetness of His Love." In the bosom of God, they would be done with their work. Seeds of sorrowing tears would yield "a joyful Crop"—a "Glorious Crown." Men would be made priests and kings to reign forever and ever (Heaven IV. 1-10; V.13).

The measure of *forever* was of course unimaginable. Every star and tree added up to a vast sum, but, if one also tried to include every leaf, every drop in every April shower, if he added all fowls, all living souls, all birds, grass blades, dew drops, grains of sand, atoms of the air, every hair on man and beast, every dust particle—he still had nothing as compared to the length of eternity. It would be as easy for a cockleshell to empty the ocean as for anything finite to give an idea of *forever* (Eternity 1-8).

With the promise of such a future, what then was to be the design of life among saints? Laying aside the problems posed by the theory of predestination—the apparent contradiction of God's rejected-before-all-worlds-were-made nevertheless willing themselves to perdition, choosing to ignore Christ's gift of merciful salvation—the poet set forth the principle that the true disciple must give up everything for a cross. He must renounce himself as center of interest, deny his own will, and expect to suffer (Meat *passim*). From the beginning Christ had said to his followers that they must "bear the Cross." He had promised no "carnal ease," no "Worldly Honour, Pleasure, Gain,/Security or Peace" (Meat IV.5). That man who forsook father, mother, and even wife for Christ's sake, who counted as of little value his houses, lands, and estates—that man would gain a hundredfold with persecution and was destined for eternal happiness (Heaven I.6).

The ideal life was an imitation of Christ, whose pattern Christians should study without ceasing (Meat VI. *passim*). No matter what men did, no matter how much they endured, their problems were as nothing compared to Christ's on earth. Innocent and just, He had suffered every conceivable misery. If men became faint, discontent, discouraged, or even terrified, they had but to recall how much more than they had Christ undergone. No mortal man could match the torments of Christ, bound as he had been, scorned, trampled,

[196]

blindfolded, spat upon, wrongfully accused, reviled, abused, buffeted. All for man's sake He had been poor, homeless, and grief-stricken. If a man was tempted, he should remember that He had been tempted with the whole world. If a man was distressed by sin and wrath, he should remember that Christ had borne the wrath of God Himself—to set men free (Meat VI.1-7; Heaven III.7; V.1).

After one had approached total self-denial of earthly property and comforts, friends, and relations, he had next to submit altogether to having his own will broken, for the "unsubdued Will" was in reality a chain. Once the will was imprisoned, the soul could enjoy "sweet Liberty." Once its tyranny had been destroyed, then any other restraints were negligible, for the soul would begin to pursue the good, as God desired—a pursuit made possible through Christ's sacrifice, since otherwise men could choose nothing but evil (Con 3,4).

Those who had been too eager for the comforts and pleasures of the flesh might find the way of the subdued will a thorny path. God must lead them into the wilderness of humility to show his love (Con II.8). Neither the journey itself nor the permanent determination to pursue it would be easy to achieve. The heart must be broken often because mere man by his very nature would stray frequently from the narrow path (Light X.2).

A true believer must cultivate utter humility. He must see God in all affliction, no matter who was the "immediate Instrument" (Meat IX.1). It was God Who created affliction—not dust, man's will, not the Devil's desire. Even if chastisement was light, a man must not despise it, for it was of God. On the other hand, if it was heavy, he must receive it gladly and with "true Repentance" as ordered in the Bible. The sufferer's most important duty was to search zealously for the offense, bemoan it, and amend it speedily (Meat IX.3,4). For that matter, suffering and patience made the soul beautiful, however unseemly one's body, for they showed man how to despise worldliness and concentrate on the divine (Meat X.5). Once a saint came to full understanding of the rewards involved, he could the more easily bring patience unto his sufferings (Meat concl.2).

One of the hardest things to bear—and Wigglesworth would know this as well as anyone—would be to recognize one's impotence in his work and to be patient in admitting that Christ meant for him to do something else. Everyone knew that it was harder to obey passively than actively. One could serve Christ now in sitting still whereas formerly he had been at least doing something. The Lord was pleased by submission, even though one was called to a lesser post. Men must recall that the Lord needed nothing at all from them, but, if they were willing though powerless, He was pleased. God honored what they did, no matter how little, provided their desire to serve was behind it. Though God expected one to do only what he could, he should not use such profound sympathy as an excuse for sloth. God expected man's best (Strength III.2-8). Wigglesworth could testify to years of bodily weakness, greater than people could know from hearing him talk. Often, he said, just as he would start to preach, his vigor would fail him. Though he would pray for strength to continue his vocation, after a sermon his powers would languish for weeks. But he would not complain, for God had the right as Potter to create vessels to serve Him in various ways (Strength II.1-7).

In truth, complaining was entirely out of line, for God could do no wrong. Justice and mercy were incapable of cruelty. It was the part of wisdom to understand that one was getting exactly what he needed for his soul's sake (Sol III. 9). And what if the afflicted one thought he was worse off than anyone else? Was it not necessary for someone to take the lead (Sol III.6)? The true believer meekly submitted to the yoke of Christ, turned the other cheek, and tried in the midst of grief and pain to think nothing but good thoughts of God (Meat IX.10) and watched that he committed no blasphemy either by spoken word or by intention. Patience was all (Meat IX.11,14). Any righteous man would choose suffering over sin. With the gift of Christ's grace he would not offend God for the sake of luxury and safety (Meat IX.16). Persecution was destined to bring the highest reward in heaven (Heaven I.4).

Humility and patience, appearing to be negative virtues, were accompanied by another passive quality—dependence. The Christian was invited to put his soul's burden on the Lord (Light X.18). Paradoxically, the more in his weakness he leaned on Christ, the stronger he became in spirit (Strength I.12). One way of deepening dependence was to expect only "daily bread," not a year's supply. In this way God would be a "present help" to conduct man to a glorious end (Poor III.7).

In the paradox of finding greatest strength in one's weakness, one could begin a positive program of action. By depending on the strength of Christ in himself (Christ could obviously defeat Satan), one could win out in the contention with the world, the flesh, and the Devil (Meat V.6). By drowning doubt and absorbing might (Light X.17), one made room for the positive choice of following the Lord's path, which led to greater riches than anything the earth could provide (Poor I.10).

What might appear to be negative sorrow, remorse, or regret now became godly sorrow which actively consumed the old "unhallowed" sorrow and brought in "Spiritual Joy." The channel dug by penitence was the channel joy ran in and made deeper (Joy intro.2,3). Not only had a Christian to *be* sorry for his misdoings, he had to *show* that he was; not only had he to lean on Christ and possess love and trust in full measure, he had to *prove* his interest in the program (Light X.3).

Faith, then, could not stop with passivity, with humility, patience, dependence, and submission, but had to be continually exercised in prayer, searching, amendment, adoration, and keeping one's brother.

The soul was sure to be depressed and shaken from time to time. The Christian was obligated at this point to look

[199]

for methods of invigorating his faith, for God was his health, his means of rising above melancholy and emotional turbulence (Light IX.5). It was his duty to make real to himself the concept that God was satisfied to forgive and forget (Light IX.4). No man could hope to repair the damage he had done; all that remained to him was to confess sincerely —and to begin again. Even though he might not be able to single out any particular sin as the cause of the present disturbance, he would do well to rise above his psychic suffering by using affliction to achieve, first, humility, then, purgation, and, finally, betterment of his celestial position (Meat IX.7).

God, he would know, would restore his soul in due season (Poor IV.8). Such faith would trust on a day-to-day basis, not expecting overwhelming results but relying on the belief that, if the Heavenly Father fed the birds—

> The Ravens, Crows, and Cormorants
> The Kites, the Hawks, the Owls,
> Also the numerous Doves,
> Whose flocks make dark the Air—

He assuredly would not neglect "his Saints" (Poor IV.1,2). If God gave crumbs to dogs, He would give His children bread, both earthly and spiritual (Poor V.1).

What would seem the passivity of physical imprisonment (whether in jail or in sickroom) could be made active in the cause of Christ. Now the soul could find liberty to praise God, the feet could be at liberty to walk in the roadways of wisdom (Con I.4; III.6,7). Now would be time to find light in darkness through confidence in Christ's kindness and the actual curative power of discomfort and disease. Those who, on the other hand, thought they were creating their own illumination—logical proof of atheism, an independence of God's generosity in sending out His light—ought to end in sorrow, for their irreverence was patent and unforgivable (Light IX.7).

It is true that the light would often be obscured; the clouds of ignorance and the mists of doubt would dim it if not altogether hide it. The Christian would understand that this obfuscation was the work of Satan (Light I.4) and would be duty bound to overcome it through vigorous prayer, counseling, and study. He should not, however, rely altogether on reason, for logic was in the long run Satan's tool (Light V.8). Religion was for the Puritans not a science in the sense that it could be subjected to formulas; there was need for contemplation—for steadily regarding the inexpressible. The word, written and spoken, was useful much of the time, but it could also work the undesirable effect of turning a soul away from consideration of God as worthy of reverence.

Wigglesworth recommended that a man try simply to forget—to drop—his wicked thoughts—even when undertaking to hate them. If he could not rid himself of these articulations, he should "run away" (Light VIII.8). Here the poet may have meant to occupy oneself with such activity as would not provide time or inclination for thinking evil. When making confession, a man should not detail the thoughts, but admit to bad thoughts in general, for to recall them in particular was to submit to stinging whips unnecessarily (Light VIII.10). Recalling evil *deeds* in detail, with an eye to avoiding repetition, apparently was another matter.

The Christian, moreover, should be grateful that he possessed the developed capacity to love God which many "worldly men" did not have. He should feel too that, having everything he needed for the present, he should not worry about the future. "Carking care" was the wrong kind of concern since it could produce only further guilt (Poor III. 5,8). If a man had lost a friend, he should think of him as having been on loan and should be thankful that God had let him stay so long (Sol II.2,3). He should pray always for the power of thanksgiving, for the ability to glorify God, to desire, love, reverence, and admire Him (Light X.27,28).

Instead of complaining when the strokes of the rod seemed heavy to bear (Meat IV.1) or when loss of property and friends seemed overwhelming, the sufferer should recall the worthy goal toward which he was working and should redirect his sadness, away from the affliction itself towards the sin—his own sin—that had brought on the necessity of punishment (Joy I.5). He should stage an active campaign to make God his Friend, to seek Him out as his Father (Sol II,4,5). If he would think of the world not as his home but merely as the road he was traveling as a pilgrim, he would begin to achieve the requisite disposition toward everything that happened to him (Meat V.5). He should be muscular in beating down his own secret murmurs, should come to hate them and to resolve to love God under all circumstances, even death (Meat IX.12). Sickness, pain, imprisonment— all would afford opportunity for active, outgoing seeking after God as his best Friend (Meat VIII.5). There should be under these conditions no reason for dreading affliction, for it all worked together for good if he realized that it was drawing him closer to God (Sick IV.12).

The Christian must take up his cross willingly (Meat VI. 8)—that is, with initiative and aggressive purpose. One could tell it in the faces of the afflicted, for example, whether they were the temples of God's indwelling—whether they exercised concern for carrying out his will daily, whether they were grieved by what grieved God, whether they were pleased to stop sinning, whether they were willing to lay down their own desires meekly. If so, they were the happiest people imaginable; the world's darlings could not match them (Meat X.3). They knew that on the Day of Wrath the only quality that would matter would be "Gospel-Righteousness." By heavenly standards the upright man was far better off than the money-mad miser (Poor II.4).

Two positions the active Christian would avoid: first, he would not act like a block, stubborn and unmoved; second, he would not mourn selfishly for his own worldly losses in ignorance or contempt of the purpose of the deprivation (Joy I.3). On the positive side, he would follow the two Great Commandments—to love God and to have concern towards man, because, tying himself to these two laws, he would experience the fullest liberty (Con II.7).

The believer must be ready and willing to admit the Trinity into his deepest love. An intellectual understanding of the principles of a tripartite God would not suffice. Irrational (emotional) acceptance would be necessary to appreciate and experience God in all His attributes, but once this admittance was achieved, the soul would never again be lonely—with the Trinity for company (Sol II.6,7).

Choosing between Christ and the Devil, however, might be a matter of great dread. To decide for penitence and suffering rather than for physical comfort as the guiding principle of one's life might, on the surface, be a hard task. Nevertheless, to remember that the reward would be a gift of free grace and an eventual crown of glory might ease the decision (Heaven III.10). There was no room for hypocrisy in this program. The conscience must remain pure, the motive undefiled (Heaven I.3). Otherwise, critics would be justified in accusing one of dishonest purpose. An unqualified love of God would purify the motive.

In his eulogy of Benjamin Bunker, Wigglesworth pointed out to his congregation that his late assistant had been a model of Christian virtue. He had grown more and more godly with the years, having had a thorough grounding in the Bible and Christian orthodox teachings. Throughout his progress in Christianity he had maintained a spirit marked by humility, contrition, and self-vilification. Small talk had not been of interest to him. He had enjoyed more than anything a discussion of the supernatural and of the traits of Christ. He had been eternally grateful for the gift of grace. Moreover, though talented beyond most men in the community, he had nurtured a meekness and sweetness of nature that any good Christian should try to emulate (Buncker 1-7).

Bunker had been one kind of saint. Another kind was the man who felt himself hopelessly entangled in the Devil's web. Blasphemous thoughts made him quake; foul phantasies stabbed his soul violently, no matter which way he turned his mind, sift and struggle as he would. The more he tried, the worse things became, especially in the midst of meditation and prayer. So the poor man dreaded to pray, meditate, or even read. Though he detested these thoughts as his own sins, actually he should recognize them as the Devil's, to be hated sincerely. Even if, then, evil suggestions came readily, the very fact should keep a sincere man humble. If he would only realize that resistance and constant strife would save the day, he might find comfort in the struggle (Light VII.1-10). He would find that God would eventually wean him from earth's distractions, help him to keep his eyes on heaven, give him a larger share of the "sweetness of His Love" (Con II.6). The point was to continue trying for the love of Christ. The very activity would squeeze out stubbornness, would melt away the most persistent evil (Light I.6,7; IV. 12-14; VII.5). Wigglesworth's own Harvard diary was a record of just this sort of battle. What a man should never forget was that God was really a gentle, loving Father (otherwise all men would be in hell) as many Biblical characters had discovered—Jacob, Moses, Joseph, Job, David, Heman (Light III.3-15). The longer a man concentrated on the eternal, the better he became and the less he would be interested in "outward things," which would now take flight from his life (Meat IX.18).

The Puritan was aware that he was a member of a community of saints towards which he should exercise concern and from whom he could legitimately gain solace (Light VII. 6,7; Joy IV. epigraph). He knew that companions could ease his grief, especially those who had suffered as he himself had. United under the Head of Christ, they would feel their common bond and could help each other in bearing burdens.

But the situation worked two ways: if one derived benefits from his neighbors, he should remember that he was obligated to mourn with the bereft and to sympathize with the afflicted. Tenderness, a gift from Christ, was a characteristic of every zealous saint. He would not only pity, pray for, and comfort his brethren, but he would actively look out for the welfare of the oppressed. It would be but a specious argument of the worldly that grief would be only magnified by sharing: the spirit of love taught differently. It would be a "blessed strife" indeed if all saints would try to outdo each other in genuine loving care. Such positive action would lead to an end of dissension and bitter quarrels. Thus absorbed outside themselves, "Souls, Towns, and Churches" would flourish. As many hands made light work, so many comforters would lighten spirits (Joy IV.1-7).

The poet wanted his readers to know that all saints were in the struggle together, including himself. His only reason for writing "Meat Out of the Eater" and "Riddles Unriddled" was to picture a saint's life and to urge the reader to copy it. He himself would be striving all along to parallel the life he had outlined, for he did not believe in merely sending out the word without digesting it and living by it himself. These poems had been written, he said, from the depths of his own experience. He realized that he was not the ideal of richness and fullness of spirit and life, that he was, rather, a poor example in spite of the opportunity for growth through adversity that had been his (Meat concl.1-7). He did take courage, however, from writing out the poems and reading what he had written (Riddles intro.).

The two sides of the Christian life, then, had been his theme. The passive side sought comfort at the source, leaned for support on God, Christ, and the Holy Spirit (Meat IX. 19). The other side belonged to the aggressive fighter, the warrior against Satan and his allurements (Light VII.intro.). In trying to show that faith and redemption were not only a matter of the receptive spirit but required sometimes violent exercise, Wigglesworth employed figures, common enough to be hackneyed, but sure of emotional response in the reader. Men on earth, he said, had work to do, a war to wage, thorns to wear, a race to run (Heaven IV.11). No such luxuries as a featherbed would carry a man to paradise; he must work hard up the stream, against wind, tide, and unending storms. The road was uphill all the way (whereas the primrose path was pleasantly downgrade). The only method of finally reaching the Celestial City was through deadly battle, fighting against the temptation to join the many acquaintances and examples who were on the broad highway to destruction (Meat I.3-7).

Michael again and again reminded his readers that the problem was not altogether an individual one. In these Puritan communities everyone was responsible for everyone else. The strife required the utmost in cooperation. Not only was a sinner expected to seek counsel from his pastor or a similarly wise person, but he could expect succor from his neighbors, the laymen who lived and worked alongside him daily, in return for his own assistance.

The poet called New England as a whole to rally to the cause. God was in righteous contention with the colony, he maintained, because of the general indifference that had increased after the death of most of the first-generation leaders. God had thought these people would always obey His commandments, but had discovered that they were easily tempted by the world and were now backsliding at a terrifying rate. As a result He was having to visit the entire region with affliction: physical ailment—"colds and coughs, Rhewms, and sore-throats" and "Agues sore & Feavers strong"; and a severe dry spell resulting in parched grain fields and pastures and in famished livestock. The community was suffering because the community had sinned (God's Con *passim*).

In the twelve or thirteen years after Mary's death, then, Michael had been a reliable propagandist for the Puritan tenets. He had made the end of the world and the Day of Judgment graphically real. He had outlined the nature of the saints and had detailed the characteristics of all sorts and conditions of reprobates. He had attempted to define God— the ultimately indefinable. He did not have to prove God's existence, for when that need arises, God *is* no more. For Wigglesworth and his compeers God was pure actuality; mere possibility would never have occurred to him. Further,

[206]

he had explained how suffering and misfortune could be used constructively for the enrichment of the soul's relation with its Creator. Man must realize that behind the puzzling frustrations of everyday life stood the eternal verities. Man's problem was to find in the daily chaos the Providential pattern. The poet had demonstrated that man's conduct on his pilgrimage to eternity must be marked paradoxically by such passive feminine traits as total submission of the will and the quiet cultivation of humility and patience and at the same time by an aggressive masculine rooting out of all evil, earnest pursuit of God's purposes through entreaty, praise, study, and active participation in the life of the community. This imposing program of checks and balances was the New England Congregational ideal toward which Michael himself was working without ceasing.

His ethic forced him into engagement in the physiological, social, economic, and spiritual life of his contemporaries, but such involvement was weighted down on the other side by subjective responsibilities. He was stirred by the necessity of choice between doing good and doing evil. His sense of guilt resulted in his constant searching out of sin, though meeting the standards of God and eradicating "naughtiness" were impossible goals and could produce only despair. Anxiety about final estrangement from God impelled him toward the incessant struggle against sin. He did not have a scientific world to fight against, but he had the terrors of a real hell to face. He lived in awareness of the imminence and possible immediacy of death and the inevitable facing of God on His throne.

IX. Martha Mudge

The little congregation at Malden had struggled along without an active clergyman for five years after the death of Benjamin Bunker, complaining, quibbling, needing a virile leadership that the invalid Michael could not supply. In 1675 the church at last was successful in securing another assistant, Benjamin Blakeman, a Harvard graduate of the class of 1663. A lively college boy, in December, 1661, he had been tried and found guilty of "abusive disturbance" of the family of Abram Smith of Charlestown—some undergraduate prank or other. Though at first not inclined toward the ministry (as Wigglesworth, too, had not been), during the four years preceding his coming to Malden he had been living around Stratford, his birthplace in the New Haven colony, and had no doubt done some reading in theology. The probability is that he was never ordained at Malden, though he did live in the "ministry house," was married to a Boston girl, and bought property in the town. He never signed himself as "teacher" or "pastor," simply "gentleman." He was probably an astute business man, but he did not help the situation much at the Malden church. The differences among the members persisted, and there was considerable unrest by the time he left town four years later for Black Point, a little farm he cultivated for a while before moving on to other enterprises.[210]

During King Philip's War (1675-1676) the town of Malden itself was apparently untouched, though twenty-three men were sent to join the other colonial soldiers in fighting the savage enemy. At Narragansett Fort, James Chadwick was wounded, Phineas Upham died of wounds, and Edmund Chamberlain was killed outright.[211] Others were sacrificed elsewhere in the defense of the New Jerusalem. The Puritan sense of community was all-pervading.

All over the colony, while the soldiery were combatting the Indian forces of the Devil, the custom rose of congregational chanting of the renewal of the Puritan covenant with God. Now, instead of individuals making public pronouncement of loyalty to the Lord, the entire church membership would come together on a stated day of humiliation, would listen to a formalized scolding, and would then rise at the minister's request to review in concert the terms of contract they had undertaken on the days of their individual conversions.[212] In these recitals the Malden church was led more often than not by Blakeman, for Wigglesworth was still frequently in bed with his ailment.

On March 17, 1676, and again on March 25, Increase Mather noted in his diary that he had been to call on the sick, including "Mr. Wigglesworth."[213] Mather's influence in the colony was beginning to be felt, for he was one of its most affecting preachers and a man with a talent for administration. In 1657, at the age of eighteen, armed with a Harvard Bachelor's degree, he had gone to his brother Samuel in Dublin, where the next year he had taken his Master's degree at Trinity College.[214] Having preached with great success in various dissenting English pulpits, he had fled the Restoration in 1661, arriving back at his father's house in Dorchester unexpectedly on August 31. Since 1664 he had been one of the ministers at the Second Church in Boston and in 1675 had agreed to be a Fellow of Harvard College. By this time he had turned unwillingly away from strait orthodoxy far enough to admit to baptism all grandchildren of the founders, even though their parents had never made the required public profession. Still strict, he could nevertheless see in part the necessity of the Half-Way Covenant for keeping the church alive at all.

Increase was aware of the influence that Wigglesworth,

his college tutor and patient friend, was wielding for the
cause through his two books, *The Day of Doom* and *Meat
Out of the Eater*. There were other ways of reaching the
children of the Lord besides pastoral care and Sabbath
preaching. With the thoroughness required of every conscientious Puritan, Michael had analyzed his potentialities
and was exploiting them with exemplary scrupulosity. Now
no longer pupil and teacher, Increase and Michael were mature defenders together of the bastion of God against the
hordes of Satan. In the coming years their friendship was
to demonstrate itself in a variety of directions.

The government of the colony was going badly. On June
10, 1676, Edward Randolph arrived from England bearing
a commission from Charles II to demand that Massachusetts send someone to his court to talk out the problems
developing from New England's growing sea trade. The
Navigation Acts tried to restrict such commerce to England;
there was to be no exchange of commodities with any foreign country, and no foreign ships were to enter a colony's
port. This was hard for Massachusetts to take. Every
year her ships were bearing pelts, flour, salt cod, mackerel,
beef, and pork to Barbados, Jamaica, and distant countries
and were bringing back hides, cloth, sugar, cocoa, and iron.
The masters of the ships were also discovering a lucrative
income in the blacks of Africa. Randolph persisted in fussing
at the colonists till at last they could ignore him no longer
and sent William Stoughton and Peter Bulkeley to London
in the summer of 1677 to answer charges of disloyalty before the Lords of Trade and Plantations.[215]

Before dispatching the envoys, the churches had for a
year prayed and fasted over the problem, Malden among
them. There were other reasons for fasting and humiliation.
In Boston in particular there were more and more fires
destroying valuable property. Increase Mather's house and
church building were burned in a great conflagration one
morning in late November before dawn.[216] These holocausts
were God's judgment for something, of course, but for what?

[210]

And who had set them? Negroes were suspected; a tailor's boy was suspected.²¹⁷ Ten days after Mather's fire the colony observed a public fast.²¹⁸ Ever aware of what was occurring in the area, Wigglesworth had made effective use of house-burning as an analogy for "unregenerate" sin.

> If in the night, when thou art fast asleep,
> Some friend of thine, that better watch doth keep,
> Should see thy house all on a burning flame,
> And thee almost inclosed with the same:
> If such a friend should break thy door and wake thee,
> Or else by force out of the peril take thee:
> What? wouldst thou take his kindness in ill part?
> Or frown upon him for his good desert?
> Such, O my friend, such is thy present state,
> And danger, being unregenerate.
>
> (PS 207-216)

Though not directly involved in the destruction of property, Malden prayed, for were they not members of the body of Christ? Were they not being punished too? And they felt concern for the colony's ocean trade. Their town was no isolated, independent settlement. Had they not earlier felt the pressures of proximity on all sides? The problems of the colony were their own immediate problems. When, in November, 1678, the General Court appointed a day of humiliation especially to pray that the charter of the Massachusetts Bay Company not be revoked,²¹⁹ they entered into the heavenly petitions with hearty fervor.

The congregation was dragging along under Blakeman, but discontent nibbled on, and differences of opinion. Michael could do little in a public way. At home he made minor changes for subsequent editions of *The Day of Doom* and *Meat Out of the Eater*. He continued to study and practice medicine, and he may have helped a few boys prepare for entrance into Harvard. The Reverend Samuel Hooker of Farmington, near Hartford, in 1677 wrote to Increase Mather about his son, who, he said, was "indisposed" for Harvard. "I hear Mr. Wigglesworth, being at greater leisure than some others (because of his rare preaching), is thought a man very Idoneous for such instruction as he needs."[220] Whether young Hooker came to Malden for tutoring is not recorded. It is quite certain that he did not graduate from Harvard.

In spite of his confinement, Michael kept in touch with events around him and even managed to cause something of a stir himself. In neighboring Charlestown in December, 1677, his friend the Reverend Thomas Shepard died of smallpox.[221] Michael had known Thomas since Harvard days. (Thomas had been one of the graduates of August 9, 1653, with the privilege of a Master of Arts degree in two years instead of the customary three.) The following March, also in Charlestown, Michael's sister's daughter was married to an Andrew Stimson.[222] At forty-six Wigglesworth was not only a grandfather, but the uncle of a bride. And he had been a widower for nearly twenty years. It was this situation that gave cause to the minor tempest he now created.

". . . The Report is, that you are designing to marry with your servant mayd, & that she is one of obscure parentage, & not 20 years old, & of no church, nor so much as Baptised." Thus wrote Increase Mather to Michael on May 8, 1679.[223] He had addressed the letter with great dignity: "These for the Revd. my respected friend Mr. W., Pastor of the church in M." He still remembered that "Mr. W." was his elder, had been his tutor, was an author of established reputation. He called him "Pastor," whether from fact or merely from esteem one cannot know. "I owe you that respect (& much more) as to informe you what I have bin told."

The situation can be reconstructed only from the periphery. Continent since the death of Mary in December, 1659, Michael could not have voluntarily discarded all passionate emotion and human urges. Prayer, energetic literary activity, and strong will power could help control his "sinful lusts," but, in a man as highly sexed as he, the desires would remain, howsoever repressed. His sister and his

daughter married and his mother dead, he would need someone to look after his household needs. How long before
this May day he had been served by his present maid—
Martha Mudge—is a matter for conjecture, but it had been
long enough for him to become emotionally involved to the
point of arranging marriage. The word had gone out.

Mather's letter argued against the union; Michael's relatives would be very unhappy; the girl was thirty years his
junior; his infirmities would put an undue burden on her
as his wife; she would no doubt be left a widow while still
a very young woman. The writer even invoked the Fifth
Commandment: "Honor thy father and thy mother." Did
he mean that Michael would be insulting his own parents,
or did he mean that Michael was old enough to be Martha's
father? Possibly both. In the pale light of his secret dislike
of and impatience with both his parents, this point may well
have given Michael guilty pause.

The arguments were not over. If Michael took such a step,
his name would go down to posterity in disgrace. Moreover,
not only Michael but the entire ministry would be blamed
for the "carnal" action of one of their number. Then, too,
Michael should remember that the law required a man to
marry in his own class, for the preservation of order and the
comfort of all concerned. Finally, Paul's first letter to Tim-
othy forbade marriage of this sort. When Michael looked up
the reference in the third chapter, he read: "Even so must
their wives be grave, not slanderers, sober, faithful in all
things."

Increase had written out of respect for "Religion, & your
credit & comfort." He had felt "bound to seeke your welfare,
& doe what I may to prevent trouble from coming upon my
neighbor, & brother, especially such an one, whose name
hath bin, & I hope may still be of precious esteem with the
Lords people." Among many other demands upon a good
Puritan's time and energy was the role of his brother's
keeper. It was this problem of how far to go in concern for
the affairs of others that had put Michael into a turmoil years

[213]

before about Mr. Mitchell's swinging barn door on a Sunday. His present reputation in the colony—if not altogether in Malden itself—was high. As a clergyman he should keep it so, for every reason.

Mather's letter concluded: "Though your affections should be too far gone in this matter, I doubt not but if you put the object out of your sight, & looke up to the Lord Jesus for supplies of grace, you will be enabled to overcome these Temptacions. The Lord be with you, I am Yours unfeignedly, I. M."

Here was language strong and earnest and candid. The tone was neither snobbish nor haughty.[224] Increase had a sincere desire to keep unsullied the reputation of the ministry, its just position and power in the face of an increasing materialism. An injudicious marriage on the part of one of its prominent members would hurt a cause that already showed signs of limping. Mather could not understand Wigglesworth's reasoning: "The like never was in New England. Nay, I question whether the like hath bin known in the Christian world."

He had not yet had time to post his admonition to Malden before Benjamin Blakeman appeared bearing a list of arguments from Wigglesworth showing why he should marry—and marry Martha.[225] Mather consulted several other ministers, who did not give him much help, for they supposed that by now Michael's passions were involved and advice would be of little use. Increase was not so fatalistic; in an appended discussion he remained adamant: "I see no cause to alter my mind." One would think he was an elder Dutch uncle trying to jerk a youngster from the brink of folly: "Indeed if the good people of Malden did approve your proceedings, & if there were an eminency of the fear of God discernable in your Damosel, notwithstanding her obscurity upon other accounts, there would be less of scandal in proceedings." It was obvious that the "people of Malden" (how "good" they were with their quarrels and backsliding would be a matter of opinion) were looking for an excuse to condemn their

[214]

ordained minister, who had not done much for them in over twenty years. The conclusion of Mather's postscript expressed the hope that the Lord would guide Michael for three purposes (were they arranged in climactic order?): "for the honour of His name, yea, & of your own name, & the comfort of those that are concerned in you." God's own name, of course, but, possibly of more demonstrable importance, Michael's reputation and, perhaps even more immediately significant for Increase, the maintenance of the dignity and influence of the clergy as a class in New England.

The bright gem of clerical aristocracy was dimming. To avoid any possible scar or smirch was beginning to consume the energies of the most vigorous and resourceful of the ministers. This letter had not been written from snobbishness but out of honest care about the condition of the colony as established nearly fifty years before. If this was to continue a Bible state, a virile Zion, the church must be kept unstained and strong, stronger than any other institution. In spite of his candid zeal Increase closed the communication on a note of manly affection: "I am yours to my power."

The effect of this letter on its recipient one can well surmise, judging from past actions: Michael spent long hours in prayer and meditation; he weighed elaborate lists of arguments on both sides. Whatever the debit side of the ledger carried, the credit side made the deeper impression on the sensitive accountant, with the result that he made Martha Mudge his bride in the late spring of 1679.[226] One is tempted to admire him for sticking to his purpose, for showing spirit not heretofore exercised in his personal life ("personal" rather than "private," for he was, after all, something of a public figure, in the body of Christ a prominent member whose individual deviations would be the plain concern of all), for being "inner-directed" rather than "other-directed," to use the jargon of today.

Whatever the place and date, to the distaste of the townspeople of Malden and the misgivings of the ministers of the Bay, Michael took to wife a girl six or so years younger

[215]

than his daughter Mercy. Martha's family had been in the neighborhood a number of years.[227] Her father, Thomas Mudge, was an honest farmer whose wife, Mary, had given him several children. The eldest, James, had been killed at Bloody Brook, South Deerfield, during the struggle with King Philip. His brothers John and Thomas and their sister Mary's husband, John Martin, had been in the rescue party that had finally driven the Indians away, too late to save the life of James. John Mudge, eventually, became a prosperous landowner and a man of some position in the town—constable, tithing man, collector, surveyor. There were younger brothers, Jonathan and George. (Among George's possessions at his death in later years were listed "8 full bottles of Rhum and 12 empty bottles.")

The Mudges, parents and children, had appeared as witnesses in various petty trials. Wigglesworth himself had been involved in one case ten years before his marriage to Martha. Her sister Mary, about eighteen years old at the time and not yet married to John Martin, had testified against James Tufts for grabbing her and bussing her against her will. She had had to call her brothers Thomas and John to intervene and send the culprit on his way. Michael and his assistant, Benjamin Bunker, had listened to Mary's complaint and had written an account of it to James's father, Peter Tufts, not in accusation but in explanation so that James would have some defense if accused of something "worse then it was, though it was bad enough." In that summary, they had not considered "it needfull nor useful to set down every circumstance (as about her holding fast by the window or some other thing, her pulling of him by the hair of his head to get rid of him, etc.)." In case she told the Court the details of the encounter, however, the two Malden ministers had written a note explaining that she would not be embroidering, that more had happened than they had committed to the Tufts paper.[228] Not surprisingly, the outcome of the trial of the stolen kiss is unrecorded, though Michael's effort to be fair to all parties attests to his desire for justice.

From the very beginning the marriage, though privately satisfactory, was publicly condemned. The townspeople, even those of high estate, sought every opportunity to insult Martha both by ignoring her and by making disdainful remarks.[229] A complex of causes stirred up the fires of their resentment. Martha, a servant girl, had by her marriage to the conventionally most important person in the town been raised in social standing above many who had heretofore not had to give her a second thought. Because she was outside the church, those who were assured of salvation felt it their Christian duty to berate her. Furthermore, Michael's only sporadic ministrations as clergyman having given rise to a growing wish for his removal, this "unsuitable" marriage provided the hopeful with another prying tool.

Meanwhile, in all the Bay the churches continued their program of days of humiliation and of thanksgiving. There were many, many fires,[230] especially in Boston, brought on as punishment for sin. On August 8, 1679, what appeared to be a deliberately set fire destroyed an estimated hundred fifty thousand pounds worth of property, the brick house of the Governor being saved by only a narrow margin.[231] This devastation was the occasion of much sweeping out of conscience among the faithful, a situation made to order for tightening the ministerial grip.

In September the ministers met in synod at Boston and voted unanimously to reaffirm as ecclesiastical policy the Cambridge *Platform* of 1648.[232] The people at the grass roots were not always happy at this "liberalizing" stand of their clergy. In Malden anything that would lead to overt statement of dissatisfaction with Mr. Wigglesworth would be taken up gladly, almost maliciously. And there were some old-fashioned conservatives still in the congregation despite the early "bad" influence of Marmaduke Matthews. Not that Wigglesworth himself was not conservative in his faith. The strictures of *The Day of Doom* were the foundation stones of his creed to his dying day. But history was bringing inevitable shifts of direction which the ministers were struggling to

[217]

cope with. Any change would have furnished fuel for the bickerings at Malden. Michael had tried a decade before to show with his pen the reasonableness of public tranquility, but to little avail.

> Help us to pity more,
> And pray for one another,
> To strive who shall in love outstrip
> And go beyond his brother.
> (Joy IV.6)

In economics and politics the colony was not doing well, either. In December, William Stoughton and Peter Bulkeley returned from the Court of Charles II to the frowns of their fellow colonists. The envoys had yielded too much. Edward Randolph was now not just an inquirer who might be ignored, but had been appointed collector of customs for all New England.[233] The interference of the throne in maritime commerce was creating an impasse. On all sides were subterfuge and secretiveness in an attempt to thwart the efforts of the officious collector,[234] whose exaggerations in London had not only increased the reports of the wealth of the colonists but had, obviously, brought him more power. Charles II was eager to recall the Massachusetts Bay charter, and the churches were determined, through concerted prayer and resulting unanimity of effort, to prevent its revocation. The congregations frequently and heartily renewed the covenant.

At Malden, in spite of the common desire to retain comparative independence guaranteed by the charter, there was such internal strife that the church all but lost sight of its position in the colony at large. Benjamin Blakeman, probably not a full-fledged clergyman, this year deserted the confusion to cultivate his farm. The people were again without pastoral care.

Michael was still not strong enough physically to do the work. Though able to make something of a living through the practice of medicine, he could not carry on the duties of the pastorate and take care of his patients at the same time.

And the church was not willing to pay him for services not rendered. At last, unable to bear the strain of opposition any longer, he drew up "Some Grounds & Reasons for Laying Down My Office Relation."[235] In fifteen sometimes thickly overlapping articles, he listed the causes for his proposed resignation. In summary, they may be stated more briefly.

He was too weak to be both minister and physician for the town. In case his work as physician did not pay enough to keep him and Martha, he wanted to be free to move elsewhere. There was much murmuring and overt objection towards him, in spite of "our Late Renewed Covenant"; many members wanted "my room rather than my company." If he were out of the way, the congregation would be free to select another, more mettlesome minister. He saw no chance of improvement in his own health as long as he was encumbered with the responsibilities of the Malden church, which was unwilling, anyhow, to support him adequately: "If they will Detain me they must maintain me (which I am far from desiring). But they cannot maintain me; Therefore must not Detain me." Near the end of the list he presented an argument very close to his heart: "I discern such an envious and spiteful disposition in some towards my wife (& those not of the meanest neither) as argueth little love or respect for me. The old proverb is, love me & love my Dogg; which if it be true, certainly they do not love me that hate my wife; & are glad when any dirt is cast upon her or affront offered to her. And indeed I see not how there can be any living amongst such, where things are thus, & such things & Persons countenanced & incouraged to more & more boldness. Therefore I desire a place for me & my wife, where we may sit with less envy & without molestation."

So far as can be discovered, no action was taken. Why Michael did not resign, why he lived on in a town that detested and tormented Martha, why the church did not accept this detailed list to the point of dismissing its author, whether in fact anyone saw the list at all—these questions must remain unanswered. That the Wigglesworths did continue to live in Malden is history. After a few years the Christians may have become used to the idea of Martha as mistress of the parson's house. That Michael, in the next twenty-five years, grew in their esteem and love almost to a degree of idolatry is one of the ironies that society is entirely capable of (in this instance, a reversal of the quickly-forgotten-celebrity formula).

The church did decide to find a replacement for Blakeman. Halfway through negotiations with Seth F. Fletcher, the members heard the preaching of Thomas Cheever, liked him, cancelled their arrangements with Fletcher, and called Cheever at fifty pounds a year.[236] The new minister was not long out of Harvard, at the head of his class. He was the son of Michael's first teacher, Ezekiel Cheever, who, after leaving New Haven years before, had been for the past ten years master of the Free School in Boston. Thomas began his work at Malden in February, 1680, and the next month was voted a fifty-pound settlement for "this year." No mention was made of Michael in the minutes of the meeting. He probably gave over the pastoral work altogether to the newcomer and devoted himself to the physical care of the people in the neighborhood.

Once Wigglesworth's marriage was a *fait accompli,* though Malden would not relax, the leaders of the colony accepted it. In no way does it appear in itself to have hindered Michael's participation in the larger activities of the Bay, to the limits of his ability. On May 19, 1680, he was one of seventy-six men (four from Malden) made freemen of the colony.[237] In his new status he was eligible to vote for the Governor, for the deputies and magistrates—a member of the political elite. This enhancing position must have made an impression on the gossiping, back-biting members of the Malden community. It must have leveled off the peaks of tension provoked by Martha's elevation to minister's wife. Michael's nomination and election as freeman would have come from his reputation as an author, from his increased estate, and, one can suggest, from his friendship with Increase Mather.

Several weeks later Martha realized that she was going to have a baby. It would be futile, if not morbid, to speculate on her tardiness in conception (well over a year after her marriage). Within the next nine years she was to have six children. Years of abstinence and physical debility had not diminished her husband's sexual virility. That the years of literary creativity were behind him might suggest that his verse-writing had been in part a compensation for loneliness, that its sometimes fearful blasts might have come in part from sexual frustration.

For the colony this was a dramatic and exciting time. In the heavens appeared a blazing comet that called forth sermons and exhortations.[238] John Hull, in a letter to Thomas Deane, was fervent: "The Lord fit us and you for all his will and pleasure!"[239]

In December the entire colony observed a feast. A letter had arrived from the King expressing dissatisfaction with the attitude of Massachusetts. He would send over agents in three months' time to discuss New England's problems with her leaders.[240] Heavenly portents; political threats—all were put to use to bring the congregations to church. The theory was that an organization that could pray together would work together, but the theory was not holding its own. Dissensions and separations were continuing. (Though at Malden Cheever had been voted in, the town was still disputing over his settlement of fifty pounds.)[241]

And fires! Many more fires destroyed a great deal of carefully husbanded property. On January 16 occurred a devastating conflagration, but, reported Hull, "nobody was found as the endeavourer of that mischief."[242] In February Mather told his diary that this was "The coldest winter that has been known these 40 years."[243] Between the untoward heat of holocaust and the bleak cold of winter the colonists were thrown into abnormal apprehension. Then when in March, 1681, Charles II dissolved Parliament and began a despotism for which his father had set the pattern, Massachusetts was feeling more than ever the pressure from the

Crown.[244] The ministers and the legislators were on the verge of hysteria.

In this month Michael became a father again after twenty-five years. Despite his frailty he would have to look out for another member of the family now. Fortunately, his wife was young and healthy and would be able to care for the needs of the little girl, Abigail.[245]

When not trying to heal the ailments of the people of Malden, Wigglesworth was at work at his desk revising his two books somewhat. In this age of menace to the purified church the ministers were doing all they could to keep it in the ascendancy. That *The Day of Doom* and *Meat Out of the Eater* were making important contributions to this effort cannot be denied when one considers their wide sale. The first book is known to have had two American and two English editions by the spring of 1681. Since the other book was in its fourth edition in 1689, there is a possibility that the third had appeared by 1681 (eleven years after the first).

In this same drive to maintain a hold on the people, on May 12 came together the prominent clergymen of the colony under Increase Mather to plan an organized garnering of accounts of heavenly intervention in the various towns. Storms and earthquakes, instances of sorcery, miraculous rescues, punishments for transgressions of the laws of God— these were to be collected and published in support of the Puritan theology. The common man was growing skeptical of the teaching that entire communities could suffer retribution. The ministers were set on proving that the will of the Lord was nevertheless mighty in acts of reward or condemnation of personal affairs.[246] The clerical hold might be weakening, but the conservatives were unwilling to admit to loss of power. The collecting of relevant anecdotes was to consume the scant leisure time of the brethren for the better part of two years.

Soon after this ministerial conference, on July 27, a year and a half after his first undertaking of the work of the church, Thomas Cheever was ordained. In addition to the fifty-pound settlement he was to receive sufficient firewood for his needs and would live in the parsonage.[247] Meanwhile, Wigglesworth stayed on in the town, living in the house constructed on his own property and attending to the bodily afflictions of the community. The members saw no reason for voting him any compensation, except a single load of firewood—in December, 1682,[248] when Martha's second daughter, Mary, was two and a half months old.

The church membership had grown to some extent, but the town would not vote in favor of enlarging the meeting house, though it did concede money for repair.[249] The waning of enthusiasm for the church was showing itself in other ways. In this same year of 1682 the town was more than two pounds in arrears for the ringing of the church bell,[250] that bell for which no tower had been provided on the meeting house itself.

On December 21, 1683, the Wigglesworths became parents of a third daughter, named for her mother, Martha.[251] Still the church would pay nothing for the support of the family of this weakling minister. With three small daughters income was an important question. Popular though *The Day of Doom* was, it was not selling during this period. There was to be no further edition in New England for eighteen years. It may be assumed that in the thirteen years following its first publication *Meat Out of the Eater* had given Michael some income. As a man of medicine, however, he would have to rely chiefly on the honesty of his patients and their ability to pay.

At this time the government of the colony was in actual jeopardy. In November Edward Randolph landed in Boston from one of his numerous trips to London with the news that Charles II would not revoke the precious charter if only Massachusetts would obey the law. Randolph was still so despised that he was even blamed for a great fire in Boston that occurred at the time of his arrival. Massachusetts remained inflexible. The following year her charter was declared null and void, and she became a royal colony.[252] For a while, with distance in her favor, she was able to operate as usual, but tensions developed; change was overhanging.[253]

When in July, 1684, the Reverend John Rogers died, leav-

[223]

ing vacant the Presidency of Harvard College, Increase Mather assumed the position on a temporary basis while the Corporation began the search for a permanent replacement.[254] Mather liked Boston too much to want to move over to Cambridge. Others refused the office, including Joshua Moody of the class of 1653.[255] In October, without question as the result of the influence of his former pupil, who wrote the letter, Wigglesworth was asked if he would be interested in the position.

One can envision the self-examination that ensued. Here would be tremendous opportunity for service, a dignified means of escaping the dissatisfactions at Malden, and—not to be ignored—a house and a salary for supporting a relentlessly growing family. (A fourth child was expected in a few months.) Also to be lifted from a fairly obscure situation in Malden to a most honorable place in Cambridge and all New England would naturally bring its gratification. But common sense ruled in the decision, and Michael declined the offer. Almost a quarter of a century before, he had written of the honest Christian view:

> For, what is Honour? What is Sov'raignty,
> Whereto mens hearts so restlessly aspire?
> Whom have they Crowned with Felicity?
> When did they ever satisfie desire?
>   (Vanity)

Everything considered, there was no reason now for him to change his attitude.

On October 27, accordingly, he wrote to Increase: "I received your Loving Lines, and having seriously considered the contents thereof, as I find great cause to thank you and other worthy friends for you and their good will & good opinion of me, yet as to my self, I cannot think my bodily health and strength competent to undertake or manage such a weighty work as you mention, if it were desired, nor have I reason to judge my self in any measure fit upon other accounts. Wherefore I hope the Colledge & Overseers will think

[224]

of and apply themselves to a fitter person."[256] It is indeed hard to imagine Wigglesworth in the chair of the President of Harvard College, even in 1684, by which year it was firmly established and highly regarded not only in New England but abroad. The college would not have run itself; and, if Michael had not been able to conduct the affairs of the little church at Malden, he would have had troubles at Harvard, wise, good, and intellectual though he might be. The following year Mather became the permanent President of his *alma mater,* a post he held, often with a diffidence spiced by out-and-out neglect, for sixteen years.

Meanwhile, in 1684 appeared Mather's *An Essay for the Recording of Illustrious Providences,* after more than two years of collecting and sorting on the part of himself and his fellow ministers. Such current phenomena as the comet known as Halley's, which had been preceded by periods of "very dreadful lightning and pretty much thunder" (to quote Hull)[257] and had been accompanied by "a dry season" (as Mather noted in his diary),[258] would enhance the effect of this curious book. It was read widely and helped revive a profound interest and belief in the agents of Satan—witches, petty devils, changelings, and other creatures of the occult.[259] In their efforts to keep faith in the supernatural a flaming issue, the ministers had created a monster which surrounded their people with all the terrors of magic and led to persecutions culminating in the frenzy at Salem less than a decade later.

In fact, the clergy were using almost any means at hand to keep the church strong. The Half-Way Covenant, liberal as it had been, was now itself being liberally interpreted. In order to maintain sizable and, hence, influential membership, churches were now admitting to Half-Way standing anyone who was of decent behavior and who could give enough of the orthodox answers to pass winking muster. Under this arrangement a still larger number of children were eligible for the all-important rite of baptism.[260]

Less than a year after Michael had said no to the Harvard Presidency occurred one of God's illustrious providences. On September 14, 1685, he went to Cambridge, entered the pulpit in the church there, and preached the annual election sermon before the Artillery Company. Samuel Sewall, indefatigable diarist, was in the congregation and took notes on the sermon. The text was obviously appropriate: "Fight the good fight of faith; lay hold on eternal life." The sermon was a success. Sewall's judgment was that Michael had done "excellently."[261]

Here was truly a mighty act—Michael, for thirty years a semi-invalid, now strong enough in body and voice to resume the preaching career he had but scarcely begun when affliction had struck. Contrary to Mather's lugubrious prognostication, marriage had brought him, not shortened life, but renewed health and the stamina to carry on the burdens of the ministry, as it turned out, for twenty more years. On this occasion the magistrates had been so pleased that, a month later, they invited Wigglesworth to preach before the voting at the next gubernatorial election, which would come the following May.[262] Delighted to see him active again, the town voted "that Mr. Wigglesworth have a highway granted to his house through the town's lands" to make passage easier to the meeting house.[263]

Michael's name began now to appear quite often in Sewall's diary. More than twenty years younger than the Malden minister, Sewall had been accumulating honors and position until at this time he was serving as Judge of the Superior Court. The diary records frequent exchange of visits between the two men.

On March 15, 1686, Michael called at the Judge's house in Boston. The conversation revealed that Thomas Cheever was in trouble with the Malden authorities.[264] The preceding August he had been heard to break the Third Commandment by using foul language in a tavern in Salem and on the road home. In spite of testimony from several witnesses the church had been inclined to forgive him at first. (Were they not all sinners? And, one might query, were not ministers hard to come by?) But when, on the next Sunday, he neglected to preserve a properly contrite countenance and carriage, the congregation began to murmur against him.[265] In the following six or seven months the gossip and allegations grew to such proportion that Malden decided it should ask for a council of churchmen from the vicinity to discuss and advise in the matter.

Two weeks after Wigglesworth's visit, Sewall heard read in meeting a letter from Malden formally requesting such a council.[266] Though jealously guarding their autonomy in most cases, the churches did make use of the wisdom of their brethren in settling difficult questions. Hartford, for example, had summoned help on various occasions to try to reach a solution to its recurring ministerial problems. Sewall and his pastor, Samuel Willard of Boston's Third Church, were selected for the conference, as were Increase and Cotton Mather (Second Church), James Allen and Joshua Moody (First Church), and nine other men, fifteen in all.[267]

Puritans doing their duty were models of self-discipline. Sewall and Willard rose about four o'clock on the morning of April 7 and set out for Malden. The way was not easy, partly up the Mystic River by boat and then a couple of miles on foot.[268]

That first day was spent chiefly in organization, Increase Mather being selected moderator. That night he and his son, Cotton, spent at the Wigglesworth house. Next morning, the group gathered to hear charges against Cheever: "light and obscene expressions (not fit to be named) in an Ordinary at Salem. . . . Also as he was travailing on the Rode. . . ." After listening to the evidence, the council decided that the young man was guilty and had not shown fitting penitence. They recommended suspension and a six-months denial of admittance to the ordinance of the Lord's Supper.

At this point, as the bell on the rock was rung, the council filed out into the open air before the assembled people, among whom was the guilty man's father, Ezekiel Cheever, still, at seventy-one, master of the school in Boston. After offering prayer, the moderator announced the decision. Sewall reported the denouement: "Mr. Wigglesworth spake, thank'd him and the Council; said had cause to condemn themselves, as for other sins, so their sudden laying hands on Mr. Cheever; and now God was whipping them with a Rod of their own making. Mr. Cheever, the Father, stood up and pathetically desir'd his son might speak, but Mr. Moderator and others judg'd it not convenient, he not having by what he said given the Council encouragement. Mr. Allin prayed; went to Dinner; Council adjourned to that day 6 weeks. Came Home well."[269] Six weeks later Thomas Cheever was discharged from the church at Malden, the council having advised "a loving dismission."[270] But Cheever was not forgotten. Half a year later, a minority of the members was in favor of reinstating him.[271]

On May 12 Michael went to Boston and, complying with his invitation, preached the election sermon. For the election itself there had not been much enthusiasm. The freemen knew that the colony was in trouble over retaining the privileges of its charter and were expecting almost daily the arrival from England of their representatives, Joseph Dudley and'John Richards, whom they had sent across the Atlantic fifteen months before to present their case. Dudley and Richards had been instructed not to yield an inch, for, if the exclusive privilege of the vote were taken away from church members and duly selected freemen, the purpose of the founders would be destroyed.[272] Rumor had it that affairs had not gone well for their envoys. If the election, then, was half-hearted, nevertheless, the colony went through the formalities. On May 6 the town of Malden, for example, had gone on record as supporting "our honoured Governor, Deputy Governor, and Assistants, elected and sworn by the Freemen of this Colony . . . together with the Deputies then sent down by the respective towns to the Court then holden, and which was never legally dissolved. . . ."[273] (A revised charter in 1684 had not been approved in London.)

Michael's sermon was built on the importance of the

founders' intent as the basic principle of settling God's controversy—formal routines being meaningless if they did not
spring from genuine concern for God and for man. His starting point had been a text from *Revelation* 2:4: "Nevertheless I have somewhat against thee, because thou hast left thy
first love." Though no copy of the sermon is extant, it is
evident that here was material for a jeremiad, now long
fashionable in New England's pulpits.[274] The word *love,*
however, was significant in Wigglesworth's approach to all
dilemmas. Despite the rigors of hell's fires in his verse the
gentler sounds of affection and engagement with his fellows
had been often audible.

> Cheer on, sweet souls, my heart is with you all,
> And shall be with you, maugre Sathan's might . . .
> (God's Con)

> Come let's return to God,
> He hath us torn, he'll heal. . . .
> (Meat concl. 15)

> Be cheerful, Suffering Saint,
> Let Nothing cast thee down. . . .
> (Heaven V. concl.)

In his prayer on this election day Michael expressed
thanks to the Almighty for guidance in the voting, asked for
bestowal of those qualities that make for genuine peace—suggesting the general feeling that the present form of government was about to end (in Sewall's words, "it may be the last
of our days"), and thanked God for "bringing forth him as
'twere a dead Man—had been reckoned among the dead,—to
preach." Since Governor Simon Bradstreet, suffering from
an attack of the gout, had been unable to come to the meeting, the company adjourned to his house for the swearing-in
ceremonies, "being much obstructed and confused by the
Drums and Vollies from which the Souldiers would not be
refrained."[275] (Anne Bradstreet had been dead fourteen
years, and her husband had married again.)

Michael's sermon had impressed his listeners. (His capac-

[229]

ity for warmth and sincerity cannot be questioned after a reading of some of the passionate passages of his college diary.) Next day the General Court ordered two of its members to thank the preacher formally and to ask him to prepare the sermon for the press as soon as possible, "adding thereto what he had not then time to deliver, the Court judging that the printing of it will be for publick benefitt." Because no copy of the printed sermon can be found, it can be assumed that it never came to press, probably because of the ensuing political events.[276]

At this distance no adequate explanation can be made for Michael's miraculous recovery and return to public life. To what degree his ailments had been psychosomatic has never been determined. Whatever the causes of recovery, one thing seems certain: he had re-entered reality from a hysteria that had silenced him nearly thirty years before. In that long-ago time he had struggled with apparently insurmountable problems rising from a high degree of sexuality and a devastating sense of religious guilt and inadequacy. Marriage to Martha for six years had given him normal adult sex experience. Committing to paper and seeing through the press two highly-approved long statements of Puritan belief had given him needed assurance in religion. At the conquest of these two major obstacles his return—at age fifty-four—to the pulpit and to active life in the colony was almost a matter of course.

Martha may have been only an unbaptized farm girl, but she had proved a godsend, nursing her husband back to health and (how important may this have been?) giving him the responsibility of a family of four daughters, (Esther had been born in April of the year before.)[277] Whatever the cause, the fact is that Michael from this point on, though never robust, was able, if ever so slowly, to win the respect and love of the townspeople and to move about in the colony at large so that at his death he was universally mourned and for long afterwards was venerated almost as Catholics would honor a saint.

Wigglesworth's was the last election sermon for three years. Two days after Governor Bradstreet's gouty induction the English frigate *Rose* landed at Boston bearing news that James II (who had been on the throne since February of the preceding year), not approving the representative form of government prevalent in New England, had set up a new council with the moderate Joseph Dudley as President. Simon Bradstreet would no longer be at the helm. The people were disconcerted, though there was nothing to do but accept the arrangement, for the time being.[278]

In spite of his regained health, Michael did not at once receive total support from the Malden church. There were grudges and memories. When the Boston churchmen had recommended "loving dismission" of Cheever in the spring of 1686, they had added: "We advise the church and Congregation of Malden duely to incourage and to hold in Reputation their Reverend and faithful Teacher [not pastor!], Mr. Wigglesworth, according as God in his word does require them to do. . . . And that they conscientiously endeavour to live and Love as Brethren, forbearing one another, and forgiving one another, if any man have a quarrel against any, even as Christ forgave you, so also do yee."[279]

But six months later discord was rampant in Malden. The town refused to vote their "faithful Teacher" any compensation. On December 3 the situation had reached such proportions that President Dudley's council appointed a committee (including among others Increase Mather and Samuel Willard) to go to Malden for the purpose of listening to the complaints and settling "the maintenance of the ministry there."[280] With Increase on the committee Michael was almost sure to get a favorable decision, but again colonial politics intervened—and to such an extent that the incumbent was not voted any kind of salary for several years. His name does not even appear in the church records until 1695. Income was important now, for Michael's four daughters were growing, and Martha was expecting a fifth child soon. (Another daughter, Dorothy, was born on the following

February 22.)[281] Dispensing of medicine and of advice on matters of health must have continued to be the chief resource, though he may even now have been working on the fourth edition of *Meat Out of the Eater* (1689), expecting further sales.

On December 20, 1686, Sir Edmund Andros arrived with a commission to serve as Governor of New England.[282] A favorite of the new King, he had only recently been knighted. His chief task was to unite all New England in an effort to resist the Indians and the French. That he was often harsh must be admitted, no matter how reasonable his purpose. His constituents were recalcitrant and looked with suspicion on every move.[283] When in March and April the liturgical practices of the Established Church were introduced at the South Meeting House, the alarm was widespread. (Andros was not requiring conformity, but was taking a step toward that tolerance which the Puritans recognized as the source of destruction of their city upon a hill.) When bonfires, sword play, fireworks, and even a Maypole in Charlestown made their appearance, the consternation of the orthodox knew no bounds.[284] Governor Andros was an openly hated man.

Despite their shared fear of the Church of England, the people of Malden would not rally around Wigglesworth. In a letter to Michael dated July 22, 1687, Samuel Sprague implied that there had been some question as to whether the minister had submitted a resignation, which Wigglesworth roundly denied.[285] One wonders about the circulation soon after his marriage of his fifteen reasons for severing his "Office Relation." Had he simply listed them for his own edification, or had he indeed transmitted them to some of his church leaders? There is no record, certainly, of formal resignation. Michael would not have lied to Sprague. The conclusion must be that through all his long infirmity and persecution he had clung to his ordination, probably hoping against hope for just such an act of God as had in actuality occurred in his restoration to comparative vigor.

Malden might be treating him coldly, but Wigglesworth was remaining firm in his faith. Whereas, as a graduate student at Harvard he had frequently entered in his diary the plea "Lord, I believ help my unbelief," now on November 27, 1687, in meditating on having recently received the elements of the Lord's Supper, he noted in a commonplace book, "I did therefore believe & I do still believe (Lord help me to believe more strongly & steadfastly) that Jesus Christ is mine with all his benefits, as surely as the bread that I eat [ate] & wine that I drank, & that he will nourish my soul to eternal life. Amen. . . ."[286] No longer here the almost hysterical outpourings of a recent convert in an effort to block out distraction or distrust. Now, rather, a more tranquil prayer for a stronger faith. Michael's years of suffering and of concentration on his Creator had carried him from the impetuous outcries of youth to the more mature petition of experience and assurance without the much-dreaded "security" that would require no more striving to do God's will.

He was traveling around in the colony with more freedom than he had known for many a year, attending various council meetings, visiting in Boston, paying last respects at funerals. On June 19, 1688, Sewall saw him at Reading (some distance north of Malden) at the funeral of the minister there.[287] He might be having difficulties with his home church and townsmen, but he was being well received elsewhere, for his writing, for his piety, and for his wisdom. That same summer, in August, when a cousin of Sewall's had brought the Judge's mother down by boat to Boston from Newbury in a little over eleven hours, Sewall had presented his accommodating relative with a copy of several items well bound together, including the Catechism and *The Day of Doom*.[288]

The colonists were seething with discontent under the hand of Sir Edmund. Their accustomed privileges had been taken away and new impositions had been levied against them. In 1688 in a cloak-and-dagger incident, Increase

Mather under disguise managed to get to England, where he pleaded eloquently before the Lords of Trade for the restoration of the democratic practice of town meetings, the recovery of rights of property, the re-establishment of courts for the probating of wills, the re-organization of a general assembly for the enactment of laws, and—ironic turn—a tax to be applied only to a man's own church.[289] Now possessing a toehold in Boston, the ritualistic Church of England was supported in large part by taxation. The Puritan churches in Massachusetts had in the beginning enjoyed this privilege, but now that there was danger of tax money going to the Established Church, the colonists were singing a different tune.

In April, 1689, Massachusetts heard that the Catholic James II had fled from London and that the Protestant William of Orange and his wife Mary had ascended England's throne. In jubilation the people revolted against the government of Andros, whom they imprisoned.[290] There was now hope of a return to the old way of life.

> On Princes poure contempt doth Hee
> Lays Tyrants in the dost
> Who proudly crush the innocent
> To satisfy their lust.
>
> (Foster)

Thus had Wigglesworth rejoiced nearly sixteen years before at the return of Mr. Foster. Thus did Massachusetts now look to God for release from bondage.

Mather, however, was not meeting with much success before the new King. When he showed that the entire concept on which New England was founded—the principle of congregational rule—depended on close relationship with the government and that it was necessary, thus, for the people to elect their own Governor, King William refused to concur: New England must not become too independent of the central government. Until a new charter could be agreed upon, though, the King would grant her the right to function under the original charter of Massachusetts Bay.[291]

Increase had another problem. As President of Harvard College, he felt the importance of maintaining the congregational influence in Cambridge. Like the colony as a whole, Harvard, too, had been operating without a charter since the return of Joseph Dudley from England in 1686. In outlining a new charter, he now proposed a self-perpetuating Corporation of ten men free of interference from "Visitors" and "Overseers." In this way, he thought, the religion and learning of the college would remain orthodox. Furthermore, he asked that Harvard be permitted to grant other degrees besides the Bachelor and Master of Arts. His pleas were unsuccessful. Such changes would give the little college in America more independence than the throne was willing to allow.[292]

While his old pupil was working at diplomacy and politics and was enjoying the cosmopolitan society of London, Michael at home was completing the revision of *Meat Out of the Eater*. In the seven years preceding, a hundred thirty-three books had been published in the Bay area, including a great many sermons and religious tracts, a few almanacs, and seventeen pamphlets against Andros. The only verse had been two elegies by Cotton Mather, Richard Steere's *A Monumental Memorial of Marine Mercy,* and possibly another edition of *Meat Out of the Eater.*[293] Clearly, the colonists had too many other things on their minds to devote any time to the writing or reading of *belles lettres*. But they did enjoy the verse of Mr. Wigglesworth, for it explained and supported their faith in easy meters and "plain style."

On September 4, 1690, Michael's servant-girl wife Martha died.[294] The cause of her death is unrecorded. It could have been from general weakness after bearing a large family. (She had given birth to Samuel, Michael's first son, on February 4, 1689.)[295] Whatever the cause, Martha was buried in the Sandy Bank "burying place" (today called Bell Rock Cemetery).[296] Her gravestone is one of several that are out of line with the others. It may be implying more than was intended to see in the awkward and seemingly careless placement of the stone one last insult to this elevated farmer's daughter.

Michael's problems were now more than doubled. So far as is known, he was still not receiving any payment from the church at Malden. And he was left with Martha's six children, the eldest not yet ten years of age.

X. The Third Marriage

Within ten months he was married again. About a month after Martha's funeral he was in Dedham, where he stayed in the home of a physician's widow, Mrs. Jonathan Avery.[297] Later, back in Malden he thought often about his hostess. Born Sybil Sparhawk in Cambridge, she was now the mother of three little daughters (a fourth having died in infancy).[298] Probably out of respect for his recently buried wife, however, Michael made no overtures until February, when on the eleventh he wrote a letter to Sybil[299] inquiring "how it fareth with yourself & children this sickly time; 2ly whither you still continue in your widdowhood, & be at Liberty or free from any Engagement, that a man may visit you without offence, 3ly And if you be free, whither a visit from me in order unto some further acquaint-ance would be welcome to you." If she would send "a brief Answer by this bearer," Michael would know God's will and would "wait upon you by a visit the first opportunity, if you incourage me so to doe." He signed himself "your lov-ing Friend." In a postscript he assured Sybil that, if she did not have time to write, she could trust the courier to bring a message by word of mouth, for he knew "upon what errant he is sent."

Before the letter had left his hands, Michael learned that Sybil's mother had died. In a lengthy addition he tried to bring comfort to "his esteemed friend." Acknowledging her bereavement as sad, he nevertheless pointed out that God "can bring the greatest good out of the greatest evils, and is wont to give us more of himself when he leaves us less of the Creature." He reminded her that the Lord "hath been with you in six troubles, & he will be with you in a seventh." (This paraphrase of a verse from *Job* was common coin in Massachusetts.) He concluded by reminding her of one of the uses of affliction—as a preparation "for peace." This was a favorite theme of his:

> Though Sorrow may abide
> And tarry for a night:
> Comfort will come at break of day,
> And Joy at morning light.
> (Joy II.5)

Sybil was favorably inclined to receive Michael, who paid her a call on March 2, no easy undertaking, for Dedham was more than twice as far southwest of Cambridge as Malden was northeast—a distance of more than thirty miles, some of it wilderness. After a decent interval of three weeks he wrote a note proposing another visit "the beginning of the next week if weather and health Prevent not." The note was actually a letter of transmittal, for the enclosed document was of much greater length, intended to pave the way for a personal interview. Doubtless the product of many hours of thorough analysis, of conscientious use of his college training in logic, and—who can deny it?—of an occasional earnest, if unconscious, descent into sophistry, "the inclosed" presented ten "considerations" for Mrs. Avery to mull over in preparation for the appearance of her suitor, who was now obviously confident that sufficient time had passed since Martha's death for him to press his case.

(I) Michael was convinced that God approved of his proposal for three reasons: (1) though he had known Sybil only a short time, he was unable to think of anyone else; (2) after long and zealous conversation with the Lord he had emerged still convinced that Sybil was his intended; (3) his desire went beyond the mere emotional: it was only reasonable to see that their marriage would be good in every way for the two families—both materially and spiritually. (II) Michael assured her that his love was solid and deep, that in his modest way he could do more for her than other "Persons more Eligible" who might propose. (After all, he was almost twenty-five years older than she, but, he probably reasoned, had he not been married for ten years— to their mutual advantage—to a woman of even greater difference in age?) (III) Since Mrs. Avery's first husband had been a physician, she might do well to marry another, for she knew the life and routines so that she and Michael could help each other. (IV) In fact, God might want her to do more for humanity than would be possible in her "Present Private capacity." If she married Michael, she would be able to turn from her afflictions toward a greater fruitfulness, a direction assuredly pleasing to God. (V) Marriage to Michael would permit her a constant proximity to "Christ in all his ordinances," which she could not now enjoy.

(VI) If she persisted in trying to manage her own affairs, she might be taken ill as she had in the past. (VII) In case of illness, if Michael were at hand, he could administer to her —an important consideration especially now that her mother was dead and she had no near relative to care for her. (VIII) The French and Indians had been causing trouble. At the coming of summer they might be an annoyance to the outlying districts. Sybil would be better off "nearer the heart of the Country." (IX) Michael longed for occasion to give her comfort after her many recent illnesses. (X) Martha had assisted him in improving his health. Likewise, Sybil might be able to help him live longer.

Wigglesworth admitted to two possible objections—his age and his six children. As for the first, he hastened to point out that God had restored his "health beyond expectation" and could give him the gift of many more years of such continuing vigor that he could provide for his new wife not only present comfort but future well-being, too, "for true love cannot be idle."

As for his many children, it might be possible to lessen the

number that Sybil would have to care for. Just how this
shrinking of the size of his family would occur he did not
suggest. It had been a custom among early Puritans to board
their children in neighboring families so that the youngsters
would learn not only reading and writing under discipline
away from home, but also the essentials of good manners and
of faith.[300] Some such arrangement as this may have been
what Wigglesworth had in mind. Whether he carried it out
is not known. Whatever the circumstance, the suitor here
promised to make the burden of the pursued as light as possible. He anticipated no difficulty, for he felt that their tem-
peraments were too compatible for trouble.

Michael concluded this orderly (and surely somewhat forbidding) arrangement with the hope that "the Consequents
will be for the furtherance of the Gospel, for the Comfort of
us both, & of both our familys & that the Lord will make us
mutual helpers & Blessings to each other, & that we shall
enjoy much of God together in such a Relation, without
which no relation can be truly sweet."

Forbidding or not, the list had influence. Michael saw
Mrs. Avery again. He gave her a lover's gift—a silver locket,
heart-shaped, about the size of a fourpence. On the front
was engraved a heart with wings on each side, the heart resting against an anchor. On the back were the words "Thine
Forever." Also, probably after they were married, he gave
her a silver box, the cover of which was a shilling. On the
bottom were engraved her initials—"S.W." Though the purpose of the box is not clear, the locket would have fitted into
it exactly.[301] These little tokens bespeak an affection often
disassociated with the Puritan in current popular thinking,
which has dwelt on the stern theology at the frequent expense
of the tender and humane emotions exhibited not only in this
charming gift-giving but further in, for example, the correspondence of Margaret and John Winthrop. In "Riddles Unriddled" Michael had testified to man's need for human companionship:

Man's Nature sociable
Delights in Company,
Declines and dreadeth Solitude,
And loves Society.
Hence to be stript of Friends
And to be left alone,
Must needs be grievous in it self,
A sore Affliction.

(Sol I.1)

Michael and Sybil were married just thirteen weeks after the would-be bridegroom had sent off his catalogue of "considerations." On June 23, 1691, the Reverend Moses Fiske performed the ceremony in Braintree, some twenty miles southeast of Dedham.[302] The clergy in New England had been joining couples in matrimony for about five years, since the summer of Wigglesworth's election sermon and the almost immediate replacement of Governor Bradstreet by a council awaiting the arrival of Sir Edmund Andros. The legality of marriage by the ministry, however, was not secured until a year after Michael and Sybil were married, under the new charter of 1692.

Michael's third bride must have been an excellent woman. Edward, her son, was to write of her that she was "an affectionate, charitable, praying saint, one who desired the good of everybody, and likewise to be herself ever doing good." Further, she "endured many sorrows and underwent great afflictions, in all which she was a mirror of patience and constancy, bearing all with true Christian fortitude. . . ."[303] Even discounting the possible overestimation of an adoring son, one is left with the portrait of an admirable person, well equipped for the variety of problems unavoidable for the wife of a parson, the helpmeet of a physician, and the mother of a large family of little children.

Her husband's participation in community and colonial activity had by this time increased considerably. On October 13, 1690 (in the month of his first meeting with Sybil in Dedham), he had convened at Charlestown with the other ministers from the vicinity of Boston to form an association that

[241]

would come together in the library at Harvard about once a month (except in the inclement weather of winter) on Mondays for discussion of mutual questions and the general promulgation of the Christian point of view in colonial life.

The first session had been held on the following Monday, October 20, to deliberate on ways and means of achieving a "Reformation of those evils, which have brought the many & heavy judgments of God upon our people. . . ." Of the seven ministers involved—Charles Morton, James Allen, Wigglesworth, Joshua Willard, Cotton Mather, and Nehemiah Walter—Morton may well have suggested the organization, for he had only recently come over from England, where a number of Independent clergymen, both Presbyterian and Congregational, had banded together in London—as the "United Brethren"—for just such a purpose. Furthermore, Cotton's father, Increase, was at that very time in the English capital trying to secure a new charter for the colony and for Harvard and had helped organize the new association. Even in his absence, in consequence, he was listed as a charter member of the Cambridge Association.[304]

The fact of the matter was that the world was creeping in at an alarming pace on this one-time spiritual Utopia, this "New-English Israel." With the expansion of trade across the seas in tobacco, fur, fish, and lumber had come a companion break-up of the agricultural village in deference to an out-and-out farm economy. At the scattering of the populace the control of the church was becoming more and more tenuous. This was the very problem that the General Court had sought to avert by forbidding Malden to expand into New Hampshire in 1662. Linked with these expansions was the growth of heresy, the strengthening of the liberal attitude at Harvard (despite Increase Mather's firm stand), a wide demand for a more democratic vote, and a frank extension of disregard for the old morality.[305] The clergy could no longer keep within bounds a careful observance of the Sabbath, the use of cards and dice, the expression of *joie de vivre* in the rhythms (and abandon?) of the dance, the worldliness of wig-wearing, the Satanic practices of drunkenness and cursing. Moreover, the statements of Isaac Newton about the mechanics of the universe were ushering in an age of rationalism that was obviously negating the supernatural structure on which the power of the ministers had been erected. Newton's *Philosophiae Naturalis Principia Mathematica,* The Mathematical Principles of Natural Philosophy, had been published in England in 1687.

The church at Lynn had been having internal differences. On November 10, 1691, a council of the churches from Boston, Malden, and Salem had gathered at the site of the offending group to settle the squabble. Though Lynn had been slow to accept the visitors as a guide, at last the meeting had begun, with Wigglesworth as moderator, and had reached agreement on the method of resolving the difficulty, Cotton Mather drawing up the articles of advice.[306] Three and a half years later, the Cambridge Association composed a letter to the troubled church at Salem suggesting a change in clergy in order to achieve comparative calm.[307] Clearly, the churches were having problems, and the ministers must have been aware of a decrease in their own power, but unwilling to go down without a fight.

On May 14, 1692 (Sybil and Michael had not yet been married a year), with Sir William Phips, Increase Mather arrived back in Boston carrying a new charter. Though it was not openly welcomed in every quarter, it was better than none at all as the colonists had learned in the preceding six years.[308] Now, except for the Governor (Phips was the first), the people could elect all officers. The franchise had been extended to all men of property. Thus the province (no longer a colony) was striding towards freedom in thinking and worship. As for Harvard, Mather had acquired first from King James a promise to confirm a charter, then from William and Mary the agreement to protect all "colleges" in the province, for the new general charter had united Massachusetts Bay not only with Plymouth but with Maine and Nova Scotia. The establishment of more institutions at the collegiate level besides Harvard did not seem improbable.

Increase was appointed "Rector" of Harvard to serve

until he heard further. But he was not happy. As a young
man he had had four stimulating years in Ireland and England. He had just now returned from another four-year sojourn abroad, after which Boston, and above all Cambridge,
seemed very slow indeed. Mather's hard-headed intellect was
matched by glowing emotion and vaulting ambition.[309] To be
stuck in a muddy village as head of a small provincial college
was no way to satisfy his craving for power and position. In
filling up the empty pages at the end of his manuscript of the
first edition of *The Day of Doom,* Mather's present colleague
and erstwhile tutor had followed the Puritan line:

> Learn what deceitful Toyes, and empty things,
> This World, and all its best Enjoyments bee:
> Out of the Earth no true Contentment springs,
> But all things here are vexing Vanitee.
>
> (Vanity)

This had not been Mather's experience, however. He had
found "This World, and all its best Enjoyments" attractive
and stimulating.

On the Sunday following Mather's seemingly temporary
appointment as Rector of the college, Wigglesworth preached
a sermon based on a verse from *Psalm* 119: "I made haste
and delayed not to keep thy commandments."[310] There is no
indication that he had his former pupil in mind. Rather, he
was joining with right good will in the clerical struggle to
keep the people aware of the awful power of God (and incidentally the power of His ministers, which the people were
beginning to ignore). In "The Day of Doom," Christ the
Judge had excoriated the procrastinators:

> You had a season, what was your reason
> such precious hours to waste?
> What could you find, what could you mind
> that was of greater haste?
>
> . . .
>
> Had you good leasure for carnal Pleasure,
> in dayes of health and youth?
> And yet no space to seek God's face,
> and turn to him in truth?
>
> (DD 110, 111)

This concept had been one of the planks in the platform of every jeremiad of the past thirty years. It had been constantly in Michael's own mind as he reworked his long poem for succeeding editions. Even now he may have been preparing what was to be the edition of 1701.

At any rate, in his sermon Michael was still warning his hearers that "man's duty" and the "practice of the godly" are "to yield speedy obedience to God's commandments." This "observation" he supported with several "reasons": that God demands obedience at once; that our own time on earth is short; that hurrying to do the will of God is a symbol of sincerity; that danger lurks in procrastination, for tomorrow may increase a man's disinclination, and, worse, a man becomes through delay a likely candidate for "God's irrevocable wrath."

From the Bible the preacher now quoted examples of unquestioning obedience, beginning with the earliest: Noah, Abraham, David (whose *Psalm* was providing the present text), Hezekiah, and Josiah. There followed the "examination" (there must be thorough spiritual testing to prepare oneself for obeying God) and the "exhortation" (one must get at it before it is too late). Finally, to the possible "objection" that man is not strong enough to do God's will, Wigglesworth returned the one sure answer: Christ would give ready support to any petitioner.

To this outline (following the pattern learned at college) Michael could bring all the honesty and sweet conviction that his years of early struggle and later affliction had yielded. The people of Malden were beginning to come over to his side. Though this sermon was probably not extraordinary, it does show its preacher to be still following the conservative doctrine of the early New England clergy. It helps to show why, too, Increase Mather held to Michael as a dear and sympathetic friend.

The following Thursday Samuel Sewall was commissioned one of the judges of the special court to try the poor souls at Salem who had been accused of witchcraft. Within five months twenty people were condemned and executed, one by the horrible device of pressing, though none were burned, as legend would have it.[311]

The collection of *Illustrious Providences* had been an effort of the ministers to combat growing rationalism. These Salem trials may in part be regarded as springing from the same cause. True, when the court requested a statement, the clergy said that, though they wanted the courts to hold to the law, they advised proceeding with "exquisite caution." How deeply involved Michael was at the time cannot be determined, but, when on October 3 the Cambridge Association gave unanimous consent to Mather's *Cases of Conscience,* as Harvard's Rector read before the brethren his detailed proof of the existence of witches (though supernatural evidence alone he declared to be inadequate), Wigglesworth was in the group.[312]

The full title of Mather's little book was *Cases of Conscience Concerning Evil Spirits Personating Men, Witchcrafts, Infallible Proofs of Guilt in Such as Are Accused with That Crime. All Considered According to the Scriptures, History, and Judgment of Many Learned Men.*[313] The theme was that devils so proved, "whoever they be, ought to be exterminated from amongst men." A humane note, however, enters the considerations: at least two actual witnesses should testify to any crime. "It were better that ten suspected witches should escape than that one innocent person should be condemned." On the other hand, the Salem judges were to be held good and trustworthy. Compiled during the terrible year of 1692 (immediately after Mather's return from England), this work grew from the determination of the ministers to keep the idea of the supernatural before the people.

A brief address to the "Christian Reader" precedes Mather's study. "That there are devils and witches the Scripture asserts and experience confirms; that they are common enemies of mankind and set upon mischief is not to be doubted; . . . that witches, when detected and convinced, ought to be exterminated and cut off we have God's warrant for. . . .

". . . That the resolutions of such cases as these is proper for the servants of Christ in the ministry cannot be denied. . . .

"The reverend, learned, and judicious author of the ensuing cases is too well known to need our commendations: all that we are concerned in is to assert our hearty consent to and concurrence with the substance of what is contained in the following discourse: and with our hearty request to God that he would discover the depths of this hellish design; direct in the whole management of this affair; prevent the taking any wrong steps in this dark way; and that He would in particular bless these faithful endeavors of His servant to that end, we commend it and you to His divine benediction." It was to this preliminary supporting essay that, along with thirteen others, Wigglesworth affixed his signature.

Having read Mather's manuscript (it was not printed till November), by October 29 Governor Phips put his foot down. The court at Salem "must fall." His wife had been accused of alliance with Satan because one day in her husband's absence she had ordered release of one of the victims. This may well have been the immediate reason for his demand. In January the court acquitted forty-seven of those indicted, the remaining three receiving pardons from the Governor.[314]

The hysteria died down, but the clergy continued to testify to the marvels of an "invisible world." In 1694 Mather and the Fellows of Harvard College proposed to the ministers to continue collecting "all unusual accidents" in nature as proof of the supernatural. Try as they would, however, the clergy, though still influential, were suffering a genuine loss of prestige. They could no longer dictate the life of their communities.[315]

In the midst of all this, Michael, ironically, was growing in esteem among his congregation. Of course, he had no way to go but up, after the years of disdain under which he had lived in Malden. Now married to a lady worthy of his position in the eyes of the townsmen, now restored to health far enough that he could lead a comparatively active life both as minister and as physician, he was winning respect, admiration, and love that were to outlast his lifetime.

His genuinely sweet disposition—albeit colored by stern orthodoxy—had shone through his poetry everywhere. Especially had the theme of *Meat Out of the Eater* with its "Riddles Unriddled" been filled with the virtues of longsuffering that culminate in a gentle, affectionate nature. If focused on growth in the love of God rather than on development of self-pity, affliction could flower only into unselfish devotion to one's fellows and adoration of God.

Though many New Englanders, including Increase Mather, approved of Wigglesworth's themes in theory, they were often beguiled by a worldliness that was to take the ascendancy in New England in the eighteenth century. A universe of purposes (apples are to eat) was being replaced by a universe of causes (why do apples ripen?). The new questions were not why God was sending troubles and blessings but what in nature was causing these things to happen. Lightning was losing its effectiveness as a weapon of the Lord as interest grew in what physical forces made the flashes. God was fading; the world was shining brighter.

At the beginning of 1693 Sybil bore her husband a son, their only child,[316] whose half-sister Mercy Brackenbury was thirty-seven years old (about the same age as Sybil) and whose father was sixty-one. If all the Wigglesworth children were still at home and if Sybil's three daughters had all come to Malden to live, there were now ten young people under twelve years of age to feed, clothe, and educate.

Fortunately, Malden now seemed willing to cooperate. On March 6, soon after the birth of Edward, the town voted that on March 21 men would cut wood and cart it to the parsonage. (One would hope that the black bugs had been exterminated.) This is the first mention of compensation for Wigglesworth in the town records after the dismissal of Thomas Cheever in 1686, the year in which Michael began doing more and more for the people.[317] Though it is hard to believe that he had served for six and a half years without

[248]

salary, this may have been the case, for the financial condition of the church and town was not strong. Beginning in this month of March, 1693, monies were voted to move the church bell from its rock to "the top of the Metinghouse," but not until over two years later were enough funds provided to finish the job.[318]

On January 24, 1694, the town voted the minister more wood, then in meeting assembled on March 12 approved a salary of fifty-five pounds, sufficient wood (thirty cords for "this present year"), and the "use of the parsonage." Just when the Wigglesworths had moved into the more commodious house is unrecorded, but here at least was formal approval. The town was at last recognizing its minister as a man deserving its support. It may be that from this point on Michael assumed the title of "pastor" with complete confidence. In 1696 the wood allowance was to be increased to thirty-five cords, the stipend placed at fifty pounds and the "strangers' money," defined in the town book as that put "into the box naked."[319]

But now in March, 1694, the relation between minister and people about to assume more nearly normal guise, Michael was called upon to sign a curious document which might appear to detract from the good will blossoming in the town. Copied out by the town clerk, the seal of the town affixed, the paper read: ". . . I, Michael Wigglesworth of Malden, doe Hereby discharg and Acquit the Town of Malden from all claims that may be made hereafter by my self, my haires executers Administrators or a signes [assigns] upon the acount of aney salary debt or dues to me for the work of the ministry from the beginning of The world until the 12 of March 1695."[320] Malden was taking no chances on back-payment! There would be trouble enough meeting current obligations to the following March.

In November, 1694, Sybil's middle daughter, aged nine, died at Malden and was interred in the burying ground near the Bell Rock. She had been the second daughter to bear the name, for Sybil's first baby, who had died within a few days

[249]

of her birth in 1681, had also been named Margaret. Having been bereft of her mother not long before, of her first husband and of two daughters, Sybil was deserving of her son's encomium, the possessor of "true Christian fortitude."

As the years began to wear away, Michael's energies appear to have strengthened somewhat. Sewall's diary mentions the Malden minister with greater frequency. On Monday, June 1, 1696, Michael preached the election sermon for the Ancient and Honorable Artillery Company, of which Colonel Nicholas Paige was captain. Sewall reported that the text was from the sixth chapter of *Ephesians*: "Put on the whole Armour of God, that ye may be able to stand against the wiles of the Devil," such wiles being interpreted as "the evil of the Times or else of Popery, or something as bad as Popery. . . ."[321] Among many other vexations the Congregational clergy were concerned over the increasing drawing power of the liturgical Established Church in their bailiwick.

Colonel Paige was a man of considerable dignity in the town of Malden. In 1692 he had been the first to whom permission had been granted to construct a private pew in the meeting house, with the understanding that, if he ever left it, it would not go to his heirs but would "returne to the towne." Later he was allowed to move his pew to the corner of the room, "by the little dore." Members in all meeting houses had from the beginning been seated on plank benches according to age and station, but this was a special privilege signalizing the rise of a new class, the well-to-do merchants, at the approach of eighteenth-century secularism. Those who could afford it went together to have a stable built for their horses "on the Sabbath days," four feet of floor space being allowed each person.[322] To the Malden of the end of the seventeenth century these rights were the symbolic equivalent of twentieth-century Cadillacs.

In the next few years Sewall saw the Malden minister often. On September 14, 1696, he accompanied his own pastor, Mr. Moody, in calling on several people, including "Mr.

Wigglesworth and his wife." They stayed to dinner with Michael and Sybil. Judge Sewall noted that "I furnished New England Salt."[323] The supply of salt had been a serious problem in the colony from the beginning. In this year of 1696 some merchants in Boston had been granted a fourteen-year patent to use the "French method" of scraping crystals from stakes driven into the salt-water ponds to await evaporation. The product was much cleaner than that taken from the clay floor of evaporated ponds. John Winthrop, Junior, enterprising as he was, had tried several ways of producing salt, as had many other colonists, but not until the time of the Revolution was it to be very plentiful.[324] Hence, Sewall's contribution to the dinner party at the Wigglesworths' was worthy of special notation.

In October Michael and Sybil stayed overnight in turn with the Sewalls in Boston.[325] Later in the month during a conversation Wigglesworth recounted to the Judge an instance of illustrious providence: a fifty-year-old inhabitant of Malden, unable to speak for eighteen years, had now for three weeks enjoyed complete restoration of voice. "He is much affected with the Goodness of God to him herein."[326] Divine intervention was of course still taken for granted. Wigglesworth's own long affliction would have made him particularly interested in this case.

On May 24, 1697, Sewall arrived back in Boston from a visit to his parents in Newbury. On the way down he had stopped in Malden long enough for a talk with "Mr. Wigglesworth." He had met a "Mr. Tappan from Reading," who had given him a lift as far as Charlestown.[327] Was this the Samuel Tappan who was to marry Michael's daughter Abigail? If so, he was beginning his suit fairly early, for Abigail remained a maiden for three and a half more years.

The following month, Increase Mather drafted a new charter for Harvard, which for over ten years had been in an unsettled state. Mather had returned from England in 1692 with nothing but promises from the Crown. Coupled with the uncertainties about a charter was Mather's restlessness in

[251]

general over his office as Rector and the unavoidable residence in little Cambridge. In 1695 he had tried twice to resign, but the corporation had insisted that he stay on. When in 1695 the Privy Council in London had cancelled the current charter because it did not provide for appointment by the King of an official Visitor, Increase set to work trying to draw up another version. He did not object to the idea of an intervening Visitor so much as did the General Court, which feared that if the King got his foot in at the college door, he would next try for control of the churches.

The 1697 charter did not last long. It called for a larger Corporation, consisting of the President, the Vice-President, the Treasurer, and fourteen Fellows—nine to be a quorum, the Fellows to be re-elected or replaced every seven years. Among the new Fellows was Michael Wigglesworth, Mather's old friend.[328] Michael had been officially separated from his *alma mater* for forty years. This new relationship being advisory, it differed a good deal of course from the office of tutor he had held those long years before. One can imagine, however, the modest pleasure (as well as the conscientiousness) with which he received this appointment.

There were later drafts of the troublesome charter, made in an effort to please the King, the General Court, and the President himself. None of them was satisfactory. Mather tried again and again to resign.[329] From 1700 to 1707 the college operated under what amounted to no charter at all. Through all the fanfare and machinations Michael served quietly as Fellow from his first appointment in 1697 until his death in 1705. This was not as rigorous or responsible a post as the Presidency he might have had in 1684, but in his miraculously recovered health he could not help feeling privileged thus to serve his college.

Sunday, January 23, 1698, was an extremely cold day. In Boston Sewall's "clock stood still this morning, and yesterday morn, which has not done many years."[330] In Malden Wigglesworth preached a topical sermon based on the text "Who can stand before His cold?" God was still causing every least change of temperature, let not the people of Malden forget it. On the following three Sundays there was so much illness among the people that no services were held at all. They must have been sick indeed! Their minister himself had succumbed to ailments induced by the cold weather. But on February 20, the day still being frigid, he was back in his pulpit preaching from another timely text: "He sends forth His word and thaws them." As proof positive of the power of the Divine Hand, Monday produced milder weather, Tuesday even milder yet, the thaw continuing for several days. The temperature was high enough that Sewall was able to come over to Malden for a conversation with his friend. He rode from Boston to Charlestown on the ice, but had to finish most of the rest of the journey slogging through deep snows.[331] Though Wigglesworth was more than twenty years his senior, Sewall obviously enjoyed being with him. The Judge loved society, but he was also a diligent Bible scholar and was always very careful about observing the Sabbath. That he so frequently sought out the Malden minister was evidence that Michael himself, despite his narrow theology and his collegiate worries over his tendency to gregariousness, had emerged a genial, gentle, and easily accessible companion. His long-lasting mysterious illness, his many children, his difficulties with the people of Malden, his coldness toward his parents, his uncertain income—these would have been enough to sour many a man against the world. But Michael, almost ideal Puritan that he was, had turned them all to good account and was now reaping the harvest of honor, respect, and admiration. In *Meat Out of the Eater* he had unconsciously forecast his own present state. After alluding to Jacob and the angel, he had concluded:

> Thus every suffering Saint
> By wrestling shall prevail,
> And having overcome at last
> Be styled Israel.
> (Meat IX.21)

How the people had changed! Though he had been able to preach again on this late February Sunday, Michael had been so enfeebled by his recent indisposition that he could not resume his duties with his customary energies. He was again bed-ridden. Instead of the gossip and disgust of earlier years, however, the congregation now turned to prayer, tears, and even fasting in their common effort to bring about his recovery. On March 31 the town voted him "sum help 4 or 5 sabath days in the work of the minestry."[332] One simply cannot imagine such solicitude in, say, the early days of his marriage to Martha Mudge.

His strength recovered, Michael was soon able to take up his preaching, his pastoral care, and his travels again. On June 5, 1699, he and Sybil were in Boston to hear Mr. Willard preach the election sermon. They spent the night with the Sewalls.[333] In August Wigglesworth requested a lean-to to be built on the rear of the parsonage. Though the town voted funds, six months later the structure was still unfinished[334]—but this time most assuredly not out of indifference to the minister.

On August 28, 1700, Michael was again in Boston attending the ordination of Ebenezer Pemberton as minister of South Church. The meeting house was filled to bulging. There were two sermons—one by Pemberton and one by Willard, who, with Increase Mather and James Allen, conducted the ceremony of the laying on of hands. Mather extended to the new minister the right hand of fellowship. Though they objected to the rubrics and rituals of *The Book of Common Prayer,* these self-styled purifiers of the Church of England had developed ceremonials of their own which, ironically, they would have been unhappy to discard. All these proceedings Michael observed from his position of vantage in the pulpit, to which he had been conducted, with Samuel Torrey,[335] no doubt out of regard for his age and health, but above all because of the general approbation of the clergy.

On December 23 nineteen-year-old Abigail was married to Samuel Tappan, nine years her senior. Her father officiated.[336] It was now lawful for ministers to perform the wedding ceremony. (Indeed Michael's own third marriage had been so blessed.) Thus had thinking changed concerning legal contracts. The original fear of confusion over the sacred and the secular had given way before the necessity of the clergy to maintain prestige. Abigail, next to Mercy, Michael's oldest child, was the first of Martha's children to marry. Her descendants, the Tappans, were destined to carry important roles in the development of New England.

The Day of Doom had not been issued in America in twenty-five years. An edition in London in 1673 may possibly have been only a reprint of the one published there in 1666. Whatever the supply, the little book had achieved an unequalled popularity in Massachusetts. Now in 1701 Michael brought out another edition, "enlarged with Scripture and marginal notes." This was to be the last during his life. The author was still patently old-school. The unbaptized babies were still allotted "the easiest room in hell" in spite of spreading opinions against infant baptism. A medieval, graphic, detailed picture of the Last Judgment was still accepted by the people, for all the inroads of science and the growth of materialism. On the final page this edition carried an advertisement for *Meat Out of the Eater,* still in its fourth edition, completed in 1789, the year before Martha's death. This, too, was to be the last edition that its author was to see in print.

Mather was continuing to have his troubles with Harvard. He so much preferred the cosmopolitanism of Boston that it was actually agony for him to stay even for a short while in Cambridge. In the hot summer months of 1700 he had forced himself to live at the college for many weeks, consulting daily with the students, preaching, lecturing, conducting discussions, but in mid-October he had returned with relief to the comforts of Boston. During that summer a new charter had been drawn up removing any religious test from the requirements for admission. This disturbed Mather, who despised the approach of liberalism anywhere, in church, state, or education. Finally, having presided at the July commencement in 1701, he returned to his Boston congregation, who were always delighted to have him back. He rather expected at this point to carry on also as President of the college, but the General Court felt otherwise. On September 6 it resolved that the administration of Harvard should now reside in the hands of the Vice-President, Samuel Willard. The conservative Mather had been dismissed. Willard remained in office until his death in 1707. Technically, the role of Vice-President did not require residence in Cambridge.[337] The college itself was without a charter all this while. Throughout the disagreements and displacements Michael continued in his capacity as Fellow.

In that same summer of 1701 Josiah Willard in Boston shaved his head for the purpose of accommodating a wig. Judge Sewall was incensed. To disfigure oneself thus in order to be fashionable was clearly yielding to the sin of pride. He listed a number of prominent men who had resisted the fad, among them "Mr. Wigglesworth."[338]

This preoccupation with the style of hair was widespread among the faithful. Hair was meant to be worn at conservative length, neither shaved off nor worn long. As early as 1649 the General Court had issued a condemnation of long hair and had urged the church leaders to discourage it. In England the Puritans' short locks had produced the nickname "Roundheads." In an outburst in his diary of 1664, John Hull had listed the evils of the day, including "pride in long hair, new fashions in apparel, drinking, gaming, idleness, worldliness, &."[339] Long hair and wigs were in the same category: they both negated the humility necessary to a true Christian. God was as much concerned over these details of daily living as over the greater issues.

In a sermon undated but attributed to him, Michael lashed out against the abominable custom of wearing the hair long.[340] In his usual methodical way, he set forth five propositions. (I) To wear the hair conveniently long is not wrong, for it should be used to prevent baldness and to keep the head warm. For this reason weaklings might need longer hair than their healthier brethren. (II) Because long hair "savors of effeminacy," it should be avoided. Here he quoted from *I Corinthians* 11, that long hair is "a shame" to a man. (III) Though permitted by custom, long hair is uncalled for if it is "an effect or a badge of pride or vanity." (IV) The least worldly men in Massachusetts wear short hair; in fact, all the best men in history eschewed long locks. It therefore behooves the sober-minded to follow suit. (V) Under the guidance of St. Paul, a man should not wear his hair long if it thus offends the weak. It might be that in the winter one could wear his hair a little longer; but, to avoid annoying his brethren, he should cut it short in summer.

After this detailed exposition the preacher then applied pressure in three considerations. (I) "God calls every christian to walk not onely sincerely but exactly." (II) "Walk safely. If there be a sin in long hair it is certain it is no sin to wear short hair; choose that which is most safe." (III) "What an evil it wil be when God awakens thy conscience."

How this sermon affected its hearers is not recorded. It does show the premium placed on outward appearance as a symbol of the inward state of grace or disgrace. External conformity has a firm foundation in American history.

In the same vein is another sermon ascribed to Wigglesworth. Based on an analysis of the third chapter of *Isaiah,* it rebukes women who conduct themselves with pride and haughtiness. Gesture, hair style, clothing, and general behavior are all potential modes of expressing pride. When inordinate and immodest in these directions, women provoke the wrath of God, not only against themselves, but against their husbands and indeed the whole land in which they live. Here was another instance of the Puritan doctrine of the responsibility of the individual for his fellows, a responsibility reaching down to such an ordinary matter as Mr. Mitchell's stable door swinging in the wind on a Sunday in long-ago Cambridge.

The town of Malden was still struggling with its public

buildings—their upkeep and expansion. In October, 1701, having raised the sum of twenty shillings to pay for the shingling of the meeting house, the townsmen voted instead to use the fund to buy materials for repairing their minister's residence. Here again was testimony to their respect for Michael, won at last after years of diffidence and open hostility. Three and a half years later they agreed to permit him to have his barn moved nearer the parsonage "to the north side of the paire tree behind the dwelling house."[341] Such consideration would have been unthought of in the early days of Michael's ministry.

The keeping of the school also presented a serious problem —and Michael and Sybil still had a brood of school age. It was actually unlawful to have a town without a school, but Malden all too frequently would find itself without masters. Possibly the difficulty lay in the fact that the salary scale was too low to attract and hold capable men. In 1691 the clerk reported in the town record, apparently with some relief, that Ezekiel Jenkins would continue "to be the Towne's scoule master."[342] Ten years later, though, there was no school, and Malden was indicted under the law. At last John Sprague was persuaded to take the job at fifteen pounds and "benefit of scholars." The chairman of the town board went over to Charlestown and paid the costs, but was not fined, since a master had been found. The same situation was to recur in 1705.[343] A further difficulty was the location of the school itself. In 1703 it was voted "that the school shall be kep in the watch hous for this yeare."[344] Admittedly with the help of the goad of the law, these people were determined to give their children at least the minimum in reading and writing. If he had had the time, of course, Michael could have given his children a better education than anyone else in town.

In the meeting house Colonel Paige's pew had set a precedent which other members soon wanted to follow. At last in 1703, eleven years after the colonel's innovation, permission was granted Samuel Sprague, John Sprague (the "scoule master"), John Dexter, and some others to construct private pews.[345] The desire for privilege and elevation was spreading. One would think that there was a fine line to be drawn between the wish for admiration and comfort, on the right hand, and the sin of pride, on the left. But the Puritans, however strict in the tenets of their faith, had never agreed to abstemiousness nor asceticism.

In addition to his work as minister and physician Michael took the time in 1703 to revise *Meat Out of the Eater,* the fourth edition of which had still been offered to the public in 1701. Could it be that the advertisement of that year had brought a spurt of sales, enough to warrant a new issue? Wigglesworth actually made only a few changes in the text, most of which were in the nature of proofreading: improvements in punctuation; omission, addition, or more accurate placement of Biblical references in the margin; minor corrections in spelling (*me* for *mee, cheerful* for *chearful*). Occasionally a misspelling in the 1689 edition had been misleading or baffling: "Our" was changed to a proper "Or" at one place; "word" to "world" at another. The swing of the lines was another of the poet's concerns: "Bravery" became "Brav'ry." On the other hand, the rhythm demanded in Meditation IV of "Poor Men's Wealth" that "childeren" remain a three-syllable word! In Meditation III of the title poem an altogether new verb was substituted to insure a steady beat. What had read "God doth chasten his own" was made to read "God doth chastise his own."

It turned out that the revised version was not published until long after the poet's death. The fifth edition, 1717, carried a notation on the title page: "Corrected and Amended by the Author, in the Year 1703." So far as can be discovered, this was the last work for publication that Michael ever did. The central thesis of the volume, turning outward in suffering rather than feeling sorry for oneself, was still good tonic. The twentieth century is beginning to see the wisdom of such an attitude. Though more often than not expressed in secular terms nowadays, Wigglesworth's idea was fundamentally healthful—one to be approved by modern psychotherapists.

[259]

'Tis better to be sick,
And have thy Soul wax whole:
Then in a Body hale and strong
To have a sickly Soul.
(Sick III.4)

The friendship with Samuel Sewall continued to the end of Wigglesworth's life. The Judge relied heavily on Michael's knowledge and ability in medicine. When on June 18, 1703, there was a community party at Muddy River to raise Sewall's son's house, the Judge sent for Michael and Sybil in the "Hackney-Coach." Michael talked at great length with Mrs. Sewall about her ailments and the health of her daughter Judith. Later in the summer Sewall brought another daughter, Mary, to Malden to stay with the Wigglesworths while Michael tried to diagnose her infirmity. He came to the conclusion that it was "of a Convulsive nature." A year later he was in Boston administering to one of Sewall's friends, Colonel Savage. Meanwhile, there was doubtless a continuation of visiting between the two families—calling, overnight hospitality, dining (as on April 18, 1704, when the Judge stopped for dinner at the Malden parsonage on his way home from a visit with relatives in Salem).[346]

The two men had come to think and feel alike about the witchcraft scandal in Salem in 1692. Five years after Governor Phips had called a halt to the outrageous proceedings, Judge Sewall had stood up in church making public acknowledgment of his sin in condemning the poor wretches. Three days later the General Court had in fact declared a day of fasting throughout the province as an expression of repentance. The conviction soon spread that the whole proceeding had been a terrible mistake.[347]

Be it forever to Wigglesworth's praise and glory that he spent July 22, 1704, composing a letter to his one-time pupil and present influential friend, Increase Mather, candidly stating his position in such a way that he kept alive the feeling of guilt in the province until 1712, when sentences began

[260]

to be annulled legally, attainders reversed, and payment made to the deprived heirs of the executed persons.[348]

In his letter Michael attempted to find the cause for God's still ongoing controversy with New England (he had first used the phrase in 1662) as manifested in the current war, drought, and famine. His opinion was that God was still wrathful over "what was done in the time of the Witchcraft. I fear that innocent blood hath been shed; & that many have had their hands defiled therewith. I believe our Godly Judges did act Conscientiously, according to what they did apprehend then to be Sufficient Proof. But since that, have not the Devils impostures appeared? & that most of the Complainers & Acusers were acted by him in giving their testimonies. Be it then that it was done ignorantly." He recommended "a public and solemn acknowledgment of it and humiliation for it, and the more particularly and personally it is done by all that have been actors, the more pleasing it will be to God and more effectual to turn away his judgments from the land and to prevent his wrath from falling upon the persons and families of such as have been most concerned. . . ."

"Moreover, if it be true, as I have been often informed, that the families of such as were Condemned for supposed witchcraft, have been ruined by taking away and making havoke of their estates, & Leaving them nothing for their relieff, I believe the whole Country lies under a Curse to this day, and will do, till some effectual course be taken by our honored Governour & General Court to make them some amends and reparations." He added that, if the objection were raised that there were already too many places to dispose of public funds, the answer would probably be that heavy taxes might well be one of God's punishments for this very thing. Payments could be made gradually: "I am perswaded God would soon make us able, if we were but willing." Michael asked Increase to discuss the situation with the other Boston ministers and then, if they agreed, to see that the Governor be informed and, with his approval, "the General Assembly at their next sessions."

[261]

His conclusion showed him physically somewhat infirm, though still vigorous in mind and conscience: "I have, with a weak body, and trembling hand, endeavored to leave my testimony before I leave the world; and having left it with you (my Reverend bretheren) I hope I shall leave this life with more peace, when God seeth meet to call me hence.

"I remain your Faithful friend & fellow Watchman in the Lord, Michael Wigglesworth."[349]

Just how fully he had supported the witch hunt remains undisclosed. That he had genuine Puritan concern for his neighbor, that he knew himself to be by vocation his brother's keeper, there can be no doubt after this letter. He had come a long way since his graduate-student days at Harvard when he would wonder and worry over his responsibilities as proctor in the college dormitory. Now he did not hesitate to speak out boldly for the cause of justice in the land. He was making the decision he would want all mankind to make. On this day he had laid a large paving stone in the road to tolerance, equity, and mercy.

He must have sensed that his end was near, for found among his papers at his death were two poems[350] composed in all probability in this final year, if their tone is any evidence. They both show the poet quite prepared to leave this life (though his love of New England, his pleasure in friends and companions, his reading and his writing would all point to a passion for living). Both poems are structured on the rhymed decasyllabic couplet he had used to good effect in the poem of thirty years before beginning "I walk'd and did a little Mole-hill view." The first, "Death Expected and Welcomed," is only twelve lines long:

> Welcome, sweet rest, by me so long desired,
> Who have with sins and griefs so long been tired.
> And welcome, Death, my Father's messenger,
> Of my felicity the hastener.
> Welcome, good Angels, who, for me distrest,
> Are come to guard me to eternal rest.
> Welcome, O Christ! who hast my soul redeemed;
> Whose favor I have more than life esteemed.

[262]

> O! do not now my sinful soul forsake,
> But to thyself, thy servant gathering, take.
> Into thine hands I recommend my spirit,
> Trusting, through thee, eternal life to inherit.

The shift in accent in the lines beginning "Welcome" and "Trusting" (four in all) relieves the potential monotony of the iambic beat, as does the concluding feminine off-rhyme of "my spirit" and "inherit." One thinks of Bach's haunting *Komm, Süsser Tod,* another Protestant hymn to death to be written a few years later, in another medium. Both have a sweetness of acceptance that would come only with complete faith. Wigglesworth's little poem has dignity and restraint. The mood is more than formal; it rises from genuine emotion.

The other piece, "A Farewell to the World," contains sixty-eight lines. Whereas the shorter poem gazes rapturously forward to a heavenly guerdon, this one takes a longer look at the present life. The tone in general is as admonitory as in "God's Controversy." Whereas, further, in the shorter poem the poet welcomed rest, Death, angels, and Christ in ascending order, here he moved from the large toward the small and personal: he addressed in turn the world, the human race, New England ("Thou mayst expect a dark Egyptian night"—the same threat he had made in "God's Controversy" over forty years earlier), the young, pillars of the church, the clergy, his friends and relatives, and finally his "vile body." Here he had more space than in the other poem to be specific and personal about his past. He recalled the ministers:

> From whose communion and society
> I once was kept through long infirmity.

He addressed those near to him:

> Who have my trials seen and great temptations.

He called his own body

> . . . to Christ's work an awkward instrument

[263]

which now would rest in the grave until the resurrection, when it would

> . . . be revived in perfection,
> Endowed with wonderful agility.
>
> . . .
>
> Meanwhile my soul shall enter into peace,
> Where fears and tears, where sin and smart shall cease.

Its second line marked by an artificer's internal rhyme and alliteration, this concluding couplet puts a satisfying cap on the poem's kindly advice to the devout and fierce warning to the indifferent. Wigglesworth was a conscientious preacher to the end.

In spite of group failures, in spite of his own weakness, Wigglesworth loved the land of New England, even though in this poem he had had to admit of the world in general:

> I have in thee enjoyed but little pleasure.

Now at the end, he was begging the majority to follow the few good souls who prayed daily and sought sincerely to follow the two Great Commandments. On the whole, New England had not fulfilled its promise as a stronghold of God, a bright and vigorous new Jerusalem. It had neglected to nurture the first generation's concept of the relevance of faith to all of life's issues, no matter how routine or how exaltedly intellectual. It had lost the feeling for creative living through any vicissitude—loneliness, poverty, suffering. It was no longer interested in the relation of the human spirit to the Last Things.

New England had wasted its chances, had become indifferent to the dreadful prospect of the Last Judgment. The dream of the first immigrants had been dissipated in human rather than heavenly desires. A growing secularism, to flutter backwards only briefly a few years later under the blasts of Jonathan Edwards, was to come to full, strong wing in the Age of Reason, growing obviously from the habitual logic of the seventeenth-century Puritans. Reason was to lead to the ascendancy of Science, and Science, ignoring in man for

[264]

generations the uncontrollable powers of the unknowable, the other Puritan trait of concern for the ultimate, was to beget senseless devastation in a series of world-wide wars.[351]

Feeble though he may have been, Wigglesworth was able to serve his community faithfully for the next ten months after his letter to Increase. On May 27, 1705, he administered the Lord's Supper to his congregation, but on the following Friday he fell sick of a fever.[352] For a full week he seemed to accept the fact of death and looked back on his life with satisfaction—not to be confused with the material "security" which he had always deplored. He called his twelve-year-old son, Edward, to his side and gave him his solemn blessing: "Thou, my son, know thou the God of thy fathers and serve Him with a perfect heart and with a willing hand. If thou seek Him, He will be found of thee, but, if thou forsake Him, He will cast thee off forever."[353] Youngster that he was then, Edward may, a half-dozen years afterward, have been embellishing his father's words, though he was accustomed to this kind of language and thought, for he was later to remark, "The instructions, cautions, counsels, & admonitions of my father, the earnest exhortations & tears of my mother, were daily putting me in mind of the things which concerned my everlasting peace & wellfare & urging me to the remembrance of my creator in the days of my youth."[354]

When Increase Mather came to call, the old man said to him, "For more than fifty years together I have been laboring to uphold a life of Communion with God, and I thank the Lord, I now find the comfort in it."[355] The Day of Doom no longer threatened him with horrors. Meat had come out of the eater: comfort and strength had burgeoned from grievous distress.

The fragile old clergyman died on Sunday morning, June 10, 1705, at about nine o'clock.[356] His frailty notwithstanding, he had outlasted all his Harvard classmates but one—Isaac Chauncy, who was residing in England. Of his daughters, Mercy, Abigail, and probably Martha were married; the other three were still at home. Of his two sons, Edward was still at school in Malden; Samuel was a student at Harvard. His widow, Sybil, was to live on at the parsonage for a little while.

He was buried at Sandy Bank, his grave close to little Margaret Avery's and next to his grandson, Samuel Brackenbury's. (A physician like his father, Mercy's son had died in 1702.) Adorned with the customary symbols of death's-head, cross bones, and hourglass, Michael's gravestone bore a brief tribute to his varied services to the community:

> Here Lies Intered in Silent Grave Below
> Mauldens Physician For Soul and Body Two.

His had been no featherbed journey to God's paradise; yet out of the doubts and agonies of his youth and the debilitating ailments of his middle age he had emerged not only a man of great importance to his vicinity as spiritual counselor and preacher and as physical healer, but a citizen of wider affairs: an often-consulted leader of strong moral fiber, an advocate of justice tempered with mercy, a writer of high contemporary reputation, extraordinary popularity, and undeniable influence. Proving that senility can be sidetracked if a man is not forced by society into idle and lonely retirement, he had been to the end a man of wisdom and spiritual strength.

Epilogue

Two weeks after Wigglesworth's death, the brilliant Cotton Mather, his father's associate at the Second Church in Boston, preached a memorial sermon. Cotton's massive historical ingathering—*Magnalia Christi Americana, Christ's Mighty Accomplishments in America*—had been published in London three years before. As he had in that collection used history to illustrate the all-pervading presence of God, so in Michael's death he found no tragedy, for bereavement of such an exemplary man was not primarily a grief to be borne but an experience designed to be turned to good account. Cotton exhorted his hearers to follow the counsel of *Revelation:* "Be thou faithful unto death, and I will give thee a crown of life." He built his sermon on the formal pattern of setting forth a "doctrine" followed by explication of two "subjects" and then a four-part "application" for the profit of the congregation. Grief was formalized, dignified, and put to use. Life indeed was for the living.

Cotton pointed to the career of the Malden pastor. "It was a surprise unto us, to see a Little Feeble *Shadow of a Man,* beyond *Seventy, Preaching* usually Twice or Thrice in a Week; visiting and Comforting the *Afflicted;* Encouraging the *Private Meetings; Catechizing* the Children of the Flock; and managing the *Government* of the church; and attending the *Sick,* not only as a Pastor, but as a Physician too; and this not only in his own town, but also in all those of the Vicinity. . . ." He advised his hearers to emulate Michael and prayed that God would "bestow such another gift upon his dear people here."

Like his father, not one to hide his light under a bushel, Cotton published his sermon later in the year under the title *A Faithful Man, Described and Rewarded.*[357] As a preface to his son's book, on July 11 Increase wrote an essay addressed "To the Church and Congregation at Malden, in New England." In the appendix Cotton collected a number of items from his subject's "reserved papers," including the two poems welcoming death. He also paid his own verse tribute to his father's friend:

> His pen did once Meat From the Eater fetch;
> And now he's gone beyond the eater's reach.
> His body, once so thin, was next to none;
> From thence he's to unbodied spirits flown.
> Once his rare skill did all diseases heal;
> And he does nothing now uneasy feel.
> He to his paradise is joyful come,
> And waits with joy to see his *Day of Doom!*

Commencement at Harvard was on July 4 that year. Sewall and some of his friends came over to Cambridge for the ceremonies, sailing "pleasantly" until wind forced them ashore, whence they proceeded by foot "over the Marsh to the Upland; and so into the Rode and comfortably to Town."[358] Edward Holyoke of the graduating class, destined to become the college President in 1727, devoted part of his Latin oration to the praise of Wigglesworth, calling him *Maldonatus Orthodoxus,* referring not only to his long residence in Malden, but also to Johannes Maldonatus, a Spanish Jesuit both learned and pious.[359] Though a Jesuit himself, with his belief that every man has the gift of grace to be good if he only will, would not have been welcome in Massachusetts, the topical complexity rising from this one's name would please a Harvard audience in 1705.

Michael's will left to his three unmarried daughters— Mary, Esther, and Dorothy—the funds "which fell to them as their own mother's portion from their grandfather Mudge's estate." To his sons, Samuel and Edward, he left his library, Sybil first to select a half dozen books she would like.[360] There is an outside chance that she chose volumes of verse, for the only poetry listed in the catalogue made the following October was a book of Horace. It is altogether possible, of course, that the Puritan Wigglesworth had permitted no English poets to contaminate his shelves, not even the work of his Massachusetts contemporary, Anne Bradstreet. Most of the titles were reflective of his absorption in medicine and theology, including several works by Increase Mather.[361]

Sybil lived on in Malden a year or two. In February, 1706, she sold all her husband's real estate to John Hutchinson of Lynn for eighty-seven pounds.[362] In March the town meeting voted to allow her four shillings a week in compensation for her hospitality to various preachers after her husband's death. She was also to receive twelve pounds in back pay on Michael's salary for the last three months of his life. (Apparently, the salary had remained fairly steady in the final decade.) But a year and a half later the sum was still owing.[363] At least, however, the heart of the town was right. In July Sybil was granted money in payment of the expense to which Michael had gone in repairing and adding to the parsonage.[364] The bickering and constant misunderstanding that had plagued the town for the first thirty years of Michael's ministry had died away in the last twenty as their pastor had grown in physical strength and consequent favor.

Samuel Sewall continued loyal to the widow of his friend. In July, 1707, he came to Cambridge to visit her. She had returned to the place of her birth to live among her relatives and to be near Edward, who was now at Harvard. The Judge found her suffering from jaundice.[365] She lived on until the summer of 1708. On August 9 Sewall went from Boston through Brookline to attend her funeral in Cambridge,[366] where she was buried near other members of the Sparhawk family at the edge of the Common across the way from Harvard. Her pallbearers were all prominent men, including the recently installed President of the college, John Leverett.

The name of Wigglesworth had become an important one in Massachusetts.

It has been important ever since. Michael's son Samuel, after following the path of his father as tutor and physician, was ordained minister at Ipswich Hamlet in 1714. Michael's younger son, Edward, was appointed first incumbent of the Hollis Chair of Religion at Harvard in 1721. Michael's grandson, also Edward, was the second Hollis professor, and his great-grandson, David Tappan, was the third.[367] Wigglesworth had built a solid foundation.

During the nineteenth century Wigglesworths were among the leaders of New England—a theologian, a geologist, a business executive. . . . Michael himself was not forgotten. As late as 1825 Deacon Ramsdell was going annually to Bell Rock Cemetery to rub the moss from the inscription of his gravestone.[368] Malden named a street after him; Boston has a Wigglesworth Street.

Today the name is still prominent. A recent Boston *Social Register* listed fifteen Wigglesworths (six Winthrops, four Cottons, two Mathers). The name has been borne by a physician in Ipswich, a composer in New York, an ambassador of the United States to Canada. . . . In two and a half centuries, a dozen Edward Wigglesworths have been at Harvard, where a year without a Wigglesworth undergraduate is rare indeed.

Its broad, red-brick walls shutting out the bustle of Massachusetts Avenue in Cambridge, Wigglesworth Hall, filled with freshmen, opens its eleven entries onto the tranquillity of Harvard Yard, where over three centuries ago Michael, up from New Haven, "far from my parents & acquaintance among strangers,"[369] paid the college steward one shilling for buttery privileges and settled down to master logic and rhetoric, Greek and Hebrew, and the "divinity catechetical."

Notes

The following abbreviations are used to make the listing less cumbersome:

AAS — American Antiquarian Society
Coll. — Collections
CSM — Colonial Society of Massachusetts
MHS — Massachusetts Historical Society
NEHGR— New England Historical and Genealogical Register
NEHGS— New England Historic Genealogical Society
NEQ — *New England Quarterly*
Proc. — Proceedings
Pub. — Publications
Trans. — Transactions

1. Michael Wigglesworth, "Diary," Edmund S. Morgan, ed., *Pub. CSM,* XXXV, *Trans. 1942-1946* (1951), 370; ms. at MHS.

2. Factual details about Wigglesworth's life may be found in various sources. See Bibliography 2.

3. *The Victoria History of the County of York,* II, William Page, ed. (London, 1912), 290, 307.

4. For interpretations of the history in this chapter, see, for example, *Life Under the Stuarts,* J. E. Morpurgo, ed. (London, 1950) ; C. Sydney Carter, *The English Church in the Seventeenth Century* (London, 1909) ; A. G. Hyde, *George Herbert and His Times* (London, 1906) ; Basil Willey, *The Seventeenth Century Background: Studies in the Thought of the Age in Relation to Poetry and Religion* (London, 1942).

5. Edmund S. Morgan, *The Puritan Dilemma: The Story of John Winthrop* (Boston, 1958), 161.

6. Godfrey Richard Park, *The History of the Ancient Borough of Hedon* (Hull, England, 1895), 6.

7. Michael Wigglesworth, "Autobiography," ms. at MHS; printed in *NEHGR,* XVII (1863), 137-139, and elsewhere.

8. Park, 2, 13.

9. *Victoria History,* 407, 432.

10. *Victoria History,* III (London, 1913), 402-403.

11. *Victoria History,* III, 418.

12. Edward E. Atwater, *History of the Colony of New Haven* (Meriden, Conn., 1902), 26.

13. Wigglesworth, "Autobiography."

14. Thomas Shepard, "Autobiography," *Pub. CSM,* XXVII (1932), 375-376.

15. Isabel MacBeath Calder, *The New Haven Colony* (New Haven, 1934), 68.

16. John Hull, "Diary of Public Occurrences," *Trans. and Coll. AAS,* III (1857), 172.

17. Morgan reviews these two cases in *The Puritan Dilemma,* 128-129, 152-153.

18. John Langdon Sibley, *Biographical Sketches of Graduates of Harvard University in Cambridge, Massachusetts,* I (Cambridge, 1873), 260, note.

19. Samuel Eliot Morison, *Three Centuries of Harvard, 1636-1936* (Cambridge, 1936), Ch. I.

20. Calder, 68-70; Atwater, 81 ff.

21. Sibley, I, 260; Atwater, 71-72.

22. For details of the beginnings of New Haven, see Calder, Chs. I, II, III.

23. *Records of the Colony or Jurisdiction of New Haven from May, 1653, to the Union* (Hartford, 1858), 518.

24. *Records of the Colony and Plantation of New Haven from 1638-1649* (Hartford, 1857), 12.

25. Atwater, 142.

26. *New Haven, 1638-1649,* 93.

27. Calder, 147 ff.

28. *New Haven, 1638-1649,* 302-303.

29. *New Haven, 1638-1649,* 17.

30. Bernard C. Steiner, *The History of Education in Connecticut* (Washington, 1893), 15.

31. Calder, 94, 130 ff.

32. Broadside at MHS; printed in Ola E. Winslow, *American Broadside Verse From Imprints of the Seventeenth and Eighteenth Centuries* (New Haven, 1930), 24-25.

33. *New Haven, 1638-1649,* 62.

34. *NEHGR,* IX (1855), 363.

35. *New Haven, 1638-1649,* 17.

36. Letter, July 18, 1653, from Edward Wigglesworth to John Winthrop, Jr., ms. at MHS; printed in *Coll. MHS,* 3rd Series, IX (1846), 296-297.

37. Wigglesworth, "Autobiography."

38. *New Haven, 1638-1649,* 137-139.

39. Calder, Ch. V, 83-105, describes the gathering of the church and a typical week's religious activity.

40. *New Haven, 1638-1649,* 191-196.

41. Calder, 93.

42. Wigglesworth, "Autobiography."

43. *New Haven, 1638-1649,* 267.

44. *New Haven, 1638-1649,* 368.

45. *New Haven, 1638-1649,* 370.

46. Sibley, I, 261.

47. Morison, *Three Centuries,* 135.

48. Sibley, I.

49. Morgan, *The Puritan Dilemma,* 170-171.

50. For full discussion of this period, see Thomas J. Wertenbaker, *The Puritan Oligarchy: The Founding of American Civilization* (New York, 1947) ; Perry Miller, *The New England Mind: The Seventeenth Century* (Cambridge, 1939) ; Samuel Eliot Morison, *Builders of the Bay Colony* (Cambridge, 1930) ; Perry Miller, *The New England Mind: From Colony to Province* (Cambridge, 1953).

51. For an understanding of the history, administration, curriculum, and student life at Harvard, three books by Samuel Eliot Morison are indispensable: *The Founding of Harvard College* (Cambridge, 1935), *Harvard College in the Seventeenth Century* (Cambridge, 1936), and *Three Centuries.*

52. Morison, *Three Centuries,* Ch. II.

53. Morison, *Three Centuries,* Ch. I.

54. Morison, *Harvard College,* Ch. IV.

55. Morison, *Three Centuries,* Ch. I.

56. Morison, *The Founding,* 319.

57. Morison, *The Founding,* 249; *Three Centuries,* Ch. II.

58. Sibley, I, 261-262.

59. Morison, *Three Centuries,* Ch. II.

60. Morison, *Harvard College,* Ch. VII.

61. James J. Walsh, "Scholasticism in Colonial Colleges," *NEQ,* V (1932), 483-532.

62. Frederick E. Brasch, "The Newtonian Epoch in the American Colonies, 1680-1783," *Proc. AAS,* XLIX (1939), 315.

63. Morison, *Harvard College,* Ch. VII.

64. Morison, *Harvard College,* Ch. IV.

65. John Ward Dean, *Sketch of the Life of Rev. Michael Wigglesworth, A. M., Author of The Day of Doom* (Albany, 1863), 5. (A second edition, 1871, much enlarged, was called a *Memoir.*)

66. Morison, *Harvard College,* Ch. VII.
67. Hull, 172.
68. Hull, 172.
69. Morison, *Harvard College,* Ch. V.
70. Morison, *Harvard College,* Ch. VI.
71. Morison, *Harvard College,* Ch. I.
72. Morison, *Harvard College,* Ch. VII.
73. Miller, *The Seventeenth Century,* develops this thesis at length.
74. At NEHGS; in enlarged photostat in the Archives Room in the Widener Library at Harvard.
75. Wigglesworth, "Autobiography."
76. Morison, *Three Centuries,* Ch. II.
77. Sibley, I, 260.
78. Morison, *Three Centuries,* Ch. II.
79. In his notebook, dated August 12, 1651.
80. H— M—, *Echoes from Mystic Side* (Boston, 1890), 49.
81. Morison, *The Founding,* 289.
82. Morison, *Builders,* 196.
83. Morison, *Harvard College,* Ch. I.
84. Sibley, I, 262-263.
85. Sibley, I, 405.
86. A tutor's situation is fully detailed in Morison, *Harvard College,* Ch. I.
87. The college library is described in Morison, *Three Centuries,* 264-270.
88. Morison, *Harvard College,* Ch. VII; *Three Centuries,* Ch. II.
89. Morison, *Builders,* 207.
90. Morison, *Harvard College,* Ch. IV.
91. Sibley, I, 323, 358, 405.
92. Samuel Abbott Green, *Michael Wigglesworth, Earliest Poet among Harvard Graduates* (Boston, 1895), 7.
93. Ms. at MHS; transcribed and edited by Edmund S. Morgan, *Pub.* CSM, XXXV, *Trans.* 1942-1946 (1951), 322-444.
94. Morgan, Introduction to the "Diary," 309-321.
95. Dean, *Sketch,* 6.
96. Morison, *Harvard College,* Ch. VI.
97. Quoted in Sibley, I, 265.
98. Mildmay, who was "transferred" from Emmanuel College, Cambridge (England), was something of a dullard. Morison, *Harvard College,* 78, 103.
99. Deloraine P. Corey, *The History of Malden* (Malden, 1899), 194.

100. Sibley, I, 265.

101. Wertenbaker, 261-262.

102. *Coll. MHS*, 3rd Series, IX (1846), 296-297.

103. A portion of this sermon (in modern spelling) is given in Perry Miller, *The American Puritans* (Garden City, 1956), 153-164. The original is in the Houghton Library at Harvard.

104. Quoted in Cotton Mather, *A Faithful Man, Described and Rewarded* (Boston, 1705).

105. Cotton Mather, "Diary, 1681-1724," *Coll. MHS*, 7th Series, VII (1911), 11, 98.

106. *New Haven, 1653 to the Union*, 90; NEHGR, LXXXI (1927), 134.

107. Wigglesworth, "Autobiography."

108. *New Haven, 1653 to the Union*, 101-102; Calder, 199-200.

109. Morison, *Harvard College*, 311.

110. Sibley, I, 551; biographical data for all Wigglesworth's classmates follow his in Sibley, I.

111. Proceedings of the *Two Hundred Seventy-Fifth Anniversary of Malden, Massachusetts* (Malden, 1925), 24-26; H— M—, 21-22; Corey, 158.

112. Corey, 186-187.

113. Sibley, I, 349.

114. Cotton Mather, *A Faithful Man.*

115. The ensuing account of Wigglesworth's courtship and marriage, the move to Malden, and the birth of Mercy is drawn from the "Diary," 399-418.

116. Morpurgo, 163-164.

117. *Bi-Centennial Book of Malden* (Boston, 1850), 146.

118. *Two Hundred Seventy-Fifth Anniversary*, 31-32, 36-39.

119. William E. Rowley, "The Puritans' Tragic Vision," *NEQ*, XVII (1944), 394-417.

120. Dean, *Sketch*, 6.

121. Sibley, I, 269-270; Corey, 196.

122. Hull, 179.

123. Quoted in Corey, 197; ms. at *NEHGS*.

124. Dean, *Memoir* (1871), 103-104; Corey, 197.

125. *Proc. MHS*, XII (1871-1873), 93-98; ms. at MHS.

126. H— M—, 14-15; Corey, 203-206; *Two Hundred Seventy-Fifth Anniversary*, 26.

127. Corey, 219; Sibley, I, 270.

128. Hull, 189.

129. Corey, 219-220.

130. Corey, 188.

131. *NEHGR*, XI (1851), 239.

132. Hull, 196-197.

133. William L. Sachse, "The Migration of New Englanders to England, 1640-1660," *American Historical Review,* LIII (1948), 278.

134. Sibley, I, 270.

135. Both in Mather, *A Faithful Man,* 42, 43.

136. The most recent edition is Kenneth Murdock, *The Day of Doom* (New York, 1929), which contains all the poems of the 1701 edition as well as a helpful introduction.

137. Sibley, I, 271.

138. See, for example, Kenneth Murdock, *Handkerchiefs for Paul* (Cambridge, 1927), which reproduces and discusses elegies by Benjamin Tompson and others.

139. *The Works,* John Harvard Ellis, ed. (Charlestown, 1867; New York, 1932).

140. *The Poems,* Donald E. Stanford, ed. (New Haven, 1960). Wigglesworth's poems are uncollected.

141. (Cambridge, 1640; facsimile, Chicago, 1956).

142. Zoltán Haraszti, *The Enigma of the Bay Psalm Book* (Chicago, 1956).

143. Samuel Eliot Morison, *The Puritan Pronaos* (New York, 1936), 210.

144. Morison, *The Founding,* 264-266.

145. "Dekker His Dream," *The Non-Dramatic Works of Thomas Dekker,* Alexander B. Grosart, ed. (London, 1884), III, 1-60.

146. Translated by William J. Irons, 1849. Hymn 468, *The Hymnal of the Protestant Episcopal Church* (New York, 1940).

147. Perry Miller, *Errand into the Wilderness* (Cambridge, 1956), 221.

148. F. O. Matthiessen, "Michael Wigglesworth, a Puritan Artist," *NEQ,* I (1928), 491-504; Thomas G. Wright, *Literary Culture in Early New England, 1620-1730* (New Haven, 1920), 23-24.

149. Moses Coit Tyler, *A History of American Literature During the Colonial Period,* II, 1676-1765 (rev. ed.) (New York, 1897), 23-35.

150. Hull, 118; George P. Winship, *The Cambridge Press, 1638-1692* (Philadelphia, 1945).

151. Corey, 233-234.

152. Miller, *Colony to Province,* 94-96.

153. *Bi-Centennial Book,* 59; Miller, *Colony to Province,* 36-37.

154. Hull, 206.

155. Matthiessen, 500-503.

156. Miller, *Colony to Province,* 30; *Errand into the Wilderness,* 2-3.

157. William Stoughton, *New England's True Interest* (Cambridge, 1670), 20. I have modernized spelling and punctuation.

158. (Cambridge, 1673).

159. From *Meat Out of the Eater.* See Ch. VI.

160. William Adams, *God's Eye on the Contrite* (Boston, 1685), 17.

161. William Barrett, *Irrational Man* (Garden City, 1957) develops this idea throughout.

162. *The Bay Psalm Book* (New York, 1914).

163. Perry Miller and Thomas H. Johnson, *The Puritans* (New York, 1938), 585.

164. Kenneth B. Murdock, "Michael Wigglesworth," *Dictionary of American Biography,* XX (New York, 1936), 194-195.

165. Kenneth B. Murdock, ed. (New York, 1929).

166. Corey, 236-237.

167. John W. McElroy, "Seafaring in Seventeenth Century New England," *NEQ,* VIII (1935), 333.

168. J. Henry Lefroy, *Memorials of the Discovery and Early Settlement of the Bermudas or Somers Islands, 1511-1687,* II (London, 1897).

169. Wigglesworth's account of his Bermuda sojourn is printed in Dean, *Memoir,* 71-76, from the ms. at NEHGS.

170. Sibley, I, 139-140.

171. Ms. at MHS, dated September 12, 1664.

172. Corey, 238-241.

173. *Colonial Laws of Massachusetts with Supplements, 1672-1686* (Boston, 1890), 79.

174. Dean, *Memoir,* 76.

175. Morison, *Builders,* 284-287.

176. See note 171, above.

177. Dean, *Memoir,* 96-97; Sibley, I, 276; Corey, 245-246.

178. *NEHGR,* XCV (1941), 206-207.

179. Hull, 216.

180. Miller, *Colony to Province,* 105-106, 130-133.

181. Hull, 219-220.

182. Ms. at MHS; *NEHGR,* XXVI (1872), 12.

183. *NEHGR,* XVII (1863), 344.

184. Hull, 227.

185. Miller, *Colony to Province,* 106-107.

186. (Cambridge, 1667).

187. Dean, *Memoir,* 76-79.

188. Commonplace book at NEHGS: see also Sibley, I, 274,

and Matthiessen, 503. Quotations from *Meat Out of the Eater* are from the fifth edition (revised by the author, 1703, published 1717).

189. Commonplace book.

190. "To Althea, from Prison," 25-26.

191. Quoted in Green, 6.

192. Murdock, *Handkerchiefs,* liii-lxxiii—an analysis of elegies by Benjamin Tompson and others.

193. Ms. at NEHGS; *NEHGR,* XXVI (1872), 11-12.

194. See the title essay in Miller, *Errand into the Wildernesss.*

195. Rowley, 417.

196. Hull, 230-235.

197. Hull, 236.

198. *NEHGR,* XIX (1865), 108.

199. *NEHGR,* LX (1906), 250.

200. Corey, 250-251.

201. See note 193, above.

202. They are now available. See note 140. Included are elegies and occasional poems, but his main work is "private."

203. See note 139.

204. *Several Poems,* a reprint of *The Tenth Muse,* with added verses.

205. Paul Tillich, *Theology of Culture* (New York, 1959), 209.

206. Tillich, 6.

207. Barrett, 244-248.

208. This is the premise on which Perry Miller works in *The Seventeenth Century.*

209. See note 182.

210. Corey, 252-255.

211. H— M—, 11, 32.

212. Wertenbaker, 116-117.

213. Increase Mather, *Diary, March, 1675—December, 1676, Together with Extracts from Another Diary by Him, 1674-1687,* Samuel A. Green, ed. (Cambridge, 1900), 27, 29.

214. Sibley, I, 410-438, supplies the outline of Mather's life. Kenneth B. Murdock, *Increase Mather* (Cambridge, 1925) gives a fuller treatment.

215. Wertenbaker, 318-319.

216. Mather, *Diary,* 47.

217. Samuel Sewall, "Diary," *Coll. MHS,* 5th Series, V (1878), 29.

218. Hull, 242.

219. Wertenbaker, 321.

220. *Coll. MHS,* 4th Series, VIII (1868), 338.

221. *Two Hundred Seventy-Fifth Anniversary*, 166.

222. *NEHGR*, LIX (1905), 246.

223. *Coll. MHS*, 4th Series (1868), 645.

224. Murdock, *Increase Mather*, 149.

225. Corey, 263.

226. Corey, 264.

227. James Mudge, "The Mudges of Malden," *The Register of the Malden Historical Society*, No. 5, 1917-1918 (Lynn, Mass., 1918), 39-54.

228. Ms. of the letter (*ca.* April 6, 1669) is in photostat at MHS.

229. Corey, 265.

230. Hull, 245.

231. Mather, *Diary*, 50.

232. Hull, 246.

233. Wertenbaker, 322.

234. Miller, *From Colony to Province*, 137.

235. *NEHGR*, LV (1901), 40-41.

236. Corey, 17-18; 257-258.

237. *Records of the Governor and Company of the Massachusetts Bay in New England*, V, 1674-1686, Nathaniel B. Shurtleff, M.D., ed. (Boston, 1854), 539.

238. For example, Increase Mather, *Heaven's Alarm to the World* (Boston, 1680).

239. Hull, 247.

240. Mather, *Diary*, 52.

241. Corey, 258.

242. Hull, 248-249.

243. Mather, *Diary*, 52.

244. Wertenbaker, 323-324.

245. *Births, Marriages, and Deaths in the Town of Malden, Massachusetts, 1649-1850*, Deloraine P. Corey, comp. (Cambridge, 1903), 322.

246. Miller, *From Colony to Province*, 142-145.

247. Corey, 259-260.

248. Dean, *Memoir*, 96.

249. Corey, 212.

250. H— M—, 14.

251. *Births . . . in . . . Malden*, 103.

252. Wertenbaker, 327-328.

253. Miller, *From Colony to Province*, 146.

254. Corey, 265.

255. Sibley, I, 275.

256. *Coll. MHS*, 4th Series, VIII (1868), 645; ms. at MHS.

[279]

257. Hull, 249.
258. Mather, *Diary*, 52.
259. Wertenbaker, 269.
260. Miller, *From Colony to Province*, 113.
261. Sewall, V, 95.
262. Sewall, V, 100.
263. Corey, 239.
264. Sewall, V, 127.
265. Corey, 266-267.
266. Corey, 268; *NEHGR*, VI (1852), 72.
267. Corey, 268-269.
268. Sewall, V, 131-132.
269. Samuel Sewall, "Diary," *Coll. MHS*, 5th Series, VI (1879), 21-23.
270. Dean, *Memoir*, 90.
271. Corey, 279.
272. Wertenbaker, 325-327.
273. H— M—, 23.
274. Miller, *From Colony to Province*, Ch. II.
275. Sewall, VI, 136.
276. Lindsay Swift, "The Massachusetts Election Sermons," *Pub. CSM*, I (1895), 407-408; *Records . . . of the Massachusetts Bay*, V, 514-515.
277. *Births . . . in . . . Malden*, 103.
278. Dean, *Memoir*, 91-92.
279. Dean, *Memoir*, 97-98.
280. Dean, *Memoir*, 99-100.
281. *Births . . . in . . . Malden*, 103.
282. Mather, *Diary*, 53.
283. H— M—, 34.
284. Mather, *Diary*, 53-54.
285. *Bi-Centennial Book*, 156.
286. Ms. at NEHGS.
287. Sewall, V, 217.
288. Sewall, V, 223. As a matter of fact, Michael's book title is entered every once in a while in the records of the time. In 1679, for example, it had been one of several volumes of verse in the library of Daniel Russell of Charlestown, catalogued after his death. Morison, *The Puritan Pronaos*, 134.
289. Wertenbaker, 335.
290. H— M—, 34.
291. H— M—, 35; Wertenbaker, 337.
292. Murdock, *Increase Mather*, 340-347.
293. Wright, *Literary Culture*, 161.

294. Corey, 281.

295. *Births . . . in . . . Malden,* 103.

296. *City Cemeteries, Malden, Massachusetts* (Malden, 1945), 7.

297. Corey, 281.

298. *The Record of Baptisms, Marriages and Deaths . . . in the Town of Dedham, Massachusetts, 1638-1845* (Dedham, 1888).

299. The letters to Mrs. Avery are in *NEHGR,* XVII (1863), 139-142 and in Dean, *Sketch,* 13-16.

300. Especially were children of habitual sinners so farmed out. See Edmund S. Morgan, *The Puritan Family* (Boston, 1944), 87.

301. Dean, *Sketch,* 9.

302. "Records of the First Church of Braintree, Massachusetts," *NEHGR,* LIX (1905), 153.

303. Corey, 281; ms. in back of commonplace book at NEHGS.

304. Corey, 281; Dean, *Memoir,* 106-107; ms. letter at MHS.

305. Wertenbaker, 291, 342.

306. Sewall, V, 352-353.

307. "Danvers, Massachusetts, Church Record," *NEHGR,* XI (1857), 319-320.

308. Wertenbaker, 338.

309. Morison, *Harvard College,* 500.

310. Ms. at MHS.

311. Sibley, I, 347 ff.

312. Dean, *Memoir,* 107; Murdock, *Increase Mather,* 299.

313. (Boston, 1692).

314. Wertenbaker, 278-279; Murdock, *Increase Mather,* 304.

315. Wertenbaker, 286-291.

316. *Bi-Centennial Book,* 155.

317. Sibley, I, 276.

318. Corey, 207.

319. Dean, *Memoir,* 101; Corey, 288.

320. Sibley, I, 277.

321. Sewall, V, 427.

322. H— M—, 17-18.

323. Sewall, V, 433.

324. E. R. Tostin, Jr., "The Story of Salt in New England," *Essex Institute Historical Coll.,* LXXXV (1949), 259-271; Morison, *Builders,* 274-275.

325. Sewall, V, 434.

326. Sewall, V, 236.

327. Sewall, V, 453.

328. Morison, *Harvard College,* 509-513.

329. Morison, *Harvard College,* 514-516.

330. Sewall, V, 467-468.
331. Sewall, V, 471.
332. Dean, *Memoir,* 101.
333. Sewall, V, 497-498.
334. Corey, 203.
335. Sewall, VI, 21-22.
336. *Births . . . in . . . Malden,* 322.
337. Morison, *Harvard College,* 530-533; Murdock, *Increase Mather,* 357.
338. Sewall, VI, 37.
339. Hull, 211-212.
340. Ewer Mss., NEHGS; *NEHGR,* I (1847), 368-371.
341. Corey, 203.
342. H— M—, 30.
343. *Two Hundred Seventy-Fifth Anniversary,* 38.
344. H— M—, 30.
345. Corey, 209.
346. Sewall, VI, 80, 83, 100, 117.
347. Rowley, 414-415.
348. Morison, *The Puritan Pronaos,* 257.
349. *Coll. MHS,* 4th Series, VIII (1868), 645-647; ms. at MHS.
350. Cotton Mather, *A Faithful Man,* 45-48.
351. Barrett develops this thesis at length.
352. Sewall, VI, 132-133.
353. Dean, *Memoir,* 110-111.
354. Note in back of commonplace book, NEHGS.
355. Corey, 293.
356. Sibley, I, 279.
357. (Boston, 1705).
358. Sewall, VI, 133-134.
359. Dean, *Memoir,* 114-115.
360. Dean, *Sketch,* 9.
361. Dean, *Sketch,* 10, 16.
362. Corey, 240.
363. Sibley, I, 282.
364. Corey, 203.
365. Sewall, VI, 191.
366. Sewall, VI, 229.
367. Sibley, I, 282.
368. Sibley, I, 280.
369. Wigglesworth, "Autobiography."

Bibliography

The books, articles, and manuscripts which I list here have been helpful in varying degrees in the writing of this book. To enumerate the thousands of other sources concerned with the Puritans would be both fruitless and endless. Authorities of our own time on whom I have leaned most heavily are Samuel Eliot Morison, Perry Miller, Thomas J. Wertenbaker, Kenneth B. Murdock, and Edmund S. Morgan, whose turning of Wigglesworth's shorthand into English has lightened my task immeasurably.

1. The Poetry of Michael Wigglesworth

An excellent bibliography has been compiled by Harold S. Jantz in "The First Century of New England Verse." (See below, 7.) The following chronological list gives some additional information. Probable date of composition is followed by the date of first publication. A third date, when indicated, is that of the last revision by the poet.

A. *"Christe, parum doleo quia te non diligio multum,"* 1660, 1705 (Cotton Mather, *A Faithful Man,* 42).
B. *"Ira premit, peccata gravant, afflictio frangit,"* 1660, 1705 (Cotton Mather, *A Faithful Man,* 43).
C. *The Day of Doom,* 1662, 1662, 1701.
    "To the Christian Reader"
    "A Prayer unto Christ the Judge of the World"
    "The Day of Doom"
    "A Short Discourse on Eternity"

[283]

"A Postscript unto the Reader"

"I walk'd and did a little Mole-hill view" (1673 ed. only)

"Vanity of Vanities; A Song of Emptiness . . ."

D. "God's Controversy with New-England," 1662, 1873 (*Proc. MHS*, XII, 83-93), ms., MHS.

E. "When as the wayes of Jesus Christ," 1665 (?), 1872 (*NEHGR*, XXVI, 12), ms., NEHGS.

F. *Meat Out of the Eater*, 1669, 1670, 1703 (revision published, 1717).

"*Tolle Crucem*"

10 "Meditations"

"Conclusion Hortatory"

"Riddles Unriddled, or Christian Paradoxes"

"Light in Darkness," 10 "Songs"

"Sick Men's Health," 4 "Songs"

"Strength in Weakness," 4 "Songs"

"Poor Men's Wealth," 5 "Meditations"

"In Confinement Liberty," 3 "Songs"

"In Solitude Good Company," 3 "Songs"

("Song III" composed *ca.* 1660)

"Joy in Sorrow," 5 "Songs"

"Life in Deaths," 3 "Songs"

"Heavenly Crowns for Thorny Wreaths," 5 "Songs"

G. "Upon the Much Lamented Death of That Precious Servant of Christ, Mr. Benjamin Buncker," 1670, 1872 (*NEHGR*, XXVI, 11-12), ms., NEHGS.

H. "Upon the Return of My Dear Friend Mr. Foster with His Son Out of Captivity under the Moors," 1673, 1871 (*American Historical Record*, I, 393).

I. "Death Expected and Welcomed," 1705(?), 1705 (Cotton Mather, *A Faithful Man*, 45).

J. "A Farewell to the World," 1705(?), 1705 (Cotton Mather, *A Faithful Man*, 46-48).

2. Biography and Analysis

In 1863, John Ward Dean printed at Albany, N.Y., fifty copies of his *Sketch of the Life of Rev. Michael Wigglesworth, A.M., Author of the Day of Doom,* a twenty-page booklet of which only pp. 3-11 constitute the life story; the other pages contain Wigglesworth's little "Autobiography," the letters to Mrs. Avery, and a limited bibliography of the poems. Ward issued a second edition in 1871, revised and much enlarged (151 pp.) and called it a *Memoir.* Samuel A. Green's seven-page pamphlet, *Michael Wigglesworth, Earliest Poet among Harvard Graduates,* was printed in 1895 in Boston.

The following sections of larger works have been indispensable:

Corey, Deloraine P., *The History of Malden* (Malden, Mass., 1899), chs. VII, VIII, IX, 186-295 (the most detailed of any of the accounts).

Murdock, Kenneth B., "Michael Wigglesworth," *Dictionary of American Biography,* XX (New York, 1936), 194-195.

Sibley, John L., "Michael Wigglesworth," *Biographical Sketches of Graduates of Harvard University in Cambridge, Massachusetts,* I, 1642-1658 (Cambridge, 1873), 259-286 (the series popularly known as Sibley's *Harvard Graduates*).

A few items were more analytical than biographical:

Matthiessen, F. O., "Michael Wigglesworth, a Puritan Artist," *NEQ,* I (1928), 491-504.

Morgan, Edmund S., Introduction to "The Diary of Michael Wigglesworth," *Pub. CSM,* XXXV, *Trans.* 1942-1946 (1951), 309-321.

Murdock, Kenneth B., Introduction to *The Day of Doom* (New York, 1929), pp. iii-xi. The title poem and the others in Murdock's edition follow the edition of 1701: hence is omitted "I walk'd and did a little Mole-hill view."

Strange, Arthur, "Michael Wigglesworth Reads the Poets," *American Literature,* XXXI (1959), 325-326.

Tyler, Moses Coit, *A History of American Literature During the Colonial Period,* II, 1676-1765 (rev. ed.) (New York, 1897), 23-35.

3. Diaries and Autobiographies

Many Puritans kept a record of their daily lives and spiritual progress. The following are pertinent here:

Hull, John, "Diary of Public Occurrences," *Trans. and Coll. AAS,* III (1857), 165-252.

Mather, Cotton, "Diary, 1681-1724," *Coll. MHS,* 7th Series, VII (1911); VIII (1912).

Mather, Increase, *Diary, March 1675- December, 1676, Together with Extracts from Another Diary by Him, 1674-1687,* Samuel A. Green, ed. (Cambridge, 1900).

Sewall, Samuel, "Diary," *Coll. MHS,* 5th Series, V (1878); VI (1879); VII (1882).

Shepard, Thomas, "Autobiography," *Pub. CSM,* XXVII (1932), 352-392.

Wigglesworth, Michael, "Autobiography," *NEHGR,* XVII (1863), 137-139; Dean, *Sketch,* 11-13.

Wigglesworth, "Diary," Edmund S. Morgan, ed., *Pub. CSM,* XXXV, *Trans. 1942-1946* (1951), 322-444.

The manuscripts of Wigglesworth's diary and autobiography are both available to investigators at MHS. At NEHGS is a commonplace book of later date (the diary extends only from 1653 to 1657) containing comment on the Bermuda sojourn and the composition of *Meat Out of the Eater,* the meditation of November 27, 1687, and, in the back, notes by Wigglesworth's son Edward.

4. Letters

The following letters (arranged chronlogically) were written by Wigglesworth or to him or contain mention of him:

July 18, 1653, Edward Wigglesworth (Michael's father) to John Winthrop, Jr., *Coll. MHS,* 3rd Series, IX (1846), 296-297.

August 25, 1656, Church at Cambridge to Church at Malden, *Christian Register,* June 29, 1850.

April 6, 1657, M. Middlebrooke to Wigglesworth, *NEHGR,* XI (1857), 110-111.

June 19, 1658, Wigglesworth to the Church at Malden, *Proc. MHS,* XII (1871-1873), 93-98.

September 12, 1664, Nathaniel White to Wigglesworth, ms. at MHS.

ca. April 6, 1669, Wigglesworth and Benjamin Bunker to the General Court, ms. in photostat at MHS.

June 5, 1677, Samuel Hooker to Increase Mather, *Coll. MHS,* 4th Series, VIII (1868), 338.

May 8 and May 12, 1679, Increase Mather to Wigglesworth, *Coll. MHS,* 4th Series, VIII (1868), 94-96.

October 27, 1684, Wigglesworth to Increase Mather, *Coll. MHS,* 4th Series, VIII (1868), 645.

October 13, 1690, Wigglesworth *et al.* to ministers of Boston area, *NEHGR,* XCV (1941), 206-207.

February 11 and March 23, 1691, Wigglesworth to Mrs. Avery, *NEHGR,* XVII (1863), 139-142.

July 22, 1704, Wigglesworth to Increase Mather, *Coll. MHS,* 4th Series, VIII (1868), 645-647.

Nearly all of those in print are also to be seen in ms. at either MHS or NEHGS.

5. Other Documentary Material

At NEHGS is a sermon notebook in shorthand and two college notebooks chiefly in Latin and English, which are available in enlarged photostat in the Archives Room in the Widener Library at Harvard. Also at NEHGS, in the Ewer Mss., are the sermon notes on the wearing of the hair and on the pride of women. In ms. at MHS is the sermon outline for May 29, 1692.

Various records have been useful:

Births, Marriages, and Deaths in the Town of Malden, Massachusetts, 1649-1850, Deloraine P. Corey, comp. (Cambridge, 1903).
City Cemeteries, Malden, Massachusetts (Malden, 1945).
Colonial Laws of Massachusetts with Supplements, 1672-1686 (Boston, 1890).
Harvard College Records, I: Corporation Records, 1636-1750, I, Pub. CSM, XV (1925).

NEHGR: IX (1855), 363 (baptism of Wigglesworth's sister, Abigail).
   XI (1857), 239 (death of Humphrey Reyner) and 319-320 (Danvers Church Record).
   XIX (1865), 108 (data on Samuel Brackenbury, Jr.).
   LV (1901), 40-41 (Wigglesworth's "Some Grounds for Laying Down My Office Relation").
   LIX (1905), 153 (Wigglesworth-Avery marriage) and 246 (Abigail Sweetser's marriage).

The Record of Baptisms, Marriages, and Deaths in the Town of Dedham, Massachusetts, 1638-1845 (Dedham, 1888).
Records of the Colony and Plantation of New Haven from 1638-1649 (Hartford, 1857).
Records of the Colony or Jurisdiction of New Haven from May, 1653, to the Union (Hartford, 1858).
Records of the First Church in Charlestown, Massachusetts, James F. Hunnewell, ed. (Boston, 1880).

6. Contemporaneous works

Election sermons, poems, and other items written in Wigglesworth's time have been useful:

Adams, William, *God's Eye on the Contrite* (Boston, 1685).

The Bay Psalm Book (Cambridge, 1640; facsimile, Chicago, 1956).

Bradstreet, Anne, *Works,* John Harvard Ellis, ed. (Charlestown, 1867; New York, 1932).

Mather, Cotton, *A Faithful Man, Described and Rewarded* (Boston, 1705).

Mather, Increase, *Cases of Conscience* (Boston, 1692).

New England's First Fruits (London, 1643).

Shepard, Thomas, *Eye-Salve* (Cambridge, 1673).

Stoughton, William, *New England's True Interest* (Cambridge, 1670).

Taylor, Edward, *The Poems,* Donald E. Stanford, ed. (New Haven, 1960).

7. Modern Studies

Materials relevant to the seventeenth century in Old and New England are legion. The following books and articles indicate only the borders of possibility in selection. My indebtedness to some of them is very deep.

Adams, James Truslow, *The Founding of New England* (Boston, 1921).

——, *Provincial Society, 1690-1763* (New York, 1927).

Arendt, Hannah, *The Human Condition* (Chicago, 1958).

Atwater, Edward E., *History of the Colony of New Haven* (Meriden, Conn., 1902).

Bailyn, Bernard, *The New England Merchants in the Seventeenth Century* (Cambridge, 1955).

Barrett, William, *Irrational Man* (Garden City, N. Y., 1958).

Bi-Centennial Book of Malden (Boston, 1850).

Boorstin, Daniel J., "The Puritan Tradition: Community Above Ideology," *Commentary,* XXVI (1958), 288-299.

Brasch, Frederick E., "The Newtonian Epoch in the American Colonies, 1680-1783," *Proc. AAS,* XLIX (1939), 314-332.

Brown, B. Katherine, "A Note on the Puritan Concept of

Aristocracy," *Mississippi Valley Historical Review,* XLI (1954), 105-112.

Calverton, V. F., "The Puritan Myth," *Scribner's Monthly,* LXXXIX (1931), 251-257.

Calder, Isabel MacBeath, *The New Haven Colony* (New Haven, 1934).

Carter, C. Sydney, *The English Church in the Seventeenth Century* (London, 1909).

Caulfield, Ernest, "Some Common Diseases of Colonial Children," *Pub. CSM, XXXV, Trans. 1942-1946* (1951), 4-65.

Corey, Deloraine P., *The History of Malden, 1633-1785* (Malden, 1899).

Eggleston, Edward, *Transit of Civilization from England to America in the Seventeenth Century* (New York, 1901).

Fiske, John, *The Beginnings of New England* (Boston, 1889).

Grierson, Herbert J. C., *Cross Currents in English Literature of the XVIIth Century* (London, 1929).

Haraszti, Zoltán, *The Enigma of the Bay Psalm Book* (Chicago, 1956).

Hart, James D., "A Puritan Bookshelf," *New Colophon,* I (1948), 13-26.

Howard, Leon, *Literature and the American Tradition* (New York, 1960).

Hyde, A. G., *George Herbert and His Times* (London, 1906).

Jantz, Harold S., "The First Century of New England Verse," *Proc. AAS,* New Series, III (1943), 219-508. Reprinted in book form by AAS (Worcester, Mass., 1945).

Lefroy, J. Henry, *Memorials of the Discovery and Early Settlement of the Bermudas or Somers Islands, 1511-1687,* II (London, 1879).

M—, H—, *Echoes from Mystic Side* (Boston, 1890).

Macy, John, "A Glance at the Real Puritan," *Harper's Monthly,* CLIV (1927), 742-750.

McElroy, John W., "Seafaring in Seventeenth Century New England," *NEQ*, VIII (1935), 331-364.

Miller, Perry, ed., *The American Puritans: Their Prose and Poetry* (New York, 1956).

——, *Errand into the Wilderness* (Cambridge, 1956).

——, *The New England Mind: From Colony to Province* (Cambridge, 1953).

——, *The New England Mind: The Seventeenth Century* (New York, 1939).

——, and Johnson, Thomas H., *The Puritans* (New York, 1938).

Morgan, Edmund S., *The Puritan Dilemma: The Story of John Winthrop* (Boston, 1958).

——, "Light on the Puritans from John Hull's Notebooks," *NEQ*, XV (1942), 95-101.

——, *The Puritan Family* (Boston, 1944).

——, "The Puritan's Marriage with God," *South Atlantic Quarterly*, XLVIII (1949), 107-112.

Morison, Samuel Eliot, *Builders of the Bay Colony* (Cambridge, 1930).

——, *The Founding of Harvard College* (Cambridge, 1935).

——, *Harvard College in the Seventeenth Century* (Cambridge, 1936).

——, *Intellectual Life in Colonial New England* (New York, 1956).

——, *The Puritan Pronaos* (New York, 1936).

——, *Three Centuries of Harvard, 1636-1936* (Cambridge, 1936).

Morpurgo, J. E., ed., *Life Under the Stuarts* (London, 1950).

Mudge, James, "The Mudges of Malden," *The Register of the Malden Historical Society*, No. 5, 1917-1918 (Lynn, Mass., 1918), 39-54.

Murdock, Kenneth B., *Handkerchiefs for Paul* (Cambridge, 1927).

——, *Increase Mather* (Cambridge, 1925).

——, *Literature and Theology in Colonial New England* (Cambridge, 1949).

[291]

Nettels, Curtis P., *The Roots of American Civilization* (New York, 1938).

Osgood, Herbert L., *The American Colonies in the Seventeenth Century*, I, II (New York, 1930).

Page, William, ed., *Victoria History of the County of York*, I, II, III (London, 1907, 1912, 1913).

Palmer, George Herbert, *The English Works of George Herbert*, I (Boston, 1905).

Park, Godfrey Richard, *The History of the Ancient Borough of Hedon* (Hull, England, 1895).

Parrington, Vernon L., *The Colonial Mind, 1620-1800* (New York, 1927).

Perry, Ralph Barton, *Puritanism and Democracy* (New York, 1944).

Porter, Katherine Anne, "Affectation of Praehiminincies," *Accent*, II (1942), 131-138; 226-232.

——, "A Bright Particular Faith, A. D. 1700. A Portrait of Cotton Mather," *Perspectives U. S. A.*, No. 7, 83-92.

Proceedings of the Two Hundred Seventy-Fifth Anniversary of Malden, Massachusetts (Malden, 1925).

Rowley, William E., "The Puritans' Tragic Vision," *NEQ*, XVII (1944), 394-417.

Sachse, William L., "Harvard Men in England, 1642-1714," *Pub. CSM*, XXXV, *Trans.*, 1942-1946 (1951), 119-144.

——, "The Migration of New Englanders to England, 1640-1660," *American Historical Review*, LIII (1948), 251-278.

Schneider, Herbert W., *The Puritan Mind* (New York, 1930).

Sibley, John L., *Harvard Graduates*, I, II, III (Cambridge, 1873, 1881, 1885).

Shipton, C. K., "The New England Clergy of the 'Glacial Age' (1680-1740)," *Pub. CSM*, XXXII (1937), 24-54.

——, "A Plea for Puritanism," *American Historical Review*, XL (1935), 460-467.

Smith, Chard Powers, *Yankees and God* (New York, 1954).

Steiner, Bernard C., *The History of Education in Connecticut* (Washington, 1893).

Stephenson, George M., *The Puritan Heritage,* (New York, 1952).

Sweet, William W., *Religion in Colonial America* (New York, 1942).

Swift, Lindsay, "The Massachusetts Election Sermons," *Pub. CSM,* I (1895), 388-451.

Tillich, Paul, *Theology of Culture* (New York, 1959).

Tostin, E. R., Jr., "The Story of Salt in New England," *Essex Institute Historical Coll.,* LXXXV (July, 1949), 259-271.

Walsh, James J., "Scholasticism in Colonial Colleges," *NEQ,* V (1932), 483-532.

Warren, Austin, *New England Saints,* (Ann Arbor, 1956).

Wertenbaker, Thomas J., *The First Americans, 1607-1690* (New York, 1927).

——, *The Puritan Oligarchy: The Founding of American Civilization* (New York, 1947).

Wilder, Amos N., *Theology and Modern Literature* (Cambridge, 1958).

Willey, Basil, *The Seventeenth Century Background: Studies in the Thought of the Age in Relation to Poetry and Religion* (London, 1942).

Winship, George P., *The Cambridge Press, 1638-1692* (Philadelphia, 1945).

Winslow, Ola Elizabeth, *Meetinghouse Hill, 1630-1783* (New York, 1952).

Wright, Louis B., *The Atlantic Frontier: Colonial American Civilization, 1607-1763* (New York, 1947).

——, *The Cultural Life of the American Colonies, 1607-1763* (New York, 1957).

Wright, Thomas G., *Literary Culture in Early New England, 1620-1730* (New Haven, 1920).

Index

[295]

passim; publication, 145-146; subsequent editions, 222, 259

Milton, John, 3

Mitchell, Jonathan: tutor at Harvard, 32; writes introductory verses to *Day of Doom,* 113; mentioned, 49

Mudge, Martha: becomes Wigglesworth's second wife, 215; family background, 216; public disapproval, 217; children born to, 222, 223, 230, 231, 235; death, 235

Mudge, Mary: trial of stolen kiss, 216

New England writers, 102, 154-156

New Haven (formerly Quinnipiac): founding of, 9; Plantation Covenant, 9; church organized, 10-11; Church Covenant, 12; social life in, 12

Newton, Isaac, 243

Paige, Colonel Nicholas, 250

Parliament: dissolved by James II, 221

Phips, Sir William: appointed governor, 243; pardons three "proven" witches, 247

Plantation Covenant (New Haven), 9; replaced, 12

Platform of Church Discipline: drawn up, 23; partial contents, 23-24

Poets, three major New England, 154-156

Publishing in the Bay area, 235

Puritanism: historical context of, in England, 2-3; in the New World, 5, 11, 160-166 *passim;* concept of marriage, 77; spiritual problem, 49. *See also* God, Salvation and judgment; "Halfway Covenant"

Quinnipiac. *See* New Haven

Quotations of Wigglesworth's poetry (note abbreviations, p. *xi*): God's Con, 2-3, 6, 16, 33, 115, 116, 229; PS, 12, 111, 156, 211; Mole Hill, 30, 150, 156; Meat, 56, 69, 135-142 *passim,* 229, 253; Vanity, 60, 112, 224, 244; Sol, 65, 99, 142, 241; Strength, 82, 141; Reader, 96, 97, 99, 109, 156; Christe, 101, 140; Prayer, 104; DD, 106-112 *passim,* 128, 244; Poor, 119; When as, 128; Virtue, 137; Riddles, 137-145 *passim;* Light, 140; Con, 141, 142; Sick, 141, 260; Heaven, 144-145, 229; Joy, 144, 238; Life, 144; Buncker (Bunker), 146-147; Eternity, 157, 158; Ira, 189; Foster, 234; "Death Expected . . .," 262-263; "A Farewell . . .," 263-264

Randolph, Edward: commission from Charles II, 210; appointed collector of customs, 218; mentioned, 223

Reformation, end of, 99

Religious observations at New Haven, 11

Remonstrance and Petition to the General Court: contents, 21-22; rejected, 21; later effects of, 22-23

Reyner, Humphrey, 99

Reyner, Mary: marries Wigglesworth, 87; child born, 91-92; joins church, 93-94; death of, 98

Richards, John: sent as envoy to England, 228

Rogers, Reverend Ezekiel, 7, 8

Salem witch trials, 245-246; Governor Phips steps in, 247; declared a mistake, colony repents, 260

Sewall, Samuel: praises Wigglesworth sermon, 226; appointed witch trial judge, 245; friendship with Wigglesworth, 250-251; acknowledges witch trials a mistake, 260

school, 17; scholarly achievements, 18; enters Harvard College, 24-25; graduates at head of class, 43; continues studies, 46; master's degree granted, 78; medical studies, 125, 131
—Professional life: joins church, 42; decides to become minister, 42; problems as tutor, 58-59, 66-67; becomes tutor at Harvard, 45; invited to ministries, 52; invitation to Malden, 79; preaches at Malden, 88, 89; moves to Malden, 91; considers resignation, 219-220; medical practice mentioned, 218, 219, 222, 223, 260; invited to presidency of Harvard, 224; declines, 225-226; preaches election sermon in Boston, 228; activities and travels, 233, 241; signs Mather's essay on witches, 247; voted salary by Malden congregation, 249; appointed a Fellow of Harvard College, 252
—Writings: declamations on eloquence, 38-41; begins diary, 48; "The Day of Doom," 101-102, 104, 107; "God's Controversy," 115-117; *Day of Doom* (q.v.) published, 120; *Meat Out of the Eater* (q.v.)

132-134; elegy on Bunker, 146-147; writings 1662-1673, 152; writing style, 152-153; imagery of, 153-154; core of meaning, 154, 156-157; fifteen articles on proposed resignation from Malden, 219; letter to Mather on witch trials, 260-262; two poems on death, 262-264
Wigglesworth, Samuel: born, 235; mentioned, 270
Wigglesworth, Sybil (Michael Wigglesworth's third wife and widow): meets Wigglesworth, 237; marriage, 241; child born, 248; daughter by previous marriage dies, 249-250; sells Malden property, 269; death, 270
Wigs and long hair, 256-257
Willard, Josiah: shaves head to don wig, 256
Willard, Samuel: succeeds Mather as president of Harvard, 256
William of Orange: ascends throne, 234
Williams, Roger, 7
Wilson, Reverend John: death, 130
Winthrop, John: mentioned, 2, 20; death, 33
Witchcraft: trials at Salem, 245-246; hysteria ends, 247; declared a mistake, 260